Also by Bernice Kanner
Are You Normal?
Lies My Parents Told Me

THE 100 BEST TV COMMERCIALS

...AND WHY THEY WORKED

THE 100 BEST

TV COMMERCIALS

. . . AND WHY THEY WORKED

Bernice Kanner

TIMES BUSINESS

RANDOM HOUSE

Library of Congress Cataloging-in-Publication Data

Kanner, Bernice.
The 100 best TV commercials—and why they worked / Bernice Kanner. — 1st ed.
    p.   cm.
ISBN 0-8129-2995-0
1. Television advertising—Case studies. I. Title. II. Title:
One hundred best TV commercials.
HF6146.T42K36 1999
659.14′3—dc21   98-47855

Book design by Robert Bull

Random House website address: www.atrandom.com
Printed in the United States of America on acid-free paper

9 8 7 6 5 4 3 2

First Edition

ACKNOWLEDGMENTS

Consider the number of commercials explored here—and the dozens more examined and not included—and you can surmise that this project's thank-you list is literally yards long. The hundreds of agency staffers, client teams, and production crews—in fact too many to single out—who dug up facts, confirmed details, and secured clearances have my deep-felt gratitude.

To Barbara Levy and her team at the London International Advertising Awards, who followed one seemingly washed-out historical chain after another to locate sources for me, sincere thanks. Thanks to Donald Gunn and Lisa Bruckner at Leo Burnett's Creative Exchange for invaluable assistance.

Deep appreciation to Karl Weber, the former Times Books editor, who breathed life into this project, and John Mahaney and Luke Mitchell, talented midwives who shaped and birthed it. And, of course, to my agent Richard Pine, who followed its course with intelligent advice and guidance.

In many ways, this book has been a true collaboration, one that would not have been possible without the diligent and devoted efforts of Burnett's team. Although many staffers helped, those on the front lines included Susan Sullivan, Amy Hoffar, and Paul Kemp-Robertson. Despite a Sisyphean workload, Cheri Carpenter led the troops on this team, solved problems with creative solutions, remained cheerful in its dark days, and was a treasured ally.

And my deepest and heartfelt gratitude to the actual parents of this project: Ella Strubel, late of Leo Burnett Company, and Wally Petersen, senior vice president and head of communications. My admiration—indeed affection—for you individually has only been heightened by the grace, competence, and ingenious creativity I witnessed in the course of this two-year odyssey. I am deeply grateful and humbled to have had this opportunity to work with you.

Last, love and appreciation to my family, my son, Andrew Cuming, daughter, Elisabeth Cuming, and husband, David Cuming, who not only listened to the triumphs and defeats of the project but gracefully forbore its intrusion into their lives.

FOREWORD

By Michael Conrad, vice chairman and chief creative officer, Leo Burnett Company, Inc.

This remarkable list began in 1995 as a request to Leo Burnett's Creative Exchange from Phil Fiebig, Burnett's managing director in Kuala Lumpur at the time. On behalf of the Malaysian chapter of the International Advertising Association, Fiebig wanted to know if the Creative Exchange had a reel of the world's greatest commercials ever. If not, could they put one together?

The Creative Exchange was the natural place to look. It had a comprehensive archive of more than five thousand of the world's best commercials since 1985. Senior vice president Donald Gunn and senior coordinator Lisa Buckner were not only familiar with the most obvious candidates—they also had the films on file.

Gunn and Buckner didn't believe any such reel existed, but that one should. So they set about making one from scratch. Considering Burnett's three key criteria of superior advertising—the concept, the fresh idea, and the execution—they generated a master list of hundreds of candidates. They consulted dozens of resources including the Clio Hall of Fame, *Advertising Age*'s "Fifty Years of Television" commemorative issue, the BBC's *Washes Whiter* advertising history series, the American Association of Advertising Agencies' Seventy-Fifth Anniversary Reel, and the U.S. Television Bureau of Advertising's historical reels, as well as Burnett's own storehouse: *Carl Hixon's Historical Reel*; Gunn's own 114-commercial *Someone Has to Get Out an Ad* reel; and *The Showreel of the '80s,* created for Burnett screenings.

That giant list was sent to Burnett creative types around the world for review and trimming. Many Burnetters contributed to the process, particularly: Oisten Borge (Norway), Carlos Chiesa (Brazil), Reiner Erfert (Germany), Phil Fiebig (Malaysia), Alessio Fronzoni (Italy), Miguel Angel Furones (Spain), Ross Goldsack (New Zealand), Bob Koslow (USA), Anny-Claude Lemeunier (France), Stan May (Australia), Nils Petter Nordskar (Norway), Juan Carlos Romero (Argentina), Ed Russell (USA), Mitsuhiko

Sasao (Japan), Bill Smith (then in Japan), and Albert Winninghoff (the Netherlands).

The list was also scrutinized by creative and advertising industry luminaries outside of Leo Burnett including Norman Berry of Ogilvy and Mather, Peter Bigg of the British TV Advertising Awards, Jeremy Bullmore of WPP Group, Michael Demetriadis and Jimmy and Ellen Smyth of the Clio Awards, Agustin Elbaile of Casadevall Pedreno & PRG, Cliff Freeman of Cliff Freeman & Partners, Walter Lurzer of Lurzer's Archive, Washington Olivetto of W/Brasil, Charles Sciberras of the International Advertising Federation, John Webster of BMP/DDB Needham, and Anthony Vagnoni of *Advertising Age*.

The Creative Exchange winnowed the choices to 193 wonderful candidates, then hijacked Leo Burnett's fourteen-member Global Product Committee to screen them. Ten commercials were instant winners. The rest were selected from those that broke through in a category, won local award shows, or made the short list at Cannes.

In December 1995, *Advertising Age*'s *Creativity Magazine* ran "The Mother of All Reels" list in a cover story. Professionals and aficionados chimed in with forgotten pearls such as Chevrolet's "Baseball, Hot Dogs, Apple Pie," which the legendary Bill Bernbach once called the greatest commercial ever made. "Edition Two" was released a year later with seven changes—some omitted pearls and some new spots.

And, of course, the current edition of this book contains several other changes. The advertising industry produces brilliant work every year: the campaigns contained in these pages will never fade in their power, but there are clearly more chapters to be written.

—Michael Conrad

CONTENTS

CONTENTS

INTRODUCTION

In May 1989, in the pale pink conference room at Saatchi & Saatchi's New York headquarters, I was a guinea pig in a psychological probe. While research types sprawled in swivel chairs behind a two-way mirror, a clinical psychologist quizzed me about how I felt when my hair looked great—and when it didn't. At his suggestion, I conjured up hair-care fairy tales and cast parts like genie, savior, and Tinkerbell (sprinkling handfuls of gold dust) in a dream-play about shampoo and conditioner. In the course of this inquiry, my interlocutor scuttled down path after mental path to learn not just how I felt when my hair looked great and when it didn't, but about *any* vestigial feelings I had about those locks.

I did not feel repelled by this cultural anthropologist, as he later identified his profession, nor by the advertising for Helene Curtis shampoo that later incorporated his findings. But I've little doubt that Vance Packard (and those he influenced) would have been outraged. In his 1957 best-seller, *Hidden Persuaders*, Packard compared this kind of motivational research to witchcraft that exploited consumers' frailties and fears, manipulated their minds, and demonically created a hunger for new products without regard to people's *real* needs and desires.

Rather than seeing commercials or the research that shapes them as insidious, I confess, I see them as artful—a no-bones-about-it reflection of our times. And I see myself as an advertising anthropologist. I've never watched an episode of *ER* or *Seinfeld* all the way through, but I could probably describe all the ads that ran on them. My addiction is not that of an ad-world insider, nor that of a layman looking for laughs between program segments. Instead, I watch because I am mesmerized by the advertising's innards, the veins and sinew that give the work strength and body. How did that ad reach out and *touch* me? How did it get me to buy?

I wasn't always eager to dissect advertising. When I began writing about the industry, first at *Advertising Age* and then the "On Madison Avenue" column at *New York* magazine, it was a good job, but it blossomed into a passion, partly fueled by the enormous impact the industry I followed had on our culture. Nick at Nite has scored with its advertising favorites from old. People watch the Super Bowl as much for the ads as for the action. And, recognizing that the advertising is often every bit as vital as the programming, in 1998 the Emmys bestowed their first award on a prime-time TV commercial.

The conundrum has always been whether advertising leads popular culture or reflects it. To my mind, however, the point is moot, like the chicken and the egg. Whichever comes first, the next follows so quickly and so inexorably that the two are incomprehensibly intertwined in an eternal pas de deux. More than movies or TV programming, advertising holds a mirror up to show us who and what we are—or long to be. The language of advertising becomes our vernacular; their dress, our wardrobes, their mores, our customs (albeit sometimes exaggerated).

So when representatives from Random House's Times Books and Leo Burnett asked me to chronicle the evolution and impact of this mother of all advertising reels, I considered it Christmas come early. Here was an opportunity to do vocationally what I'd been doing avocationally for years, and with a greatly expanded base—the world, from the earliest days of TV to now. That this assortment was selected from the industrywide Great Commercials Library and winnowed down by creative directors practically guaranteed what I'd be slurping was cream.

Much of this cream I'd never seen before, and probably most Americans won't have either. Only forty-two winners on the list were made in the USA. (Dozens more made the semifinals. I couldn't let some slip by unacknowledged, so I've tipped my hat to them in the final chapter.) The second-largest group (twenty-eight) came from the U.K., followed by France (eight); Japan and Spain (each with four); Norway and the Netherlands (each with 3); Sweden and Brazil (each with two), and one each from Singapore, New Zealand, Switzerland, and Germany. So this was for me both a walk down memory lane and an introduction to a whole new world of advertising.

Rather than serving them up chronologically, the ads are categorized by technique, proof positive there are many ways to tell a story and coax a smile. Legendary adman David Ogilvy once listed ten kinds of advertising approaches that are uncommonly good in changing people's brand preference. Donald Gunn, now head of the International Advertising Festival, who as senior vice president and worldwide creative director of creative resources at the Leo Burnett Company in London was the architect of the list, came up with his own, more contemporary categorizations.

This list honors aesthetics more than effectiveness in moving product, but this was no conventional beauty contest. Gunn said these ads expand our mind and deflate our ego and maybe change the way we think about advertising. They took a strong-selling proposition and did more than just communicate it. They translated it, enhanced it, served it to customers in a fresh, engaging, surprising, and unusually persuasive way. They moved us. These commercials have been admired and envied as breakthroughs, not just in their category but in all advertising, worldwide. In short, they've commandeered a place in our psyche. And they've done it by being both artful and artistic.

Indeed, the ads contained in this book may be to coming centuries what Giotto's paintings were to the Renaissance, the glimmering of a bold new way of expression. For most of my life, I shrank from the prospect of selling. It seemed debasing. Two decades of writing about advertising—and of living life in the modern world—has convinced me otherwise. Life today is about selling: selling products, selling ideas, selling ourselves. Selling is the language of our time and advertising is its boldest manifestation. Like it or not, it is a pure expression of the world we live in today.

If Michelangelo were alive today, he'd probably be working on Madison Avenue.

—Bernice Kanner
March 1999

THE 100 BEST TV COMMERCIALS

... AND WHY THEY WORKED

CHAPTER ONE

SHOW AND TELL

In 1998, in a one-second commercial, a bullet pierces a Master Lock: the lock remains intact. That shot-lock image is embedded in America's psyche along with Master Lock's tough-under-fire scenario. That product-as-hero story is proof positive of the power of "demo" advertising. Seeing is believing. If a picture is worth a thousand words, a well-done demonstration is often better than ten thousand verbal repetitions of the product's virtues.

Gifted marketers have gone beyond the Veg-O-Matic it-slices-it-dices and Bounty quicker-picker-upper formats to hone a single benefit and make the product the star in different ways. "Torture tests" have kept Timex ticking and Samsonite thumping. Heinz "lost" a ketchup race by being demonstrably slower (i.e.: thicker) than other brands. Johnson & Johnson proved its Band-Aids stuck by lifting an egg out of boiling water with one. An operatic tenor shatters glass with a high note—is it live or Memorex?

In side-by-side comparisons, the Energizer Bunny keeps going and going, long after rivals conk out. Years ago Scott toilet tissue unfurled two rolls until its generic rival ran out to prove it had more sheets per roll. The Pilkington glass man and VW engineers literally put their lives on the line for their products—ready to take a bullet or be run down if the glass or brakes fail. Even the prosaic before-after technique has been made enchanting in the hands of Cheer's deadpan mascot.

Artful demonstration commercials don't target a specific audience, don't rely on high jinks or argument, and are usually inexpensive to make. Their message is often clear without words, making them effective worldwide. Often they operate without a net: no background diversion, visual distractions, or extraneous elements to take your mind from the demonstration.

Sometimes, that's a disadvantage. In a 1954 live demo spot, Betty Furness couldn't pry open a jammed door of a new frost-free Westinghouse refrigerator. Ultimately the cameraman had to cut away from the fridge so a stagehand could free the door. Furness nonetheless kept her cool.

HAVE WE GOT A SUITCASE FOR YOU . . .

American Tourister's gorilla warfare on soft luggage

A gorilla in a cage is given an American Tourister suitcase, which he proceeds to violently toss around, jump on, drop from the ceiling, and ruthlessly abuse. With obvious and malicious enjoyment the gorilla grunts, howls, and roars. Meanwhile, the voice-over associates with this animalistic behavior the real-world abuse your luggage will take: "Dear clumsy bellboys . . . brutal cabdrivers . . . careless doormen . . . ruthless porters . . . savage baggage masters . . . and all butter-fingered luggage handlers all over the world . . . have we got a suitcase for you . . . American Tourister. From $20."

AMERICAN TOURISTER

GORILLA

DOYLE DANE BERNBACH, USA, 1969

Storyboard

The idea actually came to Doyle Dane Bernbach's creative director, Roy Grace, when he was in the shower. Consumers were increasingly opting for flexible, soft-sided bags that squeezed neatly under an airline seat and avoided potentially devastating baggage carousels, but American Tourister offered only heavy, molded-plastic luggage. Grace had to provide a rationale for buying such unfashionable items. The rationale turned out to be durability; the gorilla's abuse, the tool to demonstrate it. "In my youthful ignorance I had no idea that gorillas are basically not trainable, rare, sensitive, unpredictable, and very, very testy animals," Grace said twenty-seven years later.

The only "gorilla" available was actually a king chimpanzee and former circus performer, Oofi, residing in the Mexico City Zoo. A DDB team headed down for a one-day shoot. They threw the bright red suitcase in the cage and watched hopefully as Oofi picked it up by the handle and ate the luggage tag. He set it down, jumped on it—and then walked away. For hours, as the camera rolled, nothing more happened. His trainer tried to stimulate Oofi's participation with an electric prod—these were the days before the Humane Society sent agents to oversee commercial shoots—but Oofi just went into a corner of his cage.

They had a female gorilla in heat rub against the suitcase; nothing.

They packed his food into the suitcase while he watched. No effect.

The DDB team was feeling desperate when someone in the crowd that had gathered started to cheer for Oofi. The chimp perked up. The crowd began shouting "Oofi, Oofi" and, amazingly, the old circus pro began to perform. He jumped. He stomped. He beat his chest.

The spot, which cost $33,000 to produce, ran for fifteen years. All that changed on it was the super indicating the price. "Today, with computers, you could have an elephant walk on a tightrope or a building walk down a street, but back then, this was real and absurd," Grace said. "Things like this just don't happen. A gorilla doesn't take a suitcase and bang it."

The campaign ultimately became a victim of its own success: it had come to stand for all hard, molded luggage (many consumers believed the ads pitched Samsonite, whose own ads showed the Pittsburgh Steelers pummeling luggage). More to the point, by 1983, two-thirds of American Tourister's line was soft luggage. No longer top banana, and despite a closetful of awards, the "ape" went the way of the heavy, hard-sided suitcases he had thumped around during the "lug age."

GLUES EVERYTHING

Araldite sticks to a proven technique

ARALDITE

HAMMER AND NAIL

MELROPHA BASLE (DIRECT), SWITZERLAND, 1975

The scene opens on two Araldite tubes lying near a strip of plastic and a little spatula. A hand squeezes equal amounts from each tube onto a plastic strip and mixes them with the spatula. The camera cuts to a hand bringing a broken hammer on to the scene and smearing some of the mixture on broken cross sections of each piece. The only sound is the man whistling. He presses two parts of the hammer together and sets them down. Next, hands bring a nail that's broken in two into the set-up—and he similarly joins them together. The title over the same shot announces (in French) "Five minutes later." A hand picks up the hammer and nail and proceeds to hammer the nail into a wooden tabletop with five vigorous hits. The announcer says over the final shot: "Araldite glues everything—one time does it."

The *Guinness Book of World Records* lists Araldite, the epoxy-based glue from Ciba Geigy Basle AG, as the strongest adhesive in the world. Glue's main attribute is, of course, sticking power, so in this commercial for Araldite, the company aimed to drive that point home simply and dramatically.

This demonstration was stunningly effective, but it was only part of a long line of fantastical glue ads. In the U.K. in the early seventies, the same company advertised Araldite's strength by gluing a car to the girders of a building—and letting it hang there for ten days.

In France around the same time, Super Glue-3 became the brand leader with ads that demonstrated how well it bonded; the admen applied it to the announcer's shoes and hung him upside down from the ceiling, from which position he delivered his sales pitch.

And Americans have their own version of bonding magic. In 1973 Krazy Glue suspended a construction worker from a steel beam by his hard hat. He hung there for fifteen years (at least in the ads). Today, more than 90 percent of Americans recognize the hanging man. "Even though people buy Krazy Glue to make small household repairs on cups, dishes, jewelry, toys, and drawer knobs, the idea of tensile strength attracts them," said Krazy Glue senior product manager Dick LeBlanc. "People want reliability, speed, and simplicity, but because few brands advertise, glue is a low-awareness category. We need a wow factor to wake them up."

In Spain several years later, the Casadevall Pedreno agency created a "wow factor" commercial for Talen Rubber Cement flexible glue in which the adhesive must work a miracle in an extremely delicate situation. It seems two young nuns have discovered an appendage of Michelangelo's "David" has broken off: Mother Superior leads the blushing acolytes back to the scene to restore the statue's manliness.

A SPLASH OF COLD WATER

Procter & Gamble's soap opera with a happy ending

As an aria from Catalani's La Wally *grows gradually to a crescendo, a stern, bespectacled, and unremarkable-looking man whisks a dirty handkerchief into a cocktail shaker, briskly adds water, several scoops of ice, and just a small dash of Cheer, then shakes the concoction vigorously. A super reads, "We do not recommend trying this demonstration with any other detergent." The deadpan demonstrator removes the handkerchief and it is white as new. The voice-over and super both note: "Nobody cleans in cold like all-temperature Cheer."*

CHEER

DIVA

LEO BURNETT, USA, 1988

In the late 1960s, when the synthetics revolution left those doing the laundry confused about which temperatures and detergents to use for which garments, Procter & Gamble was able to carve out an "all-temperature" niche for Cheer laundry detergent. The campaign ultimately helped it become the second-best-selling detergent, but by the mid-eighties, consumers had figured out that pretty much all detergents work in most temperatures and they were being lured instead by new liquid detergents. All-temperature Cheer's share began to crumble; P&G turned to the Leo Burnett agency for help repositioning the brand.

" 'All-temperature' was no longer distinctive and therefore not persuasive," said Gerry Miller, creative director on the account. But research showed that more loads were being washed in cold water to save energy, and more colors were cropping up in each load. Cheer had a technological advance to demonstrate: the detergent could clean well even in very cold water. "After reassessing the situation, we decided to focus on cold-water cleaning with the secondary theme of color protection," Miller said.

By accident, the ad team came upon the product development group throwing a bucket of ice into a washing machine to test how it cleaned a load of laundry. "We extrapolated that to a tabletop setting, a single garment, and a before-your-eyes stain, added [*Second City* comedy alumnus] Jobe Czerny, and came up with mime theater," Miller said.

P&G was at first reluctant to use opera music, fearing it was too high-brow, but eventually came around to the idea that opera, with its overblown theatrical melodrama, was the ideal way to puncture the mock seriousness of what was happening on screen. The result was a mesmerizing, humorous way to serve up a relevant strategy to women (the target for virtually all detergent advertising). Cheer's ice-cube torture test brought new life to a category dominated by slogan advertising like "ring around the collar" or comparison commercials highlighting the intransigence of different stain types. While "Diva" adhered to the standard packaged-goods formula of product as solution, its gimmick of a little bald guy mixing detergent and water in a cocktail shaker expressed the obligatory theme of dirt versus clean in a refreshing, attention-getting way. Other iterations followed—eight in all. In the first sequel, Czerny wipes a conspicuous lipstick mark off his cheek with the white scarf he's dramatically removed from around his neck. To the strains of tango music, he does the Cheer demo. In another, he launders a clip-on tie smeared with Chinese food.

In two years, Cheer's market share grew from 6.4 percent to 7.4 percent—but by 1990, consumers had finally realized that most brands did the job. A new strategy was required: P&G relaunched the detergent with a "color guard" emphasis. Czerny remained, bemused and silently demonstrating the detergent's performance after thirty washings to the background sound of a tennis match—"Dirt goes. Color stays longer. Great for cotton." The likable Cheer Man reversed share declines, enabled Cheer to sell at a premium price, and all image ratings went up, the company says. Today Cheer remains the second-best-selling powdered detergent in the country with almost an 8 percent share of the more than $4 billion a year laundry-detergent category. Procter & Gamble says that Cheer's share has grown 25 percent since the ads premiered more than a decade ago.

BEFORE THE BUNNY

National Battery's toy fireman keeps going, and going, and going, and . . .

A National Battery is snapped into place in a plastic toy fireman while a voice announces (in Japanese) that the National Neo-Hightop challenge is to climb up a skyscraper. While upbeat music plays, the toy begins climbing up a fluorescent-yellow ladder attached to a red fire engine. As the camera pans up the ladder, we see that it extends all the way up the side of a tall building. The camera continues to follow the toy on its seemingly endless trip. Shots of city life, including traffic below and planes overhead, are interspersed until the fireman reaches the top of the building. Here he uses his water hose to put out a smoldering cigarette—then turns to the camera and says, "Did you see me? I am long lasting and strong." A super and voice-over repeat: "Long-lasting battery. National Neo-Hightop."

MATSUSHITA ELECTRIC

LITTLE FIREMAN

HAKUHODO COMPANY, LTD., JAPAN, 1983

This sixty-second spot tickled the audience with its cute approach to demonstrating lasting performance. The diminutive toy, facing a seemingly herculean task with unflagging energy, seems a precursor to Eveready's pink Energizer Bunny, the relentless hare who began drumming his way into American culture six years later.

According to the agency, the audiences most responded to the strange juxtaposition of the toy fireman and the real-life airplane. The building selected was one near Osaka Airport. The team had a hard time getting approval from the building owner and the production company, because of the possible danger in setting up a ladder on the building wall. The agency was rejected by two building owners before finally receiving an approval.

After it became a hit commercial, other versions of "Little Fireman" were developed into a series that ran for three years, very much as the Energizer Bunny became a part of American culture. The spots are still aired occasionally today. The campaign eventually extended to include a premium goods giveaway of the fireman doll. Sales and brand awareness climbed as people anticipated the next challenge for the fireman doll, and the next premium offered.

IT TAKES A LICKING

A Timex motto proves durable

TIMEX

ACAPULCO DIVER

WARWICK & LEGLER, USA, 1962

The scene opens with a respected, real-life reporter on a hilltop overlooking a cove:

"This is John Cameron Swayze reporting for Timex in Acapulco, Mexico. Just behind me you can see the rugged face of the famous La Perla cliffs, and that man is Raul Garcia, high-diving champion of the world. Strapped to his hand is a Timex waterproof watch. In a moment, that watch will take quite a jolt as Garcia hits that water at more than eighty-five miles an hour. He's ready."

Garcia arcs and dives with a resounding splash.

"How about that!" exclaims Swayze.

As Garcia swims back, Swazye primes viewers: "Now, as soon as he gets out of the water, we'll take a look at that watch. Now, there. Now here he comes to our camera."

Garcia climbs up the rocks. "Can we bring that watch up close, please. Well, there you are!" Swayze proclaims. "It took a licking and kept on ticking."

The watchwords in 1960 were precision and durability, and this ninety-second spot went a long way to implanting those ideas into watch buyers' psyches—if a Timex could take this licking and keep on ticking, surely it could survive the rigors of ordinary life. Even in the early days of TV, when people believed commercials more, Timex was careful to prove the demonstration was real, using a single long take to show that the same watch was used throughout.

As powerful as "Acapulco Diver" was at the time, however, it was not unique. In 1955, Bulova Watch Company used the same formula to lend credibility to an over–Niagara Falls torture test. In that spot, newscaster Lyle Van narrates as a Bulova is attached to a weighted ball: "Watch it; it's going over . . . down into that raging torrent . . . buffeted and jolted by the force of that terrific current . . . and here it is still ticking away!"

Nonetheless, it was Timex that made such tests its signature, with Swayze announcing "Takes a licking but keeps on ticking" through twenty-two years of torture tests, including trips through a washing machine's spin cycle and the family pet's digestive tract.

When Swayze retired in the mid-seventies, Timex advertising went off in several different directions, said C. Michael Jacobi, then company president. At first, technology and gadgetry were the craze, then the time watches told seemed less important than the status look they sold. Timex tried apple pie, special effects, and new wave approaches until, in 1989, research convinced the company to revive the slogan and the torture tests. (Virtually all of the two thousand consumers Timex asked in a survey remembered the "takes a licking" theme.)

This time, however, the campaign had a satiric twist and different ad agency, Fallon McElligott. In one spot, a native tribesman lowers a watch wrapped around a chicken drumstick into the piranha-packed Amazon River. When he lifts the concoction out, the watchband is all but consumed—but the watch is still ticking. In another, two bulging sumo masters wrestle with no discernible effect on the Timex taped to one's tummy. Timex also revived its original diver. In 1990, Raul Garcia was still plunging off the same Acapulco cliff. Timex used him in a print testimonial ad.

Timex became the best-selling watch brand within a decade of its first appearance on the market in 1950. It remained the watch to watch through the 1960s and 1970s, accounting for more than half of all watches sold for less than $100. It remains the no. 1 watch today. Today, according to ad director Susie Watson, "even with the myriad of brands and clutter" a third of all so-called mid-priced watches bought in the country are from Timex—and 98 percent of Americans still remember its name and lickin'-tickin' theme.

WATCH THE BIRDIE

Union Carbide's Super Insulation saves the day

A hand deposits a chirping chicken into a small box. An announcer says: "This little box has been built with Union Carbide's Super Insulation, which isn't much to look at. Just a layer of paper, a layer of foil, a layer of paper and so on. As thick or as thin as you need it. Enclosed in a vacuum. But when it comes to keeping something cold or hot, or keeping something from getting cold or hot, it's 25 to 100 times better than anything we've had before."

While the announcer talks, the metallic-looking box has been immersed with tongs in a cauldron of boiling water. The voice-over continues: "One inch of Super Insulation inside the walls of a railroad car can keep liquid hydrogen at 420 degrees below zero all the way from New York to Los Angeles. A half inch of it can be 2,000 degrees on one side and cool to the touch on the other. I'll tell you what: You could put a Super-Insulated container of coffee in your freezer and take it out a month later and it would still be hot."

UNION CARBIDE

CHICK

YOUNG & RUBICAM, USA, 1967

11

At this point the box is removed from the hot water. The voice-over continues, "If you don't think it's as good as we say it is, watch the birdie."

The chick emerges from the box, good as new and chirping.

A super notes: "Union Carbide: the Discovery Company."

"Union Carbide made this incredible stuff and we were seeking something fragile to prove it really did insulate," said Neil Tardio, the spot's producer. When they first talked about using live baby chicks, however, everyone was nervous, not certain if the insulation would really work. "We talked about testing it first, but decided that the rehearsal was really the test and that we should just shoot that," recalls Tardio.

The commercial was shot in thirty takes in a New York studio with 110 chicks on hand. At the end of the first two-minute shoot, when the box opened, "we were all floored and everyone in the place applauded," recalled Tardio. From the reaction of the first five chicks, the team learned that they'd only go into the box once. At day's end, all 110 of the chicks were returned, unharmed, to the farm.

"Chick" debuted on Walter Cronkite's *20th Century* TV show and, in addition to putting Union Carbide on the map, it generated thousands of orders from NASA and from research universities. "Chick" ran for a year and was retired when competitive companies discovered and advertised products that surpassed it.

Union Carbide went on to dramatically demonstrate its other products. In one spot, a beautiful deaf girl from New Jersey can hear with the help of a device Union Carbide had invented. Wearing earphones amplified by this equipment, the little girl listens to the old English song "Cockles and Mussels" and breaks into a smile. These commercials attracted attention because of their stark simplicity and all-on-the-line honesty. "There were no tricks, they were educational, and they moved people," said Tardio.

THE MAN WHO DRIVES THE SNOWPLOW

The Volkswagen's transformation into the people's car

A door opens and a man's shoe steps outside into an arc of light, breaking the snow crust. Headlights go on, an engine comes to life, and a Volkswagen Beetle surges through the snowy mist of this black-and-white-filmed landscape. A male voice asks, "Have you ever wondered how the man who drives the snowplow drives to the snowplow? This one drives a Volkswagen." He adds, "So you can stop wondering." The shoe print reappears and now the snowplow roars to life, out of its garage on its appointed rounds, leaving the VW poised in the picture-perfect three-quarter head shot that will become the norm for car advertising for the next two decades.

VOLKSWAGEN

SNOWPLOW

DOYLE DANE BERNBACH, USA, 1963

In 1949, when Volkswagen first brought the Beetle here, Americans ignored the odd-looking car. But after Doyle Dane Bernbach's legendary campaign, sales rocketed. By 1970, more than half a million "Bugs" crowded the streets, making VW the top-selling importer in America. Not one element of the car's design or engineering had changed, but the Beetle had been transformed by brilliant advertising from an oddity conceived by Adolf Hitler to a popular, lovable fixture of American life.

That transformation was not easy. The standard auto ad at the time showed artfully elongated cars in lush settings with models in diaphanous gowns draped over their hoods. Narrators boasted of superior performance or suggested visions of virility or romance. Art director Helmut Krone recalls that when he, legendary creative director William Bernbach, and copywriter Julian Koenig returned from VW's production facilities in Germany, they'd no idea how to present the stubby, clearly nonvirile car. Ed Russell, then account manager, came to the rescue by developing several counterintuitive "unique selling propositions"—the VW's simplicity and economy, its traction-enhancing rear engine, and its resistance to change. Based on those propositions, Bernbach decided on an off-beat campaign based on self-deprecating humor that turned the car's liabilities into virtues.

The spot was filmed for an (even then) incredibly low cost of $3,500, and highlighted the car's chief virtues: its reliability, durability, indeed, invincibility. "It was a time of three-toned De Sotos and American car makers bringing out new models each year to make you feel you were driving an old car, and here was Volkswagen saying it doesn't have to be that way," said Bob Levenson, who wrote "Snowplow." "There were no famous people, no big-time production values, and no inflated boasts. You would have had to say VW gets through the snow ten thousand times to sink in, but one simple scenario made it indelible."

VW approved the shoot in early spring: the production team hustled to find a locale with sufficient snow and came up with the high Alpine meadows near Geneva. All the roads had been well plowed so the team created their own, driving the car parallel to lines of utility poles that traversed open fields. In precomputer days, that meant each location could be used for one take only. That meant several days of moving around in search of trackless "roads."

"Snowplow" ran for only six months, Levenson recalled. "It was a question of money; we had basically a print campaign." But this witty, minimalist commercial was so "gettable," said Levenson, that it one-upped the snow-stalled competition and ran even in countries where it never snows. (The spot was shot with two cars: one had the American-market bumpers, trim, and signal lights, and a Michigan license plate.)

In 1979, VW stopped importing Beetles into the U.S. When a new Beetle returned in 1998, ads from Arnold Communications re-created the classic campaign for the nineties with short, powerful copy points and crisp, uncluttered product photography—and no spokespeople. One proclaimed "Less Flower, More Power." Another asked, "0–60?" and answered, "Yes."

CHAPTER TWO

THE SOUND OF MUSIC

Henry Wadsworth Longfellow called music the universal language of mankind and Thomas Carlyle described it as the speech of angels. A well-known Madison Avenue adage: If you don't have something good to say, sing it. Psychologists say people get more thrills from music than from sex, and advertisers have long recognized music's power to attract attention and carry a message. McCollum Spielman Research found that music dramatically increases the ability of viewers to remember a brand name or recall a commercial.

But more than "saying," music is about feeling. Muted in the background or delivering the actual pitch, music can indeed point out a product's benefits, but its real forte is in establishing emotional links. Music can move us to tears or to dance, to battle or to the bedroom. It can excite, relax, energize, antagonize, encourage, and even make us covetous: it can induce a mood. And it can help the medicine go down—music can help listeners process complex thoughts.

Music can turn heads, differentiate products, and punch up weak dramatic scenes ("It's the Real Thing"). It can act as a mnemonic device to help people remember a name ("Roto-Rooter, that's the name . . ."). Or remember a promise ("Just like a good neighbor . . ."). Music can add value to a product or create a winning personality for one ("When you've got the time, we've got the beer").

It can provide continuity, bridging from one marketing strategy to another ("We do it all for you" was arranged hundreds of ways). And music can change minds. When GE trilled "We bring good things to life," we no longer saw the company as an impersonal appliance manufacturer, but as a warm-hearted space age competitor who brings Mom a refrigerator for Christmas. And before Marvin Gaye's "Grapevine," California raisins were, well, simply dried-up grapes.

Used incorrectly, of course, music can backfire. It can distract from the advertiser's real message or reduce the believability of a spot. And, worst of all, if people don't like the song, they probably won't buy the product associated with it.

AMERICAN AS APPLE PIE

An automotive anthem offers America refuge from turbulent times

While country music plays, we are shown various shots of baseball games, hot dogs, and apple pie, and also shots of past and present Chevys. An unseen male singer belts out:

    "In the years that I been livin' lot of things have surely changed.
    Lots of things have come and gone, some even came back again.
    But through all the many changes, some things are for sure.
    And you know that's a mighty fine feelin', kinda makes you feel secure.

    'Cause I love baseball, hot dogs, apple pie, and Chevrolet.
    Baseball, hot dogs, apple pie, and Chevrolet.
    They go together in the good ole U.S.A.,
    Baseball, hot dogs, apple pie, and Chevrolet!"

    Voice-over: "In case you're wondering, this commercial has been brought to you by baseball, hot dogs, apple pie, and America's favorite car."

    Super: (Chevrolet logo) "Eye it; try it."

While other manufacturers were stressing their cars' features—power, engineering, economy, comfort—Chevrolet was selling emotion and trust. It didn't rap people on the head to declare that it was number one, and that one out of four new cars bought was a Chevy. Instead, Chevy chose to remind Americans that it is the car most associated with everyday American life in an upbeat way that became an anthem.

The first version of "Baseball, Hot Dogs, Apple Pie" was written as a radio spot in 1970, the heyday of the Vietnam War. The mission was for Chevy to "charge its way back into a position of trust after a year in which people believed nothing," said senior copywriter Jim Hartzell. He originally intended the spot to be a straight interview piece, and came up with an elegant script: "America, what's your favorite sport? Baseball. Sandwich? Hot dog. Pie? Apple. And what's your favorite car, America? Chevrolet." The straight format felt flat, however, so the firm called in Ed Lubanski, a New York and Nashville composer and singer who took the script to Nashville, wrote the music, and produced a demo with himself as vocalist.

The campaign evolved through several radio versions, and made the move to TV in 1974. The agency was careful never to allow the spots to contain slick sight gags, implausible situations, or exotica of any kind. "We tried to maintain a just-plain-folks attitude about the car and its public," explained David E. Davis Jr., then the director of Chevrolet creative services at Campbell-Ewald and later founder and editor of *Automobile* magazine.

CHEVROLET

BASEBALL, HOT DOGS, APPLE PIE

CAMPBELL-EWALD, USA, 1974

If you really love , , and please signal us by standing up midway through the 7th inning. thank you.

From print campaign

17

"We went for a warm, wiggly feeling rather than the belly laugh. We wanted a car that meant something to its owner, a car that had a personality. And we've been able to do that since 1955."

Campbell-Ewald had intended a big rollout of the spot, but it ran only a few dozen times. "Chevrolet management never greenlighted it, and it ran very sporadically," said Davis. "They were always uncomfortable with it, thinking that it was too lighthearted and too different from what they had been doing."

The chorus, however, lived on. Organists played it at ballparks while airplanes flew overhead with banners. And other car companies pirated it. In Australia the mantra became "football, meat pies, kangaroos, and Holden cars." Back in the USA Ford Motor Company paid homage with a similar spot featuring people at a picnic munching hot dogs and apple pies. The ad emphasized Mustang's virtues over its rival and closed with a dog eating a hot dog in the background.

BUYING COKE THE WORLD

Coca-Cola's global pitch for peace, love, and market share

COCA-COLA

HILLTOP

MCCANN-ERICKSON WORLDWIDE, USA, 1971

A veritable United Nations of young, fresh-faced people sing the well-know anthem while a helicopter-mounted camera pans back to reveal the throng.

"I'd like to buy the world a home and furnish it with love
Grow apple trees and honey bees and snow white turtle doves.
I'd like to teach the world to sing with perfect harmony
I'd like to buy the world a Coke and keep it company.
I'd like to see the world for once all standing hand in hand
And hear them echo through the hills for peace throughout the land.
That's the song I sing.
What the world wants today
A song of peace that echoes on and never goes away.
It's the real thing, what the world wants today."

Had Pan Am Flight 12 not been derailed by fog for an unexpected overnight stopover in Ireland in the winter of 1971, "Hilltop" might never have existed. It was there that young McCann-Erickson copywriter Bill Backer witnessed a large and varied group of passengers forgo their contentiousness over bottles of Coke. Moved by this cola-inspired show of solidarity, Backer jotted on a paper napkin the theme line for a commercial. The next day, at the Savoy Hotel in London, writer-musicians Billy Davis and Roger Cook helped flesh out the lyrics. And that very spring, on a hillside near Rome, young people from around the globe, clad in their national costumes and clutching bottles of Coke, and directed in sign language, sang a moving tribute to peace and love and world unity.

Actually, they lip-synched to the voices of a group called Eve Graham and the New Seekers, who had recorded the song that February for a radio spot that was met with "deafening silence from the public and with worse from the Coca-Cola bottlers," Backer recalled. The problem: "They felt it didn't sell hard enough." Backer, with senior account director Sid McAllister, reasoned that the singing had left too much to people's imagination, and the way to remedy that was by producing a commercial to flesh out the song.

The spot, which cost a then-hefty $225,000 to produce, almost didn't air. Foreign bottlers initially rejected it—indeed, Coca-Cola marketing director Paul Austin considered killing it early on because he found the words and sentiments treacly. But the united chorus of the world struck an emotional chord with the public. In the first week after the spot debuted, Coca-Cola said it received more than four thousand letters endorsing it. Many complained that the sixty-second spot was too short; some submitted their own additional verses. Other countries, dismissive at first, asked for versions in their own language. (The office in South Africa asked for a version without blacks, which McCann-Erickson declined to produce.) Local bottlers distributed 45-rpm copies of the recording, spawning two Top 40 versions, the original version, and a new version from the Hillside Singers. The two singles combined sold over a million copies by the end of 1971.

"Hilltop" ran for six years. The song was later used in a 1977 holiday commercial featuring young people holding candles in the shape of a Christmas tree on a Brazilian hillside. For a 1990 Super Bowl spot, Coca-Cola reconvened the original cast members plus their children for a nostalgic sequel. But praise was not universal. A trade magazine in London at the time bristled that the bottle of soda as social catalyst was in "questionable taste" and complained that Coca-Cola had put itself on too lofty a pedestal.

NEW BEER: GET OUT!

A sing-along salute to working-class indignation

COURAGE BEST BITTER

GERTCHA

BOASE MASSIMI POLLITT, U.K., 1979

The scene, a turn-of-the-century English pub, is shot in black-and-white in a single, uninterrupted take. All sorts of characters are drinking Courage Best Bitter Beer as a voice-over rattles off a tune:

"Now I'm a goin' back a few years, when pubners knew a bit about beer.

If it wasn't Courage Best, that's when you'd hear this strange protest."

The crowd voices its assent with a lusty "Gertcha!"

The singer continues: "Funny glasses with a little piece of ice . . ."

Again the chorus chimes in "Gertcha!"

"Anything that comes with lemon in a slice," the singer continues. Again, "Gertcha!"

"Fancy cocktails that are shaken and not stirred . . ."

"Gertcha!"

"Drinks with cherries that make you look absurd."

"Gertcha!"

"With your finger cocked to leave your friends impressed . . ."

"Gertcha!"

"Anything that ain't a pint of Courage Best."

"Gertcha!"

"Pint a pint of Best—pint a pint of Best."

"Gertcha!"

Perhaps more than any other category except automobiles, beer is sold on image more than on product benefits or attributes such as great taste—or less filling. Beer nameplates are identity badges: what you order at the bar says a lot about you. With that in mind, Courage, the second biggest beer producer in the U.K., decided to revive an old brand it hadn't been promoting, Best Bitter, with an ad that tapped into nostalgia for bygone days.

Boase Massimi Pollitt designed a campaign that seemed to be filmed in the 1930s. Shot in stark and authentic black and white, the spots used a music style called "rockney," a combination of rock and Cockney reminiscent of 1930s piano-based pub music. The lively sing-along was based on the then-current Chas & Dave hit "Gertcha," about a curmudgeonly father who doesn't like anything. It was reworded so his disdain was applied to any other drink except Courage Best. ("Gertcha" is Cockney slang for "get out.")

Courage took the pulse of its blue-collar audience with this witty-yet-pugnacious, anti-aspirational series. Despite the high production values

20

(Hugh Hudson, who'd shot *Chariots of Fire*, produced and directed it) the client had trouble accepting the spot. For one thing, it was different. "Most beer ads at the time showed lads in a pub with a joke in it. To do a musical in a pub was very unusual," said the spot's writer, John Webster. Then too, it seemed to counteract the company's recent modernization of its pubs. "They'd just spent millions refurbishing their pubs to look modern," Webster said, "and here we'd come up with a campaign that made them look like a pre-war spit and sawdust place." BMP ultimately prevailed, however, convincing Courage that they weren't selling the pubs, just the beer.

"Gertcha" was filmed in one uninterrupted take with a sweeping camera. In only three out of more than one hundred takes did all the singers join in on cue. It ran for two years, spawned a series of similar black-and-white musicals, and helped the brand flourish. The commercial was so popular, in fact, that Courage reprised it in 1992.

SNAP, CRACKLE . . . SOB!

Kellogg's operatic attention-getter

Four Italian children are seated at the dining room table as operatic music plays. "Great moments at breakfast, presented by Kellogg's Rice Krispies," the announcer says.

Mom takes her place as Dad bursts through the doors, flings himself into a chair, and booms in an operatic baritone, "Barbra, pass the Kellogg's Rice Krispies before it's all gone." But he is too late, the box is empty.

"Wha-ha-ha-ha-ha . . . No more Rice Krispies! We ran out of Rice Krispies," he sings in hilariously overwrought fashion. "My tears will not stop until I hear Snap, Crackle, and [sobbing] Pop!"

There is a knock on a glass door and Dad's intrusive mother-in-law arrives, toting a six-pack of cereal. "I've brought the Rice Krispies," she sings in a lusty soprano. "Enough to last at least two months. That's how long I'll be here . . ."

Dad, with mixed emotions, sings back, "It's her fifteenth visit so far this year!"

To his mother-in-law he groans, "Uhuhuhuhuhuh!"

To the Rice Krispies he sings happily, "Ahahahahahaha!"

Back to his mother-in-law, "Uhuhuhuhuhuh . . ."

KELLOGG

VESTI

LEO BURNETT, USA, 1969

Even with the flood of presweetened cereals in fetching shapes and colors coming on the market, Rice Krispies has prospered over the years with its animated, elfin noisemakers, Snap, Crackle, and Pop. Just as important, though, Rice Krispies also appealed to adults with a "light bounce" story. "We'd been telling people to put some 'Snap, Crackle, and Pop in their lives,' showing active people on the go, such as a policeman who directed traffic, and the benefits of rice as a good light grain that didn't weigh you down," recalls Joel Hochberg, who was copywriter for the operatic series. But with hundreds of types of cereal to choose from and on average two new ones being introduced each week, Kellogg wanted to try something else.

The safe course would have been to present the rice kernel as a good-tasting health benefit, but the Kellogg team had other ideas. "Joel and I both liked classical music and hit on the idea of trying to persuade people to think about the Rice Krispies in their pantry with a highbrow, intrusive spoof that was funny and would get their attention," remembers Don Keller, who was art director on the team. "We had no new news; this was reminder advertising." The resulting spot borrowed the melody from Leoncavallo's *Pagliacci*. The story, Hochberg says, was based on his own life—although much exaggerated. (When his then-mother-in-law saw the commercial she snapped, "I never visited you that often.")

A second spot, set to a theme from *Carmen*, featured Jamie Farr (who later turned up in *M*A*S*H*) as the matador. The last spot in the series was set to Puccini's *Madame Butterfly*. In it, a lieutenant in naval dress is offered a bowl of Rice Krispies—and chopsticks. Despite several awards and increased sales, Kellogg dropped the campaign after just a year and a half. The sixty-second spots were not only expensive to produce, they were also alienating at least a few consumers. "Some teachers and musicians thought we were exploiting wonderful music, and that it wasn't appropriate to sell cereal," Hochberg explained.

A CASE OF THE BLUES

Heineken sings a new song in an old campaign

A guy on his porch is trying to sing the blues: "Woke up this morning, the sun smiled down on me . . . 'The sun smiled on me?' That ain't the blues!"

His wife peeks out the window. "Oh, honey, that's cute," she says.

The singer strums again. "Oh, row, row, row your boat, happily down the stream . . . dang! That ain't the blues neither!"

It's hot so he opens a can of Heineken to cool himself off and thinks of new words when, miracle! his wife puts down her iron and pops her head out the window again. "What is this lipstick doing on your collar?" she asks.

"Honey, that ain't no lipstick," he improvises. "It's from shaving."

But she'll have none of it. "You're a liar," she screams as she gathers up her belongings and storms off. "I ain't never coming back," she shouts—just as the finance company comes by to repossess his car. His dog whimpers. It starts to rain.

"Sad is my first name, last name is misery," sings the man, finally finding his blues touch. "I lost my woman and the rain is coming down— oh yeah!"

His guitar string breaks.

Super: "Heineken: Refreshes the parts other beers cannot reach."

HEINEKEN

BLUES SINGER

LOWE HOWARD-SPINK, U.K., 1991

This musical celebration showed a down-and-outer and made good-natured fun of him. It also refreshed a campaign that had spanned two decades. "Blues Singer," directed by Alan Waldie, is dark but irresistible comedy, a legerdemain that swivels a mournful blues melody into a smirk of self-recognition. "Ain't life a bear?" we think as part of us identifies with the hapless masochist whose immediate problem is solved even as his life crumbles around him.

Before Heineken broke the mold in 1974, most beer advertising revolved around "blokes at the pub bantering with the beer maid or obligingly buying each other pints with lots of back slapping with manly laughter," said Adrian Holmes, chairman and CEO of Lowe Howard-Spink. "In contrast, Heineken showed beer refreshing a policeman's feet." (In 1981 Lowe Howard-Spink inherited the account from the Collett Dickenson Pearce agency.)

Actually, the first escapade in this antic campaign showed a mildly deranged piano tuner whose defective hearing was restored by a swig of Heineken. The first TV spot, shot by Vernon Howe, presented a "simple experiment" that examined "the effect of beer on the feet. Now, these feet have been walking all day and are very tired. We see that there is no movement in them . . . which is due to lack of refreshment. . . . So we administer the cold Heineken . . . wait a few seconds and we observe that the Heineken is already refreshing the feet . . . causing lively movement of the toes and activating the arches."

Dozens of variations followed showing somebody drinking a Heineken, which precipitates an extraordinary change—the more unexpected and daft the better. A flowery hat grows into a flower garden with butterflies. Humpty Dumpty's broken shell is restored thanks to Heineken. A droopy mustache turns upright; a turned-down nose turns up. And Emperor Nero, who "was unable to decide the fate of the contestants because his thumb was exhausted—after two weeks of continually watching the games," found that important body part similarly refreshed. As the campaign became more entrenched, the refreshing transformations became increasingly sophisticated.

Heineken came into the U.K. as an unknown brand, part of a new drinking lifestyle, a light lager versus a mainstay dark beer. Rather than compete in the same arena—beer as a man's end-of-day reward—Heineken took the different tact of humor, nonsense, and fantasy. "We were even able to work in a demonstration: have them drink it and something happens," gloated Waldie. Censors waved it by because the scenarios were so absurd no viewer would reasonably expect those kinds of transformations from the beer.

When Heineken client Anthony Simonds-Gooding first heard the concept on Aeroflot Flight SU 638 enroute to visit the Hermitage Museum, he declared it a breakthrough. The beer public declared it a bomb. "It completely failed research," said Holmes. "Consumers asked where are the lads and barmaids and where are the things that make us comfortable about beer advertising?" Critics charged that it wasn't beer advertising—that it was a biology lesson with its emphasis on unromantic appendages.

"But it took the main benefit of the product category—the generic commodity claim of refreshment—and made it the property of the brand," said Waldie. "That gave us a massive, enduring advantage over our competitors and added reassurance about its lager's continental origins."

The last "Refreshes the Parts" commercial came out in 1990 after more than one hundred executions. In it lonely supermarket carts that were stolen and subsequently abandoned come to life and return home. The store manager, who has been enjoying a refreshing Heineken, steps outside and discovers a parking lot full of prodigal trolleys.

The campaign spanned twenty-six years and turned a heretofore commodity beer into a brand leader. Women especially were charmed by it, said Waldie, "despite the fact that in blind tastings it never did well and people found it rather thin."

"Blues Singer" became one of the most popular of the series, but because of pricing problems, the brand share continued to slide. In 1994, after more than a quarter century, British distributor Whitbread, which saw Heineken become the brand leader on the basis of this innovative advertising, canned the campaign and the beer itself. It decided to concentrate on Heineken exported elsewhere and stopped advertising it in the U.K.

SEXY IN ANY LANGUAGE

Levi's puts the heat back into a fading brand

To the tune of Marvin Gaye's "I Heard It Through the Grapevine" a seedy, weedy youth enters a launderette, strips down to his underwear, and puts the lot, jeans included, into a washing machine. He sits down with a magazine to wait, giving his neighbor, a middle-aged housewife, a leer. She looks away in horror. Eventually he goes to get his laundry from the machine but, alas, his jeans have shrunken to toddler size and are in tatters.

The voice-over exclaims: "Translation needed."

Super: "Levi's Authorized Dealers. Garanterat Akta Levi's. Levi's 501's."

LEVI'S
LAUNDERETTE

BARTLE BOGLE HEGARTY, U.K., 1986

In 1984, Levi Strauss sales had tumbled from the glory days of the sixties and seventies, when denim was synonymous with youth and rebellion. Disillusionment had set in—along with punk rock and do-it-yourself fashion. Small, fashion-oriented brands were biting into its market share, and its image suffered from unsuccessful forays into children's wear and men's wear. Polyester Levi's Action Slacks, for example, signaled to core jeans buyers that Levi's were now their fathers' jeans.

Levi's decided to refocus on its key customers—the fifteen- to nineteen-year-old men who account for 30 percent of jeans purchases—to "insinuate the brand and its vocabulary back into the core," said John Hegarty, who art directed "Launderette."

The old lifestyle advertising had begun to seem irrelevant—and then insulting, Hegarty said. Levi's proposed using 501 commercials then playing in the United States, which had a personal-fit message for the original product from 1873. Both BBH and McCanns, Levi's agency in most of Europe, nixed them as too modern and middle-of-the-road for their markets.

Instead, they wanted advertising that addressed Europeans' interest in clothes with a genuine heritage. The original jean, indelibly associated with the birth of teenage culture in the fifties, made the slightly baggy look in the rear and the fabric bunching around the crotch the right look for today—and the only label for both the masses and trendy fashion leaders. And because the spots would run internationally they should not depend on words.

The idea to use "Grapevine" came to Hegarty as "a way of portraying the U.S. without being boring," he said. He'd hoped to recapture the zeitgeist of the 1950s but "Grapevine" was sixties music. Barbara Noakes, the agency's deputy creative director, was copywriter on the spot and Roger Lyons, film director.

BBH presented two music-based scripts in July 1985; both were approved immediately. The other, called "Bath" and set to music by Sam Cooke, featured a hero who appeared to be preparing for a Saturday night out. But the final shot revealed him lowering himself, in his shrink-to-fits, into a bath. Both ads debuted on Boxing Day, 1985.

BBH worked with the record companies to make sure singles of the music were reissued just as the commercials were launched. The label that owned the rights to "Grapevine" procrastinated, however, waiting until the ads had been running for weeks before re-releasing it. Even then it moved into the Top Ten singles charts in the U.K.

By the end of 1987, Levi's were hot again. Sales of 501's in 1987 were twenty times what they were in 1984, even with much steeper price tags, and brand share had soared.

Nick Kamen, who peeled off his clothes in "Launderette," became a star. Thousands of posters featuring him were stolen from shops. *Menswear* magazine credited the spot with making boxer shorts popular, estimating that some two million pairs were sold in 1986 as a result of the ad. The spot hit such a nerve that in its first year, twenty-three different TV programs in the U.K. aired it for free.

The advertising is very much part of the product's persona, said Hegarty. "Consumers buying a simple pair of jeans (albeit at a very fancy price) are buying a little bit of Nick Kamen, a little bit of mythical America, and a little bit of musical romance," he said.

BEFORE AND BEFORE

A Norwegian soft drink makes no promises

Olga Maria Mikalsen, a stately but eccentric older woman who fancies herself a singer, is a cappella butchering a version of "Happy Birthday" onstage when she stops to take a swig of Solo. In most commercials, the magic potion would make her a diva as melodious as Beverly Sills. But after a long draught of Solo she continues singing—in exactly the same out-of-tune way. The audience applauds. Then, the voice-over delivers the denouement: "Probably the only soft drink that cures nothing but thirst."

SOLO

SINGER

JBR MCCANN, NORWAY, 1994

I f any product is "anti-hero" it's the one in this counter-programming series for Solo. Norway's oldest soft drink (since 1934) positioned itself against the lifestyle sodas with whimsical "non-before-and-after" stories. Unhappy and untalented failures take a drink and voilà—instead of the expected dramatic transformation, nothing amazing happens: A biker pedaling feverishly is overtaken by a little old lady and other cyclists—despite sipping the orange nectar. A young man who can't get a condom on still can't after a swig of Solo. A wallflower at a dance remains solo despite drinking the stuff. An attractive woman drinking Solo in a cafe makes serious eye contact with a good-looking man at another table—until his boyfriend walks in and joins him. And the lead singer in a rock band tosses his empty Solo bottle into the audience and flings himself after—only to find that beyond the fourth row, where he lands, it's empty.

When JBR McCann took over the Solo account in 1992, Solo sales were in a skid. After seven consecutive years of slumping sales, its share had fallen to under 9 percent of the total drinks market, according to Solo's marketing manager, Jonn Arne Horpen. He said Solo had not differentiated itself from its competitors and was using the same kind of lifestyle marketing as much bigger spenders such as Coca-Cola, Fanta, and Pepsi. Frode Karlberg, the creative director and copywriter on the account, believed Solo had to do something totally surprising and completely different. "We wanted to distance Solo from the lifestyle, happiness-seeking advertising of major international brands so we came up with a promise to the people: no more lies, no more bull, the truth and nothing but the truth.

"Young Norwegians—fifteen to twenty-five year olds—who are the target audience, don't believe ad promises that any product will make them happier, prettier, or more popular," Karlberg said. "They know happiness is not to be found in a soft drink bottle. All it can do is quench the thirst."

Working with account executive Tormod Evang, art director Bjormn Smorholm, and film director Pal Sletaune, Karlberg initially produced posters alerting Norwegians to what was coming. One board showed a gloomy youth warning passersby that soft drinks cannot bring happiness

27

and that Solo would only tell the truth. "Singer" was the seventh commercial in this series.

Many people initially ridiculed the approach as "losers' advertising," according to Horpen. But things quickly turned around in Norway, the only place where Solo is sold. By 1995, two years after the campaign began, Solo's market share was back at 11 percent, the level it held in 1987, and it was growing 40 percent faster than the market in total. This was achieved with an ad budget less than one-fifth of Coke's.

"From 1993 through 1996 Solo beat Coke and the rest of the competition on all variables, including likeability, brand awareness, and brand acceptance," Karlberg said.

It also gave a boost to the career of Olga Marie Mikalsen. "Rumor has it she once rented Carnegie Hall at her own expense but success was limited," Karlberg said. Her audiences didn't exceed fifty people. But after the Solo commercial she released a CD and, now, as a resident in a nursing home in Oslo, she has had to hire a nurse to manage her appointments and appearances.

CHAPTER THREE

LIP SERVICE

W hile it's true that a picture may be worth a thousand words, it's equally true that a few well-crafted words can paint a very compelling pitch—and picture. Speech, artfully designed, can make an otherwise mundane commercial dramatic, sublime, and memorable. Indeed, if God is in the details, then advertising power is often in the dialogue.

Sometimes it's verbal legerdemain that turns an otherwise prosaic commercial into a remarkable feat, as Federal Express's fast-talking, absolutely-positively-get-it-there-yesterday executive so adroitly (and amusingly) demonstrated.

Sometimes it's the confessional and conspiratorial nature of the dialogue that lures us to eavesdrop. We listened, rapt and transfixed, by the *tranche de vie* characters and scenarios that John Hancock served up with its long-running "Real Answers" commercials.

Some scripted conversations have beguiled us into believing that what we were watching was real life. James Garner and Mariette Hartley's repartee on behalf of Polaroid's One Shot camera captured the playful barbs of a sparring couple in such an authentic way that many viewers were convinced they were actually married.

Sometimes it's the incongruous juxtaposition of words and action—the startling disconnect, as evidenced in Heineken's high-spirited "Water in Majorca" spot—that makes a commercial pop. And sometimes it's the surprise factor that keeps us cued: A Mates condoms commercial keeps us waiting, suspended with uncertainty—

will the young man escape unscathed, or die of embarrasment? And MCI clobbers us (and its rival) with the totally unexpected.

And sometimes it's the words that literally come out of the mouth that do the trick. Crest got us to focus on our mouths through our ears, presenting a starkly simple set—and a mouthful of teeth mourning their fallen comrade.

BAD TOOTH!

Crest casts out a kind character to corner the cavity market

The spot opens with men, representing teeth in a mouth, standing in a horseshoe formation dressed all in white as if they are engineers, all except one. Harold, the bad tooth, is dressed in brown.

"I'm sorry it finally happened," laments his downcast neighbor tooth. "Harold, I hate to see you go. You've been the best neighbor a tooth could have. We practically grew in together." He laughs ruefully. "At times we bit off more than we could chew."

"The caramels, the jawbreakers, the pizza pies . . ." Harold reminisces.

"Yeah, we've been through thick and thin," the neighbor recalls.

"Bitter and sweet," adds Harold.

The neighbor notes, "If only we'd been brushed."

"Yeah, yeah, I know, with a fluoride toothpaste like Crest. Maybe things would have been different."

"Harold, I'll miss yuh," the surviving tooth says, choked up. "And it all started with a little cavity."

The announcer interrupts the dead-tooth-walking scenario. "In your lifetime you can lose at least six teeth to cavities," he says as Harold steps out of the mouth. "To help fight cavities, brush with Crest. See your dentist regularly. Watch between-meal treats. Crest is accepted by the American Dental Association. Crest fights cavities so your teeth have a fighting chance."

The survivor tooth bids his final farewell. "'Bye, Harold. Things won't be the same without yuh!"

Super: "Crest fights cavities. So your teeth have a fighting chance."

CREST

GOODBYE, HAROLD (THE BAD TOOTH)

BENTON & BOWLES, USA, 1972

In 1956, Crest was introduced to the world as the first cavity-fighting toothpaste with fluoride. An ad at the time declared a "new era in preventive dental care" and that Crest, as "one of the milestones in modern medicine," was leading it.

By the time "Goodbye, Harold" rolled around in 1972, Crest had firmly rooted its position as a decay preventer into the American psyche. It had a 34 percent market share in 1972 and had been the number-one toothpaste since 1961, when the American Dental Association gave Crest's stannous fluoride formula its seal of approval. (Crest was not, however, the first fluoride toothpaste. Block Drug's Super Amm-I-Dent was, but it ultimately got lost in the Crest's hub-hub marketing blast. And Crest was *not* the only toothpaste with an ADA seal: Whitehall Laboratories' Kolynos and Colgate's Cue also had them.)

What's more, "Goodbye, Harold" was not Crest's most memorable advertising. That may have been the "Look, Ma, No Cavities" TV spot created by Benton & Bowles, the predecessor agency for D'Arcy Masius Benton & Bowles, in 1958. The 129-word commercial became both the product's positioning and claim—and a part of the vernacular. In that early advertising, a pigtailed blonde jumped out of a car in a suburban driveway, held up her dental report card, and gushed delightedly, "Look, Ma, no cavities." This was just the first of a series of different freckle-faced-kid creative approaches that Procter & Gamble used to keep Crest on top.

After the proud mom playlet came documentary demos. "Half my class used Crest and the other, ordinary toothpaste" was the proposition of one. Then the American Dental Association's Council on Dental Therapeutics came up with "Crest has been shown to be an effective decay preventing dentifrice that can be of significant value. . . ."

For the next fifteen years that "effective decay preventing dentifrice" was a part of Crest ads—even the Bad Tooth one. Despite the fact that the dialogue seemed so realistic and the tooth so anthropomorphic that the audience could believe a good tooth was really expressing regret and sadness for his boyhood chum's departure, the spot bombed in testing, recalled DMB&B chief Roy Bostock. He called it a good example of an award-winning spot that never built business.

Despite the sheer inventiveness of its commercials, the Crest story had run out of gas by the mid-eighties. At the time, rival Colgate was contending that its Ultra Brite toothpaste freshened breath as well as the leading mouthwash and that its Colgate MFP was at least equal to Crest in fighting tooth cavities. And Smithkline Beecham and Carter-Wallace claimed that their respective Macleans and Pearl Drops were low in abrasive danger.

But it was Lever Brothers that fired the most potent blasts at Crest's mast. It charged that Close-Up was more than just a cavity fighter: it was a breath-freshener, a tooth whitener, *and* a cavity fighter. And Aim warned mothers that "even children who brush with a fluoride still seem to get more than their fair share of cavities" but that, luckily, Aim's "unusually high dispersal rate" released the stannous fluoride faster than any other fluoride paste. And to encourage kids to brush, Aim's advertising boasted, "the formula was enhanced by flavoring compounds known to be especially appealing to children." Ads crowed about "astounding" results: in tests with 1,300 children, Aim was preferred more than two to one over the leading fluoride toothpaste.

Crest had cornered the cavity story and subsequent ads positioned it as "The dentist's choice. Crest protection." But when competition swarmed to appeal to mothers interested in protecting their children's teeth, and when fluoride stopped being as important and breath freshness and whiteness became more important, Crest lost its hammerlock on toothpaste sales. By

1997, Crest's share of the $1.5 billion toothpaste market had dropped to a 26.3 percent share.

In 1997 new advertising from DMB&B sought to play up the brand's all-American heritage by claiming everyone, no matter how old, is a "Crest kid."

In one spot, moms note that they are "Crest kids" who have been using the product since their own childhoods. A print ad took off on the popular "Got Milk?" campaign by asking "Got teeth?" John Nieman, worldwide creative director at DMB&B, called the new approach "more emotional and tongue in cheek than the clinical, dentists-approved approach of the recent past."

ABSOLUTELY, POSITIVELY

An air courier's new strategy arrives right on time

"Okay, Eunice, travel plans," a character named Spleen spews into the intercom at 450 words a minute. "I need to be in New York on Monday, L.A. on Tuesday, New York on Wednesday, L.A. on Thursday, New York on Friday, got it?"

Eunice gets it. Spleen confirms with a "Got it" and whirls to interview a dopey-looking job seeker: "So you want to work here, what makes you think you deserve a job?" he gushes in two seconds (seven words per, or roughly 2.5 times the normal speed of speech).

Second man, no tongue-tied lad he, surges back: "Well, sir, I think I am good at figures and I have a sharp mind."

Spleen doesn't just talk fast. He makes up his mind on the dime: "Excellent, can you start on Monday?"

The new hire adapts to his new culture: "Absolutely, without hesitation," he rattles back.

Spleen: "Congratulations, welcome aboard. Wonderful, wonderful, wonderful."

The scene then shifts in record time to the world's shortest business meeting. "In conclusion, Jim, Bill, Bob, Carl, Frank, Luke, Dork, Ed, and Ted, business is business and in order to get something done you have to do something and in order to do something you have to get to work so let's get to work. Thank you for attending the meeting."

Over a gulped lunch Spleen shuffles a subordinate's assignment.

Spleen: "P.D., you did a bang-up job, I'm putting you in charge of Pittsburgh."

FEDERAL EXPRESS

FAST-PACED WORLD

ALLY & GARGANO, USA, 1981

P.D. spurts his pleasure: "Pittsburgh's perfect."

Spleen: "I know it's perfect, Peter, that's why I picked Pittsburgh. Pittsburgh's perfect. Peter, may I call you Pete?"

P.D.: "Call me Pete."

Spleen seals the deal: "Pete."

Back at the office a rumpled-looking Mr. Schmidtler sits in the waiting room while Spleen wheels and deals, playing his phone button like piano keys.

Spleen: "Tell him to wait 15 seconds," he barks into the intercom.

Eunice: "Can you wait 15 seconds?"

Schmidtler, in a resigned and normal-paced voice—hysterical because of its contrast to the other characters'—agrees. "I'll wait 15 seconds," he deadpans in what feels like 60 seconds.

Back in his office, Spleen is bouncing from one waiting phone call to another. "Congratulations on your deal in Denver, Dave, I'm putting you down to deal with Dallas. Don, is it a deal, do we have a deal? We have a deal, gotta go, got a call coming in. Hi, doc, just tell . . ."

An announcer interrupts this gush to deliver the sales message: "In this fast-moving, high-pressure, get-it-done-yesterday world, aren't you glad there's one company that can keep up with it all?"

Back to Spleen: "You got a deal, good, I am putting you up with the deal. Are we dealing? We are dealing. Dave, it's a deal with Don, Dork, and Dick. Dork, it's a deal with Dave, Dick, and Don. Don, it's a deal with Dick and gotta go, Dave, disconnecting. Gotta go, Dick, disconnecting, Gotta go, Dan, disconnecting."

Super: "When it absolutely positively has to be there overnight."

Voice-over: "Federal Express. When it absolutely, positively has to be there overnight."

The "Fast-Paced World" ad, as well as the client-agency relationship that produced it and other ticklers, almost didn't happen. In the early 1970s, Federal Express invited representatives of the agency Ally & Gargano to Memphis, where its chairman, Fred Smith, lived, to hear about a scheme for a fleet of jets that would fly in the dead of night, take little packages from around the country to a central hub, and dispatch them again on outbound planes. "They had only $150,000 to spend on advertising and the whole thing hadn't started yet, so we were set to turn it down," recalled agency chairman Carl Ally. A mutual friend persuaded Ally to reconsider. "So we met Fred Smith, talked to him fifteen minutes, and knew he was pure gold," said Ally.

Their first commercial for the new enterprise was not amusing the way its successors were, but it was clever. "America, you've got a new airline," a solemn voice declared. "No first class, no meals, no movies, in fact, no passengers. Just packages." And it worked. The average nightly package count soared from 21 in 1973 to 11,400 by 1975. Next, FedEx laced into Emery Air Freight, the industry leader. "As research to prove we were better, we filled forty-seven packages with sand and sent them on both FedEx and Emery," recalled Mark Zizzamia, the agency's account management supervisor at the time. "The results were so good we turned them into an ad." By the time that spot stopped running, two and half years later, FedEx had wrested the lead away from Emery.

So far, Ally & Gargano had aimed its message at middle and senior management, not the mailroom supervisors or back office workers who dealt with the suppliers every day. That changed. "We focused on expanding the market with the target moving from management to every department of American business including secretaries, mailroom personnel and trainees. No one was spared," said agency president Amil Gargano.

But how to appeal to the masses? Most ad agencies present a tightly scripted storyboard to their client and outside director and then scout around for talent to bring it to life. Ally & Gargano's creative executives on the account, creative director Amil Gargano, art director Mike Tesch, and copywriter Patrick Kelly, didn't even conceive a spot first. Rather, they each saw John Moschitta perform his fast-talking specialty on the television program *That's Incredible* and decided to brainstorm an idea for him with director Joe Sedelmaier, of Wendy's "Where's the Beef" fame. Guided by the faster-is-funnier principle demonstrated by the Keystone Kops, they concocted the intense character named Spleen, who strings together dialogue at a racy hundreds-of-words-a-minute clip to demonstrate the urgency of package delivery—and the silliness of management jargon.

Sedelmaier said that at the time "people said making fun of business was a dumb way to do advertising." The company ran with it, however, launching the sixty-second spot on NFL football games in October 1981, and consumers proved that making fun of management was not at all a bad way to appeal to them. Indeed, surveys showed that working people found "Fast-Paced World" to be one of the best commercials of the 1980s.

MY FAIR LAGER

Heineken's refreshing campaign spans three decades

HEINEKEN

WATER IN MAJORCA

LOWE HOWARD-SPINK, U.K., 1986

At the "School of Street Credibility," a preppy "Sloane Ranger" (yuppies who live around chic Sloane Square) is undergoing mislocution lessons. "The water in Majorca doesn't taste like it ought to," she says in perfect English.

But the Cockney Professor Higgins tells her "no, no, no" and delivers a Cockney rendition for her to imitate. She tries and tries again to say the line his way, but without success. Frustrated, the professor summons his sidekick. "Hey, Dell, any chance of some refreshment in here?" he asks.

Dell appears with three cans of Heineken. "Here you are. Get your laughing gear around that," he instructs her.

The aristocratic student takes a sip, mumbles, "Oh, golly," and to her own amazement says the line, first tentatively and then confidently, in perfect East End diction—all Cockney. The professor grows excited—but cautious.

"She's cracked it. She's only cracked it," he warns.

But Dell, who has popped the top of his can, swigs and with a voice now gone posh announces, "You're absolutely wrong."

Voice-over: "Heineken refreshes the parts what other beers cannot reach."

Super: "Heineken refreshes the parts wot other beers can't reach."

Another highlight of Heineken's breakthrough "refreshes the parts" campaign (see page 23) was this simple subversion of *My Fair Lady*. Originally, the girl was to utter the famous "rain in Spain" line, explained Adrian Holmes, the writer of the spot and now CEO of Lowe Howard-Spink, but at the eleventh hour, a pale-faced young account lad put his head in to announce a slight problem. The estate of George Bernard Shaw, which owned the copyright to *Pygmalion*, wanted nothing to do with the Heineken campaign. Holmes thought all was lost. But another writer suggested substituting the water in Majorca line and "we were forced by circumstances into a much better piece of writing," he said.

Sylvester DeTouzell did both female voices and Victor Borge, who initially turned the job down, did the professor's voice. (He'd hoped to represent a Danish beer, but, the story goes, when his agent whispered a rumor that his friend Orson Welles could be the voice for Denmark's Carlsberg ads, Borge snapped up the Heineken offer instead.) Paul Weyland shot the commercial. Alan Waldie was creative director. (Terry Lovelock originally conceived of the campaign at 3:00 A.M. at the Hotel Mamounia in Marrakesh after holing up there with writer's block.)

VIRGIN CONDOMS

Richard Branson's comic response to a serious problem

A young man comes into a pharmacy to buy condoms, but face-to-face with an attractive young female clerk, he loses his courage. He clears his throat, excuses himself, and stammers with ahhs and agghs while script on the screen gives voice to his thoughts.

"Oh, no, it's a woman," says the super.

As the store clerk asks what she can help him with, the super reveals his mission: "I really want some condoms."

But the lad cannot bring himself to ask for them.

"I want some . . . um . . . some . . . co . . . some . . . co . . . some come co . . . cotton wool, please," he finally stutters.

The super reminds us of his real mission as the clerk asks if there will be anything else.

"Silly question," declares the super.

"Yeah," the young man says as if he has worked up his courage.

"Just ask her," prods the super.

"Have you got a packet of . . . um . . . a pack of, um . . . a packet of tissues, please?"

"Man-sized tissues," she responds and asks, "Is that all?"

"Just ask me," says the super, voicing the clerk's inner thoughts.

The announcer interrupts to note that "Mates are a new range of condoms. Like other condoms, they're reliable but they're cheaper. She sells hundreds of packets. She's not embarrassed so why should you be?"

Finally the young man musters the courage to request "a packet of Mates condoms, please," and it seems all is well.

"Of course," she replies as the super says "at last" and "no sweat."

But then the lady druggist shouts, "Mr. Williams, how much for this packet of Mates condoms?" and the young man nods, finally accepting his inevitable humiliation.

The super gets the last word: "Mates: you make love—they make sense."

MATES CONDOMS

CHEMIST SHOP

STILL PRICE COURT TWIVY D'SOUZA, U.K., 1988

Mates was the brainchild of Virgin founder Richard Branson, who determined that even with all the publicity about AIDS, not enough was being done to prevent its spread. In May 1987, the U.K. government was spending around $15 million annually to promote awareness of the dangers of AIDS. London International Group's Durex then controlled 95 percent of the condom market, a virtual monopoly. Branson decided that neither the government nor Durex was doing enough publicity to attack the problem—particularly in targeting young people and their uneasiness with buying and using condoms. He approached Ansell to manufacture a condom for him and, in November 1987, the Mates brand launched.

Mates was the first U.K. condom brand to be the subject of a TV commercial, said Chris Bell, regional manager at Ansell Personal Products. After it plowed the way, Durex took to the airwaves, urging viewers to consider condoms as a prophylactic against the AIDS virus. Until then, condoms in the U.K. had been promoted as family planning products. (In the U.S. in November 1991, just before Magic Johnson announced that he is HIV-positive, Fox became the first major TV network to allow prime-time ads for prophylactics, but only if they are promoted as a disease preventive. Before this, affiliates of the networks ran condom commercials only in local time slots, not nationwide.)

Branson insisted on offering Mates for less money than Durex, to get more young people to use condoms, and he arranged to sell them more where young people shop: at The Body Shop, in his own Virgin record stores, and in some clothing stores.

(By aiming for teens, Branson avoided a problem plaguing other condom makers, who'd pitched their brands largely to Cassanovas. Despite brighter colors, ribbing, and thinner latex, many men dislike condoms, claiming they interfere with sex. The rubbers also trigger memories of adolescent awkwardness—and many men never truly admit the possibility of pregnancy.)

"Branson wasn't interested in making a profit on Mates. Any money he made from it went to charity," said Bell. But he wanted retailers to join him on this charity mission and most balked when he asked them also not to take a profit. Advertising, however, didn't escape his scrutiny. Branson scrapped several unmemorable approaches suggested by the agency and ultimately approved six approaches that he thought would put youngsters at ease. Apparently they did, for within six months Mates had captured 25 percent of the condom market.

The spots ran for a year. In the second half of its run, Mates's share started to slip. Bell said it was because the government stepped up its anti-AIDS effort and portrayed the disease as affecting the overall population. At the same time, competitors fought back on the pricing front. And its early lower price actually worked against the brand, said Bell. "People equated lower price with lower quality," he noted. Currently Mates has around a 20 percent share of the U.K. condom market.

When "Chemist Shop" was retired, Virgin began more literal treatments of safe sex. In one spot a man lies in bed with several women: "Every time you sleep with your boyfriend you sleep with all his old girlfriends," one proclaimed. Another reversed the sexes and talked about sleeping with the girl's old blokes. The commercial noted that condoms are "awfully silly to put on but that's half the fun."

"We don't need to tackle the acceptability of condoms anymore; they're accepted," said Bell. "Now we approach beginning users in different ways, briefly acknowledging the safety reasons for it, but focusing on the fact that condom use is fun—worry-free enjoyment.

"But when an eleven-year-old boy fathers a child with a fourteen-year-old girl in London," he added, "people [still] accuse you of encouraging promiscuity among underage children."

MAMA CRIED

MCI reaches out to AT&T's customers with a spot-on takeoff

The commercial opens on a sobbing middle-aged, middle-class black woman as her husband tries to comfort her. "Have you been talking to our son on long distance again?" he asks. She nods affirmatively.

"Did he tell you how much he loved you? And did he tell you how well he's doing at school?" he asks. She affirms all through her tears.

"All those things are wonderful," he exclaims. "What on earth are you crying for?"

Speaking for the first time, she bawls, "Have you seen our long-distance phone bill?"

An announcer adds, "If your long-distance phone bills are too much, call MCI. Sure, reach out and touch someone, just do it for a whole lot less."

Super: "MCI: the nation's long-distance phone company."

MCI
PARENTS
ALLY & GARGANO, USA, 1982

In 1981, N. W. Ayer & Partners created the memorable and heart-tugging commercial "Joey Called" for AT&T. That vignette of an aging mother moved to tears by her grown son calling "just because I love you" reached out and touched us. It also inspired Ally & Gargano to create an aggressive, funny, and shrewd parody for MCI.

At the time, AT&T had more than 98 percent of the market—"so we attacked it," said Tom Messner, now a principal at Messner Vetere Berger McNamee Schmetterer/Euro RSCG, who was then senior vice president at Ally & Gargano and copywriter on the spot. "It was part of a total effort that went for the jugular and that brought MCI from a $95 million company to $2.5 billion and changed its personality from a mild-mannered to venomous competitor. It was the first pitch in an ad war that lasted until 1997."

Back then, long distance meant bad news; people only phoned to report an accident or somebody dying. (Calls then were more expensive: since

1980, they've fallen in price by 70 percent.) As the kingpin in the market, AT&T wanted to broaden long-distance phone usage and make it more casual. And, preparing for divestiture, AT&T saw competition on the rise.

MCI had a different problem: it had to introduce the first new long-distance phone company since the invention of the telephone to a public that had grown up on AT&T. "People felt it might be illegal to change phone service and feared if MCI didn't work they'd be without any," said Messner. "AT&T spent one hundred times more than MCI did and it was a legend. We had to convince people that MCI was a credible, low-cost alternative to AT&T."

Messner, working with creative director Amil Gargano and art director George Euringer, decided to target heavy residential long-distance users and aim to convince them that MCI could save them up to 60 percent on long distance and that it was a reputable company that required no installation to switch. "We positioned MCI as a David versus Goliath," Gargano said.

It was actually Bill McCowan, the late chairman of MCI, who galvanized the agency into creating "Parents." He praised AT&T's "Reach Out and Touch Someone" campaign for helping to turn the long-distance call into a commonplace event and singled out "Joey Called." Messner suggested MCI do a version where the woman holds up the bill and cries because the "greedy, blood-sucking monopoly had drained the family resources." McGowan thought a moment, recalled Messner, "then asked us to find a stronger word than blood-sucking."

Director Bob Giraldi shot the commercial in two hours. It cost $70,000 to produce.

"Parents" ran from mid 1982 through 1983 in spot markets during the day when women, who make a disproportionate number of residential long-distance calls, were the prime audience. (Sisters are the single most important long-distance phone connection, followed by parent to child.) Initially the MCI team worried whether a casual viewer would understand that this wasn't a Bell commercial but a takeoff on one, and that the satire would backfire. As it turned out, there was no need to worry.

"The advertising paid out in less than thirty days," said Gargano. "By 1985, MCI had the highest revenues growth rate versus a year ago of any major company in the history of American business—with a tenth the ad budget of AT&T. It branded MCI as feisty." AT&T did not react until MCI and others' market share had reached 12 percent. Then it pulled the commercial that started it all.

CLASS WARFARE

Parker takes the high-status ground with a low-priced pen

It is the last day at the prestigious Zermatt School for Young Ladies. A group of obviously well-to-do young ladies is preparing to take their final lesson—"how to spend Daddy's lovely money"—from a very proper teacher.

"Checkbooks open, girls," the teacher instructs her charges. "Pens at the ready."

One of the students makes the egregious error of pulling out an improper pen.

"No, no, no, Felicity," the teacher scolds. "You couldn't possibly go shopping in Knightsbridge with one of those." She then gives Felicity a Parker Lady in white rolled gold and demonstrates how easy it is to write a check with, "a pen with style, a pen with elan. A Parker Lady in white rolled gold. Words just seem to roll from its tip. Signatures just flow with a flourish. Now, then, altogether girls."

Her attention is diverted by a confused girl. "Yes, Celia?" she asks.

Poor Celia blurts out her problem. "Madame, does one spell pence with an 's' or a 'c'?"

The teacher wryly retorts: "I don't think you need worry about that, my dear."

Voice-over: "The Parker Lady in white rolled gold. £9.95."

Super: "The Parker Lady. £9.95."

PARKER PEN

FINISHING SCHOOL

COLLETT DICKENSON PEARCE, U.K., 1974

In a world where fancy fountain pens are respectfully referred to as "writing instruments," Parker was tops among the Brahmins. Theirs was *the* pen to give as a gift. "The Parker name had a high level of status," said John Salmon, president of CDP, the agency that crafted the archly droll "Finishing School" commercial.

Waterman, Parker's archrival at the time, was gaining on its once stalwart competitor. Waterman kept updating its designs, while Parker styles never changed. "The company considered its designs to be classics. The public considered them old-fashioned," said Salmon.

Waterman advertising had also written its way into consumers' consciousness. Its ads, which used beautiful photography to present the pens as jewelry, bestowed a feeling of emotional well-being on owners, suggesting rich rewards justly earned. The combination of product and pitch eroded Parker's position.

In the very tongue-in-cheek "Finishing School" Parker punched back. After a visit to the factory, the ad team discovered how well the pens were made and so decided to emphasize quality. But the recitation of attributes was served up with a humorous twist.

41

In "Finishing School," the U.K. company aimed to suggest that Parker Lady was the same high quality as Parker's other coveted writing implements—but that it was available at a very reasonable price.

Copywriter David Brown wrote the subtle spot quickly. CDP cast up-and-coming stage actress Penelope Keith as the very upright teacher. "Finishing School" ran for a year and was replaced by "Parking Wardens," starring English actor Leonard Rosto. That commercial's plot revolved around a meter maid writing out a parking ticket.

In 1993, Gillette purchased U.K.–based Parker Pen. Four years before that it had acquired rival France-based Waterman.

CHAPTER FOUR

DREAMSCAPES

I f the job of a commercial is—as some marketers believe—to dazzle viewers (especially those likeliest to buy a product) with the original and unexpected, then dreamscape imagery may be the ticket.

Marketers have used evocative settings for different reasons—and rarely exclusively for their aesthetic impact. Certainly, presenting visuals that consumers have not seen before—or not seen in a particular style—entertains and engages them and is a way to raise the voltage on a low-interest category. But there are less obvious motivations, too. Some advertisers, like Chanel, opt for fantastic imagery to forestall wear-out, so that viewers could watch their commercial repeatedly without getting bored. Others strive to make the scenes timeless, partly to keep the setting from being tied to a particular market or time frame. Others do the opposite: Marlboro became the best-selling cigarette in the world partly because it tied its product to a very specific and authentic, yet idealized and mythical country "where the flavor is." The cowboy, that shorthand of masculinity in command of its destiny, is almost a prop in beautifully photographed, even poetic settings. And by showing an idealized, fictive past, Hovis implied that its nostalgia-tinged bread was different from—and better than—the bread of its competitors. To buy it would be to buy a piece of the past.

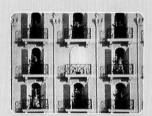

In some cases, either because of regulatory scrutiny or lack of competitive advantage, there's little marketers can say about their product. Scenery operates as a smokescreen to draw attention away from the lack of a rational product benefit. And sometimes the imagery says things that can't politely—or legitimately—be voiced. Dunlop took on its unnamed rival Michelin, implying evil, just as Nike's forces battled troops from Hades.

Other times, all the traditional ways of delivering the sales message—and imagery to illustrate it—have been said and done to death, leaving little but clichés to present. Smirnoff's "Message in a Bottle" relied on distinctive imagery to break through clutter and present its vodka as the drink with which people would want to identify. But that imagery was also designed to stretch viewers' imaginations and suggest that things aren't always what they seem.

Or conversely, that they are. Jeep intentionally never showed the car in "Snow Covered" so as not to tie it to any particular model. Instead, its thirty-second silent commercial showed just majestic terrain that, in viewers' minds, Jeep alone could conquer, branding Jeep owners as masters of their destiny. The setting did the sell.

CECI N'EST PAS UNE CIGARETTE

A cigarette manufacturer skirts the rules of advertising with Dadaism

A helicopter transports what looks to be a large tin of sardines to a remote and dangerous desert locale, complete with lizards, where a swimming pool is filling. To a backdrop of rhythmic rock music, suggesting undertones of danger, the helicopter drops the tin into the pool. A scuba diver approaches with a large key, which he uses to peel back the corner of the can, revealing human-sized Benson & Hedges cigarettes. The aperture of the camera closes and then reopens to reveal a billboard featuring a partially opened can of cigarettes in a swimming pool. The super announces, as required by law, that: "Cigarettes can seriously damage your health."

BENSON & HEDGES

SWIMMING POOL

COLLETT DICKENSON PEARCE, U.K., 1978

Directed by Hugh Hudson, written by Mike Cousins, and art directed by Alan Waldie, "Swimming Pool," with neither words nor obvious message, was one of the most expensive commercials ever produced. It aired in the cinema at the same time as a surreal campaign for Benson & Hedges cigarettes was running in magazines and outdoor billboards.

Before "Swimming Pool," Benson & Hedges had been running elegant, stylish, opulent lifestyle ads. One showed a gondola going down the Grand Canal and asked what attracted the merchants to Venice. The answer was obvious and funny: the pack was on the front of the boat.

Benson & Hedges always associated that pack with solid gold, positioning it as an "aspirational device like a Dunhill lighter, the paraphernalia of a man of style," Waldie said. "People saw it as strong, hefty, and valuable."

That premise led to subtle and funny TV commercials featuring comedians such as Terry-Thomas and Peter Sellers. In one, on a boat in the Mediterranean, Peter Sellers chucked the pack onto the boat—which promptly sank under its weight.

Following this, Benson & Hedges began a surreal print campaign. One ad in the series showed a birdcage hanging from a ceiling with a cigarette pack instead of bird on the perch. Another featured a room with a giant mouse hole in the skirting board; outside it leaned a pack of Benson & Hedges. A third showed a sardine tin resembling a cigarette pack.

"I was thinking of Dadaism and decided to combine many of these elements in a surrealistic way," Waldie said. "But in the days before computers we had to construct it all."

"Swimming Pool" was shot in Death Valley, where it had not rained since 1913. As such, neither client nor agency pushed for weather insurance.

45

As soon as the production crew arrived, however, the heavens opened. "It then rained nonstop for a week," Waldie said. Production costs soared from just waiting out the monsoon.

The Collett Dickenson Pearce team asked the rock band 10cc to use a track from one of their records. The band re-recorded it so the music matched every nuance of action in the Benson & Hedges film. (Band leaders Lou Trene and Kevin Godley later gave up music and went into directing commercials.)

"Swimming Pool" broke at a time when tobacco regulations were tightening. With regulatory scrutiny, there was little one could safely say about the product, so the commercial was designed to draw attention to the packaging. That was valued for itself and, consistent with Benson & Hedges advertising, was always made the hero. The pack was made to look expensive but cost the same as any other king size. "The suggestion was that if you want to smoke, smoke the best," Waldie said.

"Swimming Pool" ran for a year in theaters as part of a surreal campaign that helped push Benson & Hedges, once deep into the pack, into being the number-one cigarette in England. The company abandoned the surrealistic look "after other companies started doing it and it became devalued," said Waldie. "The imitators became more successful than what they were imitating because we had restrictive rules. Chocolate boxes and perfumes and liquors could rip it off without restrictions."

EGO TRIP

Chanel's immodest proposal for a new product launch

CHANEL EGOISTE

BALCONIES

CHANEL DIRECT, FRANCE, 1990

A beautiful and angry woman appears on a shuttered balcony—behind which you can barely glimpse a lavishly decorated room—and screams in French, "Egoiste, ou es-tu? (Selfish, where are you?) Montres-toi. Prends garde a mon courroux! Je serais implacable! (Reveal yourself, you miserable worm! My heart is shattered!) O rage! O désespoir!" She writhes in torment and slams her shutter.

The film turns from black-and-white to color as a man's muscular arm extends out into one of the balconies to grasp a bottle of the fragrance and place it on the balustrade of his balcony. The camera pulls back to reveal the horizontal sweep of a baroque palace. The man's room is right in the middle. Six, then twelve Furies join the original complainant in her strident, over-the-top melodramatic condemnation. The camera pans back and another thirty beautifully gowned, black-gloved,

46

raging women roar "Egoiste! Egoiste! Egoiste!" *to protest the caddish be-havior of the unseen man. Shutters snap open and clamp closed as music swells in the background. He was their man and he done them wrong.*

Voice-over: "Egoiste, Chanel for Men."

"The job of a commercial is to get viewers, especially prospects for the product, to say 'holy cow. I've never seen anything like that in my life,' " said Arie Kopelman, president of Chanel. "We could have produced a commercial that would have been very predictable, show-ing a man winning over a lady, but we wanted something different and this spot does the job. We went for a shockingly arresting attention-getter that viewers could see a thousand times without getting bored. They may not un-derstand it all but they'll know they saw something."

What they saw is classic French theater, adapted from Corneille's *Le Cid,* directed by Jean-Paul Goude (the creator of the famous 1989 parade commemorating the bicentennial of the French Revolution), and set to the swelling theme from Prokofiev's *Romeo and Juliet.*

It was the foundation of what Kopelman called "the biggest get-out for any men's fragrance ever." It certainly could have been the most elaborate commercial set ever built. "Even before the dry cleaning bills for the dresses came in we'd spent considerably more than one million dollars" Kopelman said. All told, the company was said to have spent over $20 million on the launch campaign.

The commercial was shot in Rio de Janeiro, where a crew of 150 labor-ers worked for weeks to construct a fin de siècle Parisien hotel, modeled after the Carlton in Cannes. It had the same rows and rows of thirty-six identical French windows, white shuttered and balconied, with spired domes on the roof. Chanel tried but couldn't rent the Riveria hotel for the two-week shoot so the team chose Rio for its supposedly perfect weather. The production, budgeted at $1 million, was plagued by rain.

When Chanel introduced the pricey ($28.50 for 1.7 ounces) men's fra-grance in Europe in April 1990, the launch was so successful it seemed Ego-iste would rival Opium's debut thirteen years earlier. (It was actually conceived to take on Ralph Lauren's Polo and Calvin Klein's Obsession for Men.)

Chanel did groundwork to seed the hype. The month before the com-mercial began it planted stories in magazines, profiling its master perfumer and soliciting readers' definitions of egoism. A week before the launch, teaser ads in newspapers used the word "I" in the handwriting of cele-brated egoists including Beethoven and Confucius. The day before the launch, full-page ads pictured the bottle. And on the eve of "E" day, Chanel sponsored a TV special during which the commercial made its debut. Meanwhile, windows of perfumeries throughout France featured the bot-

47

tle. Au Printemps in Paris erected marquees and arches and hung banners and posters of outtakes from the commercial. Video monitors showed a film on the making of the spot, while a video sound wall broadcast it out on the street until 10:00 P.M.

Chanel tried to inspire the same word-of-mouth excitement for its New York introduction by duplicating many of the marketing steps: the pre-launch magazine stories, an exquisite pied-à-terre for l'homme Egoiste and a sitting room and bath designed for an AIDS benefit in which the commercial played constantly. Scent strips decorated with the shutters from the spot were sent to everyone on Bloomingdale's mailing list. An hour-long documentary on the making of the ad was released and for two weeks that April, every room in Bloomingdale's was turned into an Egoiste haunt, where the making of the commercial was continuously shown.

Many viewers seeing this enigmatic spot mistook it for a promotional clip for a new foreign film. "The pace moves so quickly in super-edited frames with surreal close-ups of the women screaming that you don't know what's going on," admitted executive director of creative services Lyle Saunders. But then, you don't need to know, he said. "The message was the intrigue . . . and that whoever this guy is he must be fabulous in any number of ways."

Chanel created a persona for the fictitious l'homme Egoiste. Professionally he was an architect with one apartment in company headquarters in Neuilly and another in New York. Both were decorated by Christinas Benais and featured a self-indulgent diary with such scribbled notes as "All of me I give except myself" and fanciful sketches.

Kopelman fretted that Americans would see "ego" as a dirty word. But Chanel's market research showed high recognition and acceptance of the name among Europeans, so the company stuck with it, taking care to explain the French connotation of the word: "Egoiste: To assume he's uncaring or aloof is to misread him. He walks on the positive side of the line, separating arrogance and self worth," explained some promotional material. Kopelman said the man doesn't represent "self centered-ness so much as confident masculinity. Men will say 'That's me, or the guy I'd like to be.' Women will say 'That's my guy or the guy I'd like to have.' We've created a new hero for the nineties."

The "hero" is intentionally not shown—although the product name is mentioned a lot. "The image of a young guy trying to be cool has been stretched to its limit in men's fragrance advertising," said Goude. He said the commercial worked on many levels. "Macho men think the women are begging for more. And the women who have been betrayed by this egoist hate him but are still under his spell. Wounded women are the ones buying the stuff. They think men are egotists but feel it tenderly and with indulgence."

Part of the mystery was preserved by not using subtitles. In Italy the women shrieked passages from Goldoni and in Germany they ranted passages from Goethe and Schiller. Chanel's team had considered using Shakespeare's *Merchant of Venice* in the English version but scrapped it because the archaic language sounded too phony, Saunders said.

Within months of Egoiste's touchdown, the company said the campaign was generating 35 to 40 percent more business than expected and was well on its way to doing what Chanel No. 5 had done in the women's market. *Women's Wear Daily* called it differently, however, reporting that Egoiste returned just $7 million in sales after an initial $9 million promotional flurry. According to the trade paper, sales fell to $2.5 million in 1993. (A top-selling men's fragrance rakes in $80 million in annual retail sales.)

Chanel tried to revive the brand later with Egoiste Platinum and another thirty-second TV spot, also produced by Jean-Paul Goude. In it, viewers saw beyond the clattering shutters into the bedroom of the man who uses Egoiste. His shadow punches him and steals his bottle of Platinum only to have the man take it back. Women's cries of "*Egoiste! Egoiste!*"—echoes of the first commercial—are heard at the end. Goude called that commercial less ambiguous than the first ad.

SHARE THE FANTASY

Chanel creates a fantasy world Freud would be proud of

The Ink Spots' rendition of the classic "I Don't Want to Set the World On Fire" plays as a long shot of the gardens at Versailles fades to become an elongated view of piano keys playing themselves. That view in turn becomes a mirrored building with the reflection of a plane overhead. The scene again morphs, this time into a sumptuous woman walking between trains. In the next scene she is in a room walking toward the silhouette of a man.

"Charles," he announces.

"Catherine," she replies, with her eyes saying more.

". . . and that's what you do," we catch a snippet of his conversation. "Do you mind if I ask you a personal question?"

"No, what is it?" she asks.

The camera closes in on Catherine and then sweeps back to the building with the shadow of a plane emerging from it. The camera again reverts to Catherine, a beatific, slightly smug expression on her face—and then lingers on a bottle of Chanel No. 5.

Voice-over: "Share the fantasy. Chanel No. 5."

CHANEL NO. 5

POOL

CHANEL DIRECT, FRANCE, 1979

Chanel's first perfume (despite the No. 5, there's no Chanel No. 1, 2, 3, or 4) has become a byword for sophistication. But by 1980, women had grown up associating the formerly radical Chanel No. 5 with their mothers or grandmothers. The brightly colored, quick-cut, new-wave spots replete with optical illusions and extensive production values aimed to bridge the age gap and make Chanel contemporary.

"We wanted to reach out to a younger group, a woman twenty-five to thirty, to say, 'Here's what Chanel's about today,' " said Arie Kopelman, president and chief operating officer of Chanel Inc. "We wanted what is alluring, what is seductive and sexy to her."

Sex, seduction, romance—even poetry, elegance, and lavish and suggestive imagery are what's served up in "Pool" and the two other spots in the trilogy conceived by Chanel's Paris-based creative director Jacques Helleu and directed by Ridley Scott (who also directed, among other movies, *Alien* and *Thelma and Louise*.)

In the first spot, "Piscine," a languorous beauty (Catherine Deneuve) dramatically posed at poolside gazes dreamily at the water into which she has just tossed her stiletto heel. She arches her back rapturously as an airplane's shadow floats over her. An Adonis at the other end of the pool cleanly slices the water with a perfect dive, retrieves the shoe, and ever-so-suggestively emerges from underwater between the V of the blonde's knees. All this is tantalizingly orchestrated to a melody by Vangelis.

Then came a spot in which the airplane's shadow glided erotically up the phallic symbol that was the TransAmerica pyramid in San Francisco while a woman inside closed her eyes and experienced ecstatic fulfillment.

"The shadow of the plane was an accident" whose effect was so startling that "Ridley Scott incorporated it and it became his signature," said Lyle Saunders, executive director of creative services at Chanel. The production team tried to match the piano key movement to the song but it didn't look good, said Saunders, so they used other music whose note sequence was more visually arresting.

While competitors were using sex to sell perfume, Saunders said Chanel's goal was to "stay subtle . . . sexy but never sleazy. If anything we tend to pull back rather than go too far, which is the opposite of the rest of the business."

The commercials, with their stark graphics, ran for three years—the traditional run time for Chanel spots. But because there was such interest in the commercials, especially "Pool," it was resurrected in 1994 for the U.S. Open.

Chanel never tested its far-out, new-wave commercials, but even though the sixty-second versions didn't mention Chanel No. 5 until the end, viewers remembered the spots and their lingering sensuality. And while Chanel says it's hard to peg the strong sales for its fragrance to the commercial, that advertising did help keep Chanel the world's most recognizable name in perfume, still going strong at seventy-five.

THE ROAD TO HELL

Dunlop paves the way to a new image for its tires

The music is "Venus in Furs" by the Velvet Underground, the cult pop group from the 1960s, which had re-formed and allowed its music for the first time to be used in a commercial. A surreal nightmare netherworld unfolds where a bloated bald demon—a malevolent magician—and his colorized hobgoblins set a diabolical obstacle course to threaten a car traveling a desert highway with purple trees and vivid orange skies.

In surreal scenes, vicious imps and their ghoulish leader set two motorized pianos driven by crazy pianists to charge the car and cascade off a bridge while demons chortle and singers croon of "Shiny shiny shiny boots of leather . . . whiplash girl child in the dark . . . come in bells. Your servant [sic] don't forsake him. Strike his mistress and cure his heart."

A minefield bursts into flames and a river percolates soap suds while the lyrics tell of "Dowdy sins, of street life fancies chase the costumes she shall wear . . . ermine furs, adorn, impervious, severan, severan awaits you there."

Fantasy creatures scrub the road with soap, and twisted ghouls spill mountains of marbles and ball bearings in the car's path—all to a pulsing beat and driving colors—while a car with Dunlop tires speeds through it all with never a hint of a skid. That's because the tires are, as the super explains, "Tested for the unexpected."

DUNLOP

TESTED FOR THE UNEXPECTED

ABBOTT MEAD VICKERS/BBDO, U.K., 1993

In a typical tire ad, a family in a car on a dark night suddenly faces a truck careening toward them. This avant garde Mad Max meets Dali landscape, written by Tom Carty, art directed by Walter Campbell, agency produced by Francine Linsey, and directed by Tony Kaye of Tony Kaye Films, travels a different road altogether.

"Tested for the Unexpected"—more a mini-film sequence of interrelated vignettes—demonstrates the tire's reliability and flexibility on all kinds of surfaces and shows that it can grip in the wet and resist punctures along prickly paths. It is a battle of good against shadowy, sinister evil; viewers interpreted the demon, who embodies the evil that drivers and their tires might face, as representative of Dunlop's key rival, Michelin. The tagline is the only clue to the product.

Previous spots had emphasized Dunlop's quality credential and contemporized the brand, but "none were as creatively original or ambitious as this mold-breaking idea," said Stuart Wyss the marketing services manager at Dunlop. "It made tires interesting and worth talking about."

What tires are really all about, according to art director Walter Campbell, is "the moment when something horrible happens—like a child running out in front of you or finding yourself on ice or going into a bad corner fast and the only thing that will keep you on the road is the quality of your tires. That's the moment when suddenly everyone thinks about their tires." It's the moment that led the team to the line "Tested for the Unexpected."

But all the imagery the agency had in mind to illustrate its selling proposition had been done repeatedly—the car braking because a child ran into the road scenario, said Campbell. "Our goal was to take those clichés and make them new."

They did that by tying the hazards to a weird and diabolical character with the unexplained mission of attacking the car with Dunlop tires. "The concept was a nightmare or crazy dream, so we needed to film it to mirror the images of a dream," said Campbell.

The shoot itself had many nightmarish aspects. The team flew into Los Angeles on the day of the verdict in the Rodney King trial. (The set was an hour's drive north in the hills off Route 5.) "We didn't know whether we'd be flying into a war zone," said Stefan Hohmann, account director at Abbott Mead Vickers/BBDO in London.

Several elements from the original script didn't work—because it was raining, for example, they couldn't use banana skins on the road—"so we had to keep inventing on the set," said Hohmann. The "script" was actually a series of ideas or suggestions rather than binding details, he said, so the creative team fluidly evolved the production on the spot.

The road-scrubbing scene required eight models to be dressed, body painted, and coiffed, a process that took six hours. To look striking and unusual the actors wore special contact lenses that gave them an eerie, glazed, snake-eyed effect. Some of the outfits needed real rigging—the green-eyed witches and Buddha in a bondage corset with metal hooks on his nipples; others required gluing bits of shattered mirror on a frame. The explosions and pyrotechnics were real. There were ten different cameras shooting at different angles. "It was a genuine traveling circus," said Hohmann.

Eleven months from the day the creative team was briefed and after six days of shooting with a cost overrun of 20 percent, the film was ready for colorization. Tony Kaye had shot it in black and white. To achieve that weird colored landscape, the commercial was sent to CST Entertainment Imaging in Culver City, Los Angeles, which used the same process that adds color to old black-and-white films.

"Unexpected" aimed to reach men who have traditionally been the primary premium-brand tire buyer or specifier. It also was designed to appeal to corporate and business drivers who "need to feel good about the brand credentials of the tires that have been factory fit," said Wyss. "The tire trade needs to be impressed too."

Its competitors were advertising heavily at the time. Market leader Michelin was focusing on its research and development with a "color of your driving" commercial. Dunlop was running second on par with Goodyear

Rubber & Tire and Pirelli. Goodyear focused on its Formula 1 racing heritage as a credential and Pirelli was using sex to sell with a spot featuring Sharon Stone in the rear of a Mercedes wanting to get in front to drive. Continental Tires was playing up its German engineering with scientific-oriented demonstrations, said Wyss.

"We were trying to elevate and modernize Dunlop's image and shake up people's perceptions of the brand, making it top of mind while demonstrating the performance credentials of the tires," said Wyss. "We needed a big and unusual idea to make that happen and in the process rewrote the rules of advertising in this country." Research showed all key image criteria were positively affected by "Unexpected": quality, performance, high tech, and value, he said.

Still, Wyss admits he had sweaty palms. SP Tyres acquired Dunlop in 1984; Wyss hadn't shown the Japanese owners the eighty-second film and admitted he didn't know what they'd make of it.

Many English people made something Dunlop hadn't intended of it. They complained to the Independent Television Commission about the racy nature of some of the imagery, the themes of bondage and sadomasochism that seemed to percolate in this hellish, Dune-like horizon.

Despite its expense—the commercial cost more than £500,000—and the complaints of some that the idea got lost in the "half-million-pound pop promo," Dunlop "rated it as good value for the money," said Wyss. "Most brands beat us on share of voice but we beat them hands down on cut through, memorability, and the sheer impact of the imagery, which started a new genre of TV advertising in the U.K. Our advertising became a cult. Five years later we still get requests for tape," he said.

Unprompted, brand awareness for Dunlop was the highest of all tire brands in the U.K. during the campaign's run, and the advertising achieved more consumer-awareness rating points per dollar than any piece Dunlop has ever aired, said Wyss. "This is a low-interest, distress-purchase category and we really didn't expect a sales blip and frankly you can't prove a relation to sales because of many variables, such as what was the original equipment on the car and black market imports, but Dunlop was trading in the black for the first time in over a decade and we felt we were influencing the tire trade and fleet car and company managers to stock Dunlops. And mysteriously our market share has grown steadily over the past four years. Funny that," mused Wyss.

"Unexpected" stopped running in 1996 after four years. The company determined that it had worn out, that its impact had been exhausted. Abbott Mead is now working on a successor.

Tony Kaye attempted to have the commercial exhibited as art at London's Tate Gallery. When his plea was rejected, he protested by setting up a screening on the pavement outside.

AS GOOD AS IT GOT

A breadmaker's promise of paradise by the oven light

HOVIS

BIKE RIDE

COLLETT DICKENSON PEARCE, U.K., 1973

The scene is an English town in the 1800s, shot in mellow hues of golden brown. As Dvořák's "Planets" from the New World Symphony plays, a young boy pushes his bicycle mightily up a steep hill. He is making his final delivery of bread for the day.

His thoughts are spoken: "Last stop on't round would be old Ma Peggotty's place. T'was like taking bread to the top of the world."

After his great effort he rides his bike back down the hill as fast as he can.

"T'was a grand ride back though. I know t'baker'd have t'kettle on and doorsteps of hot Hovis ready."

When he returns to the baker he is given a loaf of Hovis bread and he recalls what the baker told him: " 'There's wheat in that loaf,' he'd say. 'Get it inside you, boy, and you'll be going up that hill as fast as you go down.' "

Announcer: "Hovis still has many times more wheat germ than other breads. As good for you today as it's always been."

The super repeats the message: "As good for you today as it's always been."

Legendary adman David Ogilvy once singled this commercial out as "among the most persuasive I've ever seen." Its effectiveness, he said, resided in its large content of nostalgia, charm, and sentimentality.

The commercial aimed to stimulate empathy by showing an idealized, fictive past and implying that the intangible benefit of its nostalgia-tinged bread was different from—and better than—the benefits of the bread of its competitors. The proposition was that to buy this bread was to own a piece of the past and its time-honored values, that paradise bought is paradise regained.

"Bike Ride" was the third commercial in a campaign shot by Ridley Scott at a time when Hovis made just one product, bread with wheat germ, that it had been turning out since 1885. "We decided that because people thought of white bread as artificial, we'd emphasize the unchanging, old-time goodness of Hovis, that it's as good today as it's always been," said John Salmon, chairman of Collett Dickenson Pearce, which created the series.

Originally, the line was supposed to be that the bread was good "for you" but television censors in the U.K. made the agency scrap that claim. It was a fortunate hurdle: the substituted phrase—"as good as it's always been"—was more emotional and nostalgic.

54

Hovis management was skittish about the commercial at first. "Every bread marketer wants a commercial showing stuff spread on their bread and the bread made into thick sandwiches and happy children smilingly eating them," said Salmon. The "Bike Ride" imagery was of a different order.

It was imagery the public loved. The ad was filmed on Gold Hill in Shaftesbury in Dorset, which has subsequently become a tourist attraction. (At the top of the hill there's a facsimile of a Hovis loaf.) Another spot in the campaign, "Postman," used Dvořák music, establishing it in many consumers' minds as "the Hovis music."

"Bike Ride" ran intermittently for nineteen years and was last shown in 1992. Because Hovis did not have a large advertising budget, commercials tended to start and stop, with sales sparking when advertising was running, but having little residual impact when the advertising stopped, said Salmon. "People remember this campaign fondly, but with such a small profit in bread, there was a constant debate whether they could afford to advertise, whether they should milk it and stop."

That happened before, in the 1950s, when Hovis brought the famous "Don't Say Brown, Say Hovis" campaign to TV screens. That line—"Don't say Brown, say Hovis"—became such a part of popular culture that children called Brown were nicknamed Hovis. And when George Brown, the foreign secretary in the 1960s, made yet another political gaffe, one headline read, "Don't say Brown, say useless." Hovis, named in a national competition in 1890, is a shortened form of *Hominis Vis,* which means "strength of man."

Eventually Hovis produced a loaf made from entire grain and also a white loaf, and commercials promoting these breads followed. Collett Dickenson Pearce lost the account three years after "Bike Ride" first aired—and went on to work for competitor Kings Mill.

In 1994, Hovis began a new series of advertising, still using Dvořák's New World Symphony but with a new line, "Raised the Hovis way." That was designed to reflect the fact that Hovis no longer makes just brown bread but a family of breads, including white. These were done by the DMB&B agency and feature the voice of Julie Walters, the comedian/actress.

The most recent spot for Hovis Brown, the new name of the original Hovis wheat-germ loaf, features a sixteen-month-old baby boy, Noah Brooke. He is happily enjoying time with his dad, giggling with excitement as he awaits his toast soldiers. The announcer explains that Noah is very fussy about his soldiers: they must be very neatly cut and, of course, have to be made from Hovis bread with wheat germ.

In one of two commercials for Hovis white bread, twenty-year-old Susan Oliver demonstrates how to make the perfect bacon sandwich. The bacon has to be crisp, the sauce has to be brown, and the bread has to be Hovis white. The other spot features Charles Stebbings revealing how to make the ultimate summer pudding.

A WINTER'S TRAIL

Jeep breaks new ground in auto advertising

JEEP

SNOW COVERED

BOZELL WORLDWIDE, USA, 1994

The spot opens with a bird's-eye view of a wide open winter expanse—fresh snow covered mountains under a pink sunrise. Suddenly, a crunching sound breaks the serenity. Something is moving rapidly beneath the surface of the snow, as if burrowing or tunneling, leaving a molelike trail over the mountains and across the plains under the snowfields, and leaving a wake of broken snow behind it.

It pulls up at a half-buried stop sign and suddenly viewers see the glow of red brake lights through the snow, then a flashing yellow turn signal blinking on and off. The object, not yet identified, turns left—and out of the frame.

A title card notes: "There's only one Jeep."

"This may have been the most arrogant commercial ever made," said Gary Topolweski, creative director at Bozell North. "Style is as important in a new car as it is in a new wardrobe, and we didn't even show the car."

"Snow Covered" violated other "tell 'em and sell 'em" auto advertising traditions than not showing the metal. There are no actors or announcers, no glamorous model draped over the hood, no "hero" plowing through woods or pulling the competitors over a stream to upbeat music. Indeed, there are no people at all.

Nor is there talk of horsepower, braking systems, or air bags, nor of lease rates and warranties, and no suggestion of friend envy. In fact, there's no talk at all, just thirty seconds of silence.

The spot came about after Bozell, which had been doing Jeep advertising for thirty-five years, was surprised when sales soared in the mid-eighties. To intensify whatever elements were causing it, the agency hired a cultural anthropologist.

He identified four unique threads tying consumers to Jeeps. The first is that Jeeps are "integral to the experience of nature, not just a conveyance for getting to nature," said David Kerr, former advertising and market planning director for American Motors Corporation. Jeep owners say their fishing trip begins when they load the car, not when they get to the cabin. The second element is that Jeeps are the authentic, original go-anywhere, do-anything vehicles, unmatched in ruggedness, durability, and technical superiority (even though, Kerr said, most Jeep owners take their cars off the highway less than 10 percent of the time. The attraction, he said, is that Jeep brands the owner an outdoorsman, rugged individualist, a macho Marlboro man.). Then too, Jeep affords its owner mastery—the ability to control life

56

and leave little to chance. And Jeeps are versatile, easily able to fit in anywhere in a lifestyle from casual to elegant, from the opera to the outback.

"Snow Covered" dramatized three of those threads: nature, mastery, and authenticity. And it did it in a way that suggested that Jeep alone had conquered this terrain. "You can't visualize any other vehicle in that spot," said Topolweski.

The way to execute those threads began as a late-night doodle. Senior art director Andy Ozark was watching the movie *Tremors*, featuring subterranean earth-displacing creatures, and thought of Warner Bros.' Bugs Bunny cartoon characters burrowing underground, leaving piles of dirt above their path. He drew a Jeep like a cartoon gopher.

Copywriter Peter Pohl essentially pressed himself out of service: voices or voice-overs would diminish the impact of the spot, he argued. Motion and strong visual imagery would better make the case. And because it's wordless, it could run globally, he suggested.

Bozell hired director Eric Saarinen of Plum Productions, Santa Monica, to shoot helicopter footage of glacier landscapes in Kluane National Park, Yukon Territory, Canada, on the Alaska border, and Durango, Colorado. And they hired Digital Domain in Venice, California, to create the special effects. It was Digital's first job ever.

Digital devised software that animated a computer-generated snow mound, eliminating the need for Saarinen to use a motion-control camera. They created a two-thirds scale model of a Jeep they named the Snow Sub, and with a 100-foot cable attached it to a Sno-Cat, which grooms ski areas. The Sno-Cat literally pulled the baby Jeep under the snow for that burrowing effect. Digital composited real mounds of snow along with computer-generated mounds into the glacier background.

Initial filming attempts near Jackson, Wyoming, failed: the snow was too crunchy. The team moved to a site 10,900 feet above Molas Lake Pass, north of Durango, Colorado, where the snow was four feet deep and light enough to burrow through.

Some $1 million and three months later, after many literal "snow days" and production slowdowns due to the Los Angeles earthquake, Bozell had wrapped its subtly humorous and quietly majestic spot that demonstrated the car's Jeepness, heightened its image as a status symbol, and appealed to the yuppie audience spending their discretionary dollars on this gentlemen's truck, this weekend trophy.

"Snow Covered" initially aired during the 1994 Winter Olympics. Because the commercial does not feature a specific product its life was not limited to one model year and it still airs. It also still works. Since the spot began, Jeep's Wrangler, Cherokee, and Grand Cherokee have had record sales, up 97 percent. In 1994 alone, Grand Cherokee posted a 25 percent gain—its highest ever—compared with an overall 12.6 percent growth of all sport utility vehicles. It was the only domestic compact SUV to post a sales and market share increase in 1994.

" 'Snow Covered' enhances the Jeep legend and lets viewers complete the scene with whatever Jeep model they think most fitting," said Ed Brust, Jeep and Eagle general manager. "Not many brands can build brand image without showing their product."

COWBOY CHIC

One cigarette's journey from femininity to masculinity to ignominy

MARLBORO

FOGGY MORNING

LEO BURNETT, USA, 1967

Soft strings play. Cowboys camped out by their herd of horses on a foggy morning wake up to coffee that's been brewing over an open fire and savor the first cigarette of the morning. They've let their horses graze in the wilderness and then they start to harness them up, getting them ready to go.

The announcer says, "Come to where the flavor is. Come to Marlboro country."

One cowboy gets on his horse and rides off as the music crescendos.

The glorious, graceful cinematic commercial is part of what may be the longest-running modern campaign with one of the highest brand identification and recall scores in advertising. It took a relatively obscure product aimed at women, tied it to rugged individuality and masculinity, and made Marlboro the best-selling cigarette in the world.

For the first quarter century that Philip Morris made Marlboro, it limped along as a women's cigarette. Since its introduction in 1920, the pack was white and bore the slogan "Mild as May." It had a red paper "beauty tip" initially to keep the cigarette paper from sticking to a woman's lipstick and later to mask smudges—and a "tearoom" or woman's image. Men steered clear. By the early 1950s, fewer than one quarter of 1 percent of U.S. smokers smoked Marlboros.

It was then that Philip Morris set about transforming the brand. It redesigned the blend to increase the flavor, and replaced the white pack with a flip-top box with strong red and white colors and a new logo. And it fired the now extinct New York–based Cecil and Presbrey ad agency—even though the account supervisor on Marlboro was the son of the chairman of the board at Philip Morris—and hired the Chicago-based Leo Burnett.

Agency founder Leo Burnett, reviewing research wherein people regarded filters as for sissies, suggested repositioning Marlboro as an icon of machismo. To defeat effete, he said, go bold. He had proposed using the cowboy as its messenger to win the account. Burnett had a file of magazine images and, rummaging through them, came across a 1933 issue of *Life*. A feature in it glorified the American cowboy.

The agency's first ad for Marlboro ran in a newspaper in Miami, one of the few markets in 1954 where Marlboros could be bought. In fashioning the ad, art director Lee Stanley featured the cowboy as the centerpiece, and proclaimed that the redesigned cigarette ("new from Philip Morris") "delivers the goods on flavor."

By January 1955 the restaged cigarette was available nationally. So was the advertising. Some commercials featured the cowboy relaxed and savoring the smoke. Others used similar rugged-looking, steel-eyed men with sleeves rolled up to reveal tattoos: a navy lieutenant, a car mechanic, football players, a diver, a yachtsman, a radio operator, and lots of pilots. They were ideal, the original photographer of the series, Constantin Joffe, once mused, because many had a little wrinkling around the eyes. Their mission was to stress the filter, flavor, and flip-top box.

The tattoo, which suggested a romantic past and a man who had come up the hard way and is enjoying the fruits of his labor, soon disappeared— as did all the other emblems of masculinity except the cowboy. He consistently had the highest recall of all vocations depicted.

The advertising showed the man most men want to be, the fiction we create about ourselves, said Owen Smith, a vice president on the account at Burnett. He called the cowboy an almost universal symbol of admired masculinity and one that also appealed to women, who generally buy what they consider to be "a man's cigarette."

Sales began to climb—by 1956 Marlboro was the tenth biggest cigarette in the country with sales 107 percent ahead of 1955. But then in March 1957, *Reader's Digest* published a report on smoking's harmful effects on health. It said filtered Marlboros contained even more tar than unfiltered Camels.

Jack Landry, retired marketing director at Philip Morris, claimed that article increased people's awareness and consciousness of health and filter cigarettes, and drove smokers to Kent, which the article had rated low in tar and nicotine. For the next two years, Marlboro sales stagnated while Kent sales more than doubled.

Burnett tried to reignite the brand, even producing a series of commercials in which Julie London seduced Marlboro Men by warbling "Where there's a man, there's a Marlboro" in their ears.

After several other unsuccessful attempts, Burnett reverted to the cowboy and Western imagery and its appeal to individualists. In 1962, the agency bought the rights to Elmer Bernstein's score for the motion picture *The Magnificent Seven* and copywriter Tom Laughlin and art director Neil McBain conceived of "Marlboro Country." When the initial campaign line ("Marlboro Country—Come to Where the Flavor Is") was tested, it bombed. "Too macho and not enough female appeal," testers said. One study even predicted that the ad line would kill the brand within five years.

Even with such a dark prognosis, Landry urged the Burnett team to go ahead. After trying hundreds of poses and postures, they settled on real cowboys at the 475,000-acre Four Sixes ranch in Guthrie, Texas, as the physical representation of the mythic Marlboro Country. When the Burnett creative team came into Philip Morris's fourth-floor conference room at 100 Park Avenue with a recording of the theme of *The Magnificent Seven* to accompany footage shot there, "the whole thing jelled," Landry has said.

He expected the beautifully photographed, poetic series would slowly build the brand rather than motivate people to switch right away. And, initially, there was little effect on sales. But by 1971, when the TV industry voluntarily banned cigarette advertising, the simple, strong image–based campaign easily transferred to print (even without its memorable music) while competitors had a much harder time. By 1972 Marlboro had become the top-selling brand and surpassed Winston in 1976 to become the best seller in the U.S.

During that time, the shorthand symbol for tough-guy masculinity continued to resonate because it was both authentic and aspirational. When Ken Krom became creative head of the team he was instructed to set the tight-lipped cowboy in "any positive place where it looks like Marlboro Man commands his own destiny," he recalled.

The spots were also formulaic. Jim Braddy and Joffe, as the principal photographers of the Marlboro campaign in the past two decades, had more than three hundred special hats in their prop bin. Many were made from the silky hairs on the bellies of beavers with four-inch brims and six-inch straight-up creases so that the head from the chin to the top of the hat was an oval. That made it look like the hat is part of the model's face, as if he'd been wearing it all his life, said Krom. The hat, ropes, chaps, and rain slicker, the way the cowboy walked and rode, all had to express authenticity. (The team did take the liberty, however, of furnishing him with a clean hat.)

Part of the Marlboro Man's appeal is that he's "lived his life by his own rules and principles and wasn't dictated to," according to David Dangoor, executive vice president of marketing at Philip Morris. "It's believable that a man like that would only smoke a cigarette he likes."

Dangoor said the cowboy—or even just his boots and spurs, which were used to introduce Marlboro Mediums—also reinforces the fierce independence of smokers in an antismoking era and that the "communication device for freedom and enjoying what you enjoy most to do" works worldwide.

Since "Marlboro Country" landed on the advertising map, more than three trillion of its cigarettes have been smoked and Marlboro has become the world's best-selling puff, marketing some 300 billion cigarettes a year. It has around a 26 percent market share today—three times second-placed Winston—and the Marlboro brand had retail sales of more than $10 billion in 1997.

It has also been on the firing line. A quarter century after copywriter Draper Daniels contributed ad lines to the Marlboro Campaign, he wrote editorial ones seeking to eradicate smoking. The widow of Marlboro Man David McLean, who died of lung cancer, sued the tobacco giant for damages. And the government's ban on characters representing cigarettes in commercials has consigned the mythological tough guy who epitomized glamour and independence to the advertising archives.

STRANGE FRUIT

A bright idea for making lightbulbs a lifestyle choice

The scene opens on a very tight close-up of an orange in a man's hands. Slowly, he peels the orange to discover a lighted round bulb inside—illuminating the fruit in a transcendent way. Then the camera cuts to the hand pulling a pineapple into two halves—to reveal a big lighted oval bulb.

Voice-over (in Japanese): "Light brings to life those things in the evening that the sun brings to life during the day. It's no longer light's function to simply illuminate our surroundings. It's now light's function to present the various shades of the night . . . Light by National."

While gentle music plays, the camera continues to embrace this fruitful still life. It sidles up to peas in a pod and miraculously, the peas alight as six little bulbs. Similar things happen with a leek revealing a slender tube light, an eggplant, and finally a bunch of red grapes.

Voice-over: "National Light can assume many moods. Its Pana Ball bulb can be gentle for a soft light. Its silica bulbs can conserve energy and save electricity. Our fluorescent lightbulb Paluk show colors more naturally. We also have small U-shaped fluorescent lightbulbs for the evening. National's menu of light comes in three hundred varieties."

NATIONAL LIGHTBULBS
MENU OF LIGHTS

HAKUHODO COMPANY, LTD., JAPAN, 1982

The camera cuts to a fruit basket filled with lightbulbs of different shapes and forms and ends with the bulbs lighting up in a gracefully choreographed sequence.

Voice-over: "National has been lighting your world for fifty years."

Other lightbulb manufacturers have portrayed their bulbs as longer lasting, brighter, or more trustworthy, but none before Matsushita Electric Industry Company's arresting commercial had suggested you can see the world more artfully, indeed, more artistically through them.

Hakuhodo broke ground with a commercial whose language was as poetic as Japanese flower arrangements—perfectly matching visuals startling both for the way the fruit was lighted and the way that the light transformed it.

Yuzuru Mizuhara, Keiichi Watanabe, Nobuhiko Mega, and Masaya Shibata conceived this ninety-second commercial to demonstrate that illumination is no longer the only function of lights, that they can be as effective a mood accessory as a fragrance. Their goal was to make this utilitarian product a desired life enhancer, justifying a premium price. They didn't realize that in the precomputer age, they'd be cutting a new technological path.

"When Yuzuru Mizuhara of Hakuhodo showed a presentation board of three colorful pictures, I wondered if I could possibly do it," said director Masatake Satomi. But as he drew sketches of fruits, "they gradually began to form a clear image. I then realized that one could feel the freshness of fruits only from real fruits." He then began a series of tests to find the best way to achieve the glow. Ultimately, Satomi achieved the astonishing effect by scooping out the fruits and wiring them with power cables and adjusting the lighting exposure. It was painstaking detail work, but in the end, he said, "a small green apple grew larger and ripe."

HUNGRY NO MOA

A Japanese noodle manufacturer's prehistoric take on convenience food

NISSIN CUP NOODLE

MOA/WINTERELIUM

HAKUHODO COMPANY LTD., 1993

In "Moa," a pack of tiny tribesmen, waving spears and gibbering wildly, chases a giant purple moa, a cross between a monster ostrich and a dinosaur, across primal terrain. The moa speeds up, then comes to a screeching halt at the edge of a cliff; then the ostrisaurus jumps into the air. The mob of tribesmen chases on right under it—and hovers. He stamps his feet. They all fall out of sight. The ostrisaurus stomps back out of the scene. All of this computer-generated imagery occurs to lots of grunting, falling, and thumping.

In "Winterelium," an enormous mammoth stamps onto a primeval desert landscape, its whole bulging body covered with tiny brown objects that look like leaves. It is groaning and thumping and bellowing with rage. The megalithic monster shakes itself like a dog out of water. The tiny objects fly off and fall to the ground, all except for one, which smacks off with its tail. The tiny objects turn out to be hundreds and hundreds of Lilliputian cavemen. They get up and race off, yelling in pursuit of the giant beast.

Both spots end with the same tag:

A macho voice grunts "Hungry?" with a super asking the same question (both in English). "Cup Noodle," they both respond, "Nissin."

They close with a product shot of Cup Noodles, the easier meal option.

Most Japanese advertising appears incomprehensible to outsiders and Nissin's bewildering scenes are no exception. Yet in their fanciful way they serve up a hearty message: cup noodle is convenient and easy to make.

The ads are aimed to associate Nissin with hunger satisfaction, to indicate that good food can be obtained anytime without hassle in this modern era. They were also designed to increase brand loyalty to the world's leading instant noodle. Nissin Food Products Company was founded in 1958 by Momofuku Ando, who invented the world's first instant noodles after noting customers lining up at Japanese ramen, or noodle, shops.

The campaign was conceived by Susumu Miyazaki, chief creative director of a Hakuhodo creative division. In mid-1991 Nissin had decided to replace a campaign created by Dentsu, featuring Arnold Schwarzenegger, that had run for three years but which, Nissin determined, wound up promoting Schwarzenegger more than the noodles. Nissin asked Hakuhodo, the second-biggest advertising agency in Japan behind Dentsu, to come up with a new campaign to compete with Dentsu's. Miyazaki and ten of his team camped out at the Harumi Grand Hotel for a two-day nonstop brainstorming session that resulted in the birth of the cavemen.

The first commercial, which aired in January 1992, showed the tribe of tiny cavemen chasing a mammoth. In later commercials, the tribe's pursuit of a pterodactyl, brontosaurus, and giant squid in futile searches for fresh food always ends in defeat.

Miyazaki, who has worked on Nissin for twenty years, said they miniaturized the cavemen and made them a little less smart than their prey to allay the client's concerns that viewers might be threatened by cavemen.

In 1994, Nissin zeroed in on a Stone Age family. Hakuhodo created a spoof on dinnertime in which a Stone Age wife sends her husband, armed with his club, out for food. Crashes and bangs are heard outside. A mammoth's trunk then opens the door and tosses in a disheveled husband. The prehistoric animals still have the upper hand.

The theory goes that because Japanese consumers assume that all goods produced there are high quality, it's pointless to dwell on a product's benefits. Image wins the day, but breaking through the clutter on TV often results in baffling ads that stick in consumers' minds mostly because they're still trying to figure them out.

The Moa and Winterelium spots, like much Japanese advertising, relied heavily on the soft-sell, fantasy approach and use of cartoon characters to create a mood. There's little selling or product usage demonstrations or touting of unique features in Japanese ads. Just as Japanese clerks greet customers in their department stores by thanking them for coming, soft-sell advertising invites the consumer to kindly take a closer look at the product. Japanese advertisers feel the need to justify why their commercials are interrupting the show.

Nissin noodles, which spends about $118 million a year on advertising in Japan and an additional $24 million in other markets, saw sales climb as a result of the commercials. By 1995, total domestic sales had surpassed 10 billion cups. And even as competition increased, the Cup Noodle brand maintained its 80 percent sector share and Nissin its 35 percent share of the overall market.

"Hungry?" secured "the goodwill of a vast number of consumers," said Norio Sakurai, Tokyo-based assistant manager of Nissin's advertising division. But recently the company has focused more on the product itself and the place it is sold. "It's time to shift attention to the distributors and retailers and reward their painstaking efforts by emphasizing the stores," Sakurai said.

GRRRL POWER

Perrier tries to regain the lion's share of the market

Moving on all fours across a parched landscape in the African savannah, a parched, determined woman and big thirsty lion toil up opposite sides of a mountain and unexpectedly come face-to-face at the top. Between them stands their quarry: a bottle of Perrier. The ferocious lion bares its yellow fangs and roars; the woman roars back even more mightily. As rock classic "I Put a Spell on You" plays on the soundtrack, she points a commanding finger at the lion, who skulks off. The woman lifts the bottle skyward, and drinks greedily as a voice-over declares, "Perrier—Earth's first soft drink."

PERRIER

LE LION

OGILVY & MATHER, FRANCE, 1991

In early 1990, Perrier's bubble had burst. Researchers discovered traces of benzene, an industrial solvent and carcinogen, in its bottles. Although Perrier had sold its water as a luxury item, the "champagne of table waters," and not as a substitute for tap water or health-giver, consumers in the health-conscious 1980s went ahead and assumed that the world's best-selling bottled water was absolutely pure and therefore healthy.

The adult soft drink had hit troubled waters. The French manufacturer withdrew every bottle from worldwide circulation, and when it reintroduced Perrier three months later, sought to reestablish its credibility. At first, Perrier made light of the benzene incident. Then, recognizing that rivals were swooping vulturelike, it switched gears to focus on the innocuous concept of refreshment with lion and lioness.

"Le Lion," art directed by Christian Reuilly and overseen by creative director Bernard Bureau, presented "the very meaning of Perrier—its naturalness, purity, and emotion—in a daring and dramatic way," said Richard Girardot, director of marketing for Perrier Vittel, S.A., in Paris. "The beauty overcame great odds to reach her life-giving refreshment. And the sparkle of Perrier, which is essential, was reinforced through a mix of originality and humor."

The new strategy was to present Perrier as a refreshing thirst quencher and the Perrier bottle as hero, said Frederik Zimmer, managing director of Source Perrier. "Le Lion" also aimed to attract younger drinkers and bring the brand's disparate approach to advertising in Europe under a common theme. Wordless (apart from the voice-over at the end), and dominated by simple imagery, the showdown was exportable. It also ran in the U.S., replacing the interim post-benzene spots and the long-running, whimsical "It's perfect. It's Perrier."

"Le Lion" was not universally admired. Environmentalists complained that the woman won over the beast on his own terrain and ascribed neocolonial overtones to the spot. When it won the Grand Prize at the Cannes

Advertising Festival, the audience booed and jeered. Director Jean-Paul Goude, who also directed Egoiste's "Balconies," booed the crowd back and purposely dropped the statue on the stage as he exited.

Despite a massive advertising effort, Perrier never quite regained its sparkle in the U.S. Deprived of Perrier for at least six weeks, yuppies discovered the fizz in San Pellegrino, the clean taste of Saratoga, and the relative cheapness of seltzer. (In the U.S. alone there are some seven hundred brands of bottled water.) Perrier's share dropped to half its previous high. But in France, Perrier's biggest market, people appreciated what they saw as lighthearted charm in "Le Lion." Sales returned to the bubbly's precrisis market share of around 38 percent.

VODKA GOGGLES

Smirnoff offers a young audience a new perspective on drinking

SMIRNOFF

MESSAGE IN A BOTTLE

LOWE HOWARD-SPINK, U.K., 1993

The commercial opens in a cocktail bar on a prewar ocean steamer. A surreal, Edward Gorey-esque atmosphere prevails. The crowd murmurs as a pianist croons a love song. The camera follows a waiter carrying a Smirnoff bottle and two frosty glasses on a tray. He sets the tray down and goes off to serve the drinks. Then, strange things happen to objects seen through the bottle.

A flower becomes a Venus's-flytrap. A lady's fox stole comes fearsomely to life and snarls. Seen through this peculiar filter, a smoker spews fire and a necklace turns into a hissing snake. Two portly gentlemen wearing tuxedos are transformed into penguins while a demure young woman is revealed to be a veritable Medusa. A couple playing shuffleboard become a dominatrix in black leather and her slave—we hear the crack of the whip. And a harmless black cat sneaking past the bottle changes into a panther—its meow into a growl. The spot ends on a shot of the Smirnoff bottle as script on the screen notes: "If Smirnoff can do this still in the bottle, just imagine what happens when you drink it."

In 1992, Smirnoff was the best-selling vodka in the U.K., but its supremacy was being challenged by such rivals as Absolut and private label vodkas. "Message" was conceived to reassert Smirnoff as hip and happening, leading edge, to prompt and provoke a complete reappraisal of the Smirnoff brand, especially among younger drinkers who may have been swayed by rivals' cases and less wedded to the Smirnoff heritage. There was no obvious persuasive sales pitch.

"Message in a Bottle," created by art director John Merriman and copywriter Chris Herring of London's Lowe Howard-Spink and directed by Tarsem through Spot Films, was the first global campaign for Smirnoff. By the end of 1993, the commercial had been aired in twenty-five markets around the world and the campaign it spawned had appeared in fifty. Indeed, "Message" had a staggered launch so it continues to run in some countries even today.

"Message" launched the TV version of a campaign that had previously run in print. Magazine ads had suggested that nothing is quite what it seems when viewed through the medium of the bottle by depicting visual transformations that startled and amused. Before "Message," various disparate ad campaigns had stressed lifestyle, product purity, and Smirnoff's Russian heritage.

The ad was aimed at eighteen- to thirty-five-year-olds, said Alistair Wood, art director and board director at Lowe Howard-Spink. The campaign deliberately set out to break classic spirits advertising conventions that portrayed young affluent people in social situations having a good time while drinking the advertised liquor. The pitch was not literal or rational, but was instead designed to engage and stretch consumers' imaginations. The desired response, Woods said, was for the viewer to want to identify with this highly distinctive advertising and, therefore, also with Smirnoff.

"Message" moved cases "and motivated consumers to associate Smirnoff with purity, excitement, style, and fun," Wood said. Smirnoff's volume share climbed to 61 percent from 55 percent. From January 1993 through January 1994, consumer awareness of the campaign soared from 29 percent of the population to 93 percent, and correct brand association was up to 76 percent from 51 percent. Two-thirds of those surveyed (68 percent) said they were "highly involved" in the advertising while seven out of ten said the advertising "stands out as different" from all other advertising. And, perhaps most tellingly, almost half (46 percent) considered it "radical."

CHAPTER FIVE

BLOCKBUSTERS

Whether the goal is to take viewers' eyes off the ball, declare themselves in the game big time, or signal a radical change, the highly stylized, expensive technical tour de force is a surefire way to snag attention.

Citroën dazzled viewers with an outlandish, flashy commercial as an elaborate smokescreen to divert attention from the fact that its cars had no new models or features. The mission of Apple's "1984," probably the best-known commercial of the twentieth century, was grandiose in its Homeric proportions. The Macintosh, whose arrival it boded, was leading a revolution to change the world, taking computers (and power) from the elite cabal of big business and big government and transferring them to the people. Seizing the anti-Big sentiment of the day, "1984" fought fire with fire to stop the world in its tracks and bellow that something major was happening.

Nike has often used huge-budget spectaculars to declare it's a player. Grand-scale advertising also let Nike link itself to the energy, excitement, and nobility of sports and sportsmen. In oversized strokes, its momentous painting made heroes of its celebrity athletes and morally uplifted viewers who (by design) empathized with them.

British Airways went in for eye-popping visual effects initially to refocus the world on its strength—not the pricing or equipment advantages it had previously touted but its eminence and popularity. What better way to trumpet that this is the airline that flies more people to more countries than any other than via a costly, startling extravaganza?

Its single-minded mission was to tell the world that British Airways had changed from an undistinguished, uninterested bureaucracy to the world's foremost airline using visual (rather than verbal) cues instantly understandable to cultures throughout the world—and that size was the barometer.

And when British Air wanted to warm up its image, it produced a peace-love-we-are-the-world epic that reaffirmed its grandeur while emotionally reflecting people's desire to connect with other people. The blockbusters gave wings to British Air—not just by turning around a money loser but by creating what's been hailed as the advertising equivalent of man walking on the moon.

BIG BROTHER

In one stroke, a computer company changes advertising forever

"1984" opens on a gritty vision of the future—a monumental structure with an aura of doom. Blue-tinted, zombielike, gray-uniformed people with shaved heads and mouths agape ritualistically shuffle in lockstep into a huge assembly hall dominated by a huge screen. Big Brother orates from the huge TV screen: "For today, we celebrate the first glorious anniversary of the Information Purification Directives. We have created, for the first time in all history, a garden of pure ideology . . ."

The devolved zombies sit compliantly, staring straight ahead while Big Brother delivers the party line: ". . . where each worker may bloom secure from the pests of contradictory and confusing truths. Our Unification of Thought is more powerful a weapon than any fleet or army on earth."

As the crowd stares, unseeing, at the video screen, a young, athletic blond woman in red shorts charges in wielding a sledgehammer, pursued by ominous-looking "thought police."

The harangue continues: "We are one people. With one will. One resolve. One cause. Our enemies shall talk themselves to death. And we will bury them with their own confusion. We shall prevail!"

The woman runs toward the screen as the guards close in. She swings the sledgehammer over her head and throws it with all her strength into the oversized, menacing face. The screen explodes in a blinding flash of light, which sweeps over the staring, awed automatons.

Announcer: "On January 24, Apple Computer will introduce Macintosh. And you'll see why 1984 won't be like '1984.' "

APPLE MACINTOSH
1984

CHIAT/DAY, USA, 1984

"1984" the ad attracted more attention than the 1949 book by George Orwell on which it was based. Apple paid $500,000 for the sixty-second spot to run just once but it was repeatedly shown on news programs and was probably the most publicized moment in advertising history. It launched the genre of advertising as an event, transformed the Super Bowl forever from a football game to an ad spectacular, made Chiat/Day a formidable national creative force, and helped drive $4.5 million in sales within six hours.

People may not have understood the intended message entirely—that Apple was the computer for the masses, that the woman represented youth rebelling at oppression, and that what she was smashing symbolically was IBM, playing David to Big Blue's Goliath. But they knew that this eerie engrossing spot, which never showed the product or said what it was, spoke to them.

The day after it ran, according to Apple, 200,000 consumers flocked to dealers to view the Mac, and 72,000 bought the computers in the first 100 days, exceeding Apple's goals by 50 percent.

Before the Macintosh was introduced, Apple's future was shaky. IBM had swept past it to take the lead in the PC market in 1983 and its two most recent introductions had bombed and its stock was depressed. Macintosh could change both Apple's fortune and the way the world worked. "Computing had been in the hands of a close-knit elite and we were going to bust up that cabal and give the power to the people," said copywriter Steve Hayden (now working on IBM at Ogilvy & Mather). Macintosh was leading a revolution, he said, taking power away from big business and big government and putting it in the hands of the people.

Chiat/Day's mission was to get viewers to want something they'd never had before—a twenty-pound machine that cost $2,495 in 1984. It aimed to speak to college students and office workers, to appeal to those intimidated by competitors. But most important, its mission was "to stop the world in its tracks, to let everybody know that something terribly important has just happened," Hayden said. They had mused about a commercial that would play into the issues of the day: the anti-government Reagan revolution, fears over factory closings, the rise of automation, the ubiquity of Big Brother.

All that fell in place in the office of Lee Clow, Chiat/Day president and executive creative director. Clow was meeting with Brent Thomas, then art director, and Hayden, when he doodled a storyboard on a scrap of paper. It showed a guy watching Big Brother, when a girl bursts in with a baseball bat and smashes the TV.

Brent later shaped the vision, making Big Brother a dark and sinister monolithic corporate force that threatens to enslave us. He was aided by British filmmaker Ridley Scott, who directed "1984" after having just filmed the futuristic movie *Blade Runner*. The commercial was shot on a London soundstage, Shepperton Studios, and cost $400,000 to produce. (It cost another $500,000 to broadcast in its single national paid airing.)

In 1983, Apple marketing director Michael Murray (now at Microsoft) says Apple cofounder Steve Jobs handed him a newspaper clip about how George Lucas had marketed *Star Wars*. He'd made it seem like an instant and spontaneous hit but actually it was a marketing event meticulously orchestrated months before. Jobs pushed for the same strategy.

Initial plans were to run "1984" on New Year's Day college football games. Air date was ultimately pushed back to the Super Bowl to be closer to Macintosh's official introduction at Apple's January 24 annual shareholders' meeting. Jobs, not a football fan, worried whether computer buyers actually watched the game.

Apple tiptoed into running the spot: it was ready to bail out if another advertiser used an Orwellian theme. Chiat chief Jay Chiat worried so fervently about that possibility—particularly from a phone company, like Sprint, celebrating the January 1 breakup of AT&T—that it won permission to air the commercial in an obscure market in late 1983 so it could enter the commercial in award shows. Apple's directors were another threat. After a screening for them "the room went silent," recalled Murray. They couldn't believe the agency wanted to run that. One director, Mike Markkula, suggested the agency sell the reserved ad time. Chiat/Day did sell one of the two spots it had booked—and pretended it couldn't unload the second minute in the second half of the game.

The rest is history. Almost 100 million viewers—46 percent U.S. households—watched Apple's populist message. Its spectacular minidrama on the most-watched TV program of the year focused more attention on a new product than perhaps any commercial ever. IBM was not caught with its terminals down, however; Charlie Chaplin continued to tramp, an emissary from the undisputed leader.

The Cupertino, California–based Apple tried for another touchdown with feature film production values on the 1985 Super Bowl with "Lemmings." In that bleak and macabre commercial, a caravan of blue-suited, blindfolded, conformist executives trudge after one another through a bleak, surreal landscape, right off a cliff, whistling "Heigh Ho (It's Off to Work We Go)." In the end, one lifts his blindfold as a somber voice says, "The Macintosh office. You can look into it or you can go on with business as usual."

"Lemmings" took as big a plunge as the IBM minions it spoofed partly because it prematurely introduced Macintosh office automation products. A disastrous year followed in which Apple closed three of six factories, cut 20 percent of its employees, and in May 1986, after nearly seven years together, fired Chiat/Day and moved its account to BBDO. Soon after, the company fired Jobs.

In fall 1997, thirteen years after making history with "1984," Steve Jobs rejoined Apple and reassigned the computer company's advertising account to Chiat/Day, now TBWA/Chiat/Day.

Before he left Chiat/Day, Hayden mused about the mixed blessing of "1984." Despite the glory it brought to the company, some Apple executives rue running the spot because the image it created conflicted with today's more mainstream Apple. "It froze time in people's minds," he said.

WE'LL TAKE MANHATTAN

Size matters in the global air wars

BRITISH AIRWAYS
MANHATTAN LANDING

SAATCHI & SAATCHI, INTERNATIONAL, 1983

The scene is a NASA-type control room where engineers are guiding in for landing the aircraft "Manhattan." The scene shifts from the flying replica of New York island to astonished civilians, who note the humongous mass overhead.

Control Tower: "Roger, Manhattan. Continue descent to flight level eight zero."

Manhattan: "Roger. Descent to F.L. eight zero."

In the background are ominous sounds, as well as crunching feet on a sidewalk and a dog barking.

Control: "Manhattan, that's correct. Contact radar direction on one, two, zero. Roger, Manhattan. Continue to two thousand feet, reduce speed to one seven zero."

Voice-over: "Every year more people choose to fly with British Airways to more countries than with any other airline."

Ominous music swells along with a roar of engines.

Manhattan: "Manhattan is established needing two thousand feet on the glide path."

The voice-over continues: "In fact, every year we bring more people across the Atlantic than the entire population of Manhattan."

Control: "Manhattan, you are cleared to land. Two eight right."

Voice-over: "British Airways. The world's favorite airline."

Super repeats, "British Airways. The world's favorite airline."

On Sunday, April 10, 1983, British Airways ran a six-minute commercial during a weekend talk show in England. In it, Lord Kind, chairman of the "world's favorite airline," crowed about the airline's recent achievements and for the first time showed a futuristic *Close Encounters*–like ninety-second spot with eye-popping visual effects.

In "Manhattan Landing," as the spot was called, the well-lighted borough soars across the Atlantic to Heathrow in London like an aircraft, to the amazement of people below.

This expensive and startling blockbuster was designed to highlight how British Air was bringing the world's major cities and peoples together, how it "flies more people to more countries than any other airline," and more over the Atlantic than the total population of Manhattan. (Ironically, at that time Aeroflot actually carried more passengers, but because its flights were primarily domestic, BA's international claim held.)

Saatchi & Saatchi saw its mandate as creating a campaign that was simple and single-minded, dramatic and groundbreaking, instantly understood throughout the world, visual rather than verbal, long-lasting, likeable, and confident. In short, it would be quite different from all other existing airline advertising.

Apart from its extravagant effects, "Manhattan Landing" was unusual at the time because, unlike other airline spots, it did not feature airports, planes taking off in the sunset, or smiling stewardesses. It cost almost $2 million to make and simply promoted the image of British Airways as a major airline. The ninety-second spot had no voice-over during the first forty seconds—and only thirty-five words of announcer copy in all.

"Our goal then was to reposition British Airways as a world-class airline and as a worldwide carrier," said John Lampl, public relations manager for British Airways U.S.A. British Airways had been running in the red and in the rear: people quipped that BA stood for Bloody Awful. The carrier was considered cold, routine, shabby, and uncaring, a shambling bureaucracy lacking in imagination and disinterested in its passengers. Research conducted in July 1982 showed that consumers saw BA as a large, experienced airline with modern equipment, but it rated poorly on friendliness, in-flight service, value for money, and punctuality.

But it had one major strength: it flew more passengers to more places than any other airline, and Saatchi & Saatchi decided to play to that strength—thus "World's Favorite Airline" was conceived—and to worry about warming up the airline later. Another goal was to help the carrier take a larger chunk of New York-to-London air traffic, one of the busiest international routes in the world and the world's most profitable route.

Before "Manhattan Landing," British Air advertising was inconsistent from country to country. In the U.K. a flight attendant promoted the patriotism aspect of flying the national flag carrier. In the U.S. from 1971 to 1980, droll English actor Robert Morley extended the welcome mat, promising "We'll take good care of you" in a series that emphasized traditional British values. (Sir Laurence Olivier was originally offered the endorsement role but he turned it down.)

The Morley ads were designed to soften the carrier's stern image. But British Air scrapped it after its executives complained that the campaign caused problems by overpromising customer service. Its at-home "Fly the Flag" spots reinforced BA's Anglocentric image and worked against its claim to be seen as an international carrier.

Overall, before "Manhattan Landing," BA advertising urged passengers to choose the carrier based on product feature advantages such as better equipment, pricing, scheduling, competencies, and in-flight entertainment. Many of these earlier ads included the price.

Because 42 percent of BA's revenues were made in the United Kingdom, the company based its epic commercial there, but ran it in seventy countries around the world, helping to justify its hefty cost. At the time, BA flew to eighty-nine cities in sixty-two countries outside the United Kingdom.

Not everyone in these countries greeted the blockbuster warmly. Former British colonists scoffed at the "World's Favorite Airline" theme. The Japanese country manager refused to run it outright. Managers in some countries fretted that it wouldn't sell seats. Others worried that there wouldn't be enough money left over to fund fare and tactical advertising. (BA subsequently raised the budget and allocated 40 percent of the new budget to the worldwide concept campaign and 60 percent to local market advertising.)

GLOBAL FACE

British Airways looks at the big picture

BRITISH AIRWAYS

FACE

SAATCHI & SAATCHI, INTERNATIONAL, 1990

A triathlon's worth of swimmers in red caps and costumes emerge from the ocean to an island-type drumbeat that turns into opera-style hymnlike singing with an international flavor. An aerial shot shows the massed bodies moving up the beach in the shape of human lips.

Another overhead view shows hundreds of figures in blue, gliding through a city in the shape of an eye.

In a field, other people, clad in white, form an ear. As the jigsaw assembles a voice-over announces:

"Every year, British Airways brings twenty-four million people together."

After shots of men and women of all nations embracing across the image of the British flag, we return to an entire face made of tiny figures coming together in the Utah salt flats. It smiles. It winks. It turns into a map of the world.

Voice-over: "British Airways. The world's favorite airline."

A super, "British Airways," is accompanied by the zooming noise of an aircraft flying by.

British Airways, which brings 24 million people together each year, produced a marvel of human choreography in bringing together hundreds of colorfully dressed people in breathtaking synchronization to form a human visage that winked and smiled.

The spectacle, directed by Hugh Hudson, who'd also directed the movies *Chariots of Fire* and *Greystoke,* used four thousand people, largely high school and college students who were enticed by the competition of winning ten flights to London as prizes.

The score "Flower Duet" from French composer Delibes's French opera *Lakme* soundtrack was arranged by Malcolm McLaren, former manager of the punk band the Sex Pistols. It ran with revised music—Pavarotti singing "Nessun Dorma"—within the U.K. broadcast of the World Cup. The scenes were choreographed by American Judy Chaboia, who engineered the opening and closing of the Seoul Olympic Games in 1988.

Filming took nine days in Utah's flats, cities, and mountains with several retakes. This extravagant film, brimming with universal emotional experiences and no dialogue, and costing $2 million to make, was watched by more than 600 million viewers in seventy countries and fifteen languages—twice as many as who'd watched E.T., then the most popular film of all time. Millions more watched the making of the commercial in a video shown on BA flights and even at the Wall concert in Berlin.

From 1982 through 1985, the mission of "Manhattan Landing" was to establish the airline's new theme line and impress consumers with the size, stature, and internationalization of BA. It told the world there was a change at BA—and that size was the barometer.

Beginning in 1985, BA shifted tactics from image-building to more pragmatic advertising aimed at the business traveler, crowing about new service changes. In 1988, a year after British Air was privatized, Club World was launched. Ads touted the wider club-class seat, promised the airline would "take super care of you" and that it would "deliver you ready to do business."

By 1989, research showed British Air that it needed to bring more warmth and humanity to its brand personality—especially competing against Virgin, which had positioned itself as "friendly"—and that it was in danger of becoming too targeted at business class. BA decided to refocus on a wider customer base. Eager to disassociate the airline from people's attitudes about Britain, BA management decided to reaffirm the size of its international network while bringing more warmth and humanity to the brand personality with a peace-love-we-are-the-world message on the scale and grandeur associated with its earlier blockbuster. "Face" emphasized BA's size while reflecting the real end benefit of flying—that people do it to meet other people.

A follow-up commercial in 1992 emphasized how "All around the world British Airways makes millions of people feel good." By 1993, BA was back emphasizing its Club World that "helps you recharge."

In 1995 the newly formed M&C Saatchi agency had wrested British Airways' $100 million advertising account away from Saatchi & Saatchi after an eleven-year run and a boardroom coup that jettisoned Maurice and Charles Saatchi from the agency they'd founded.

Their first work: another $2 million resplendent extravaganza directed by Hugh Hudson and backed by a haunting soprano voice accompanied by strings and percussion. In a five-week shoot on an island off Australia's Great Barrier Reef, Hudson organized 300 actors, 40 boats, an assortment of helicopters and stunt pilots to cover the island in 40,000 square feet of red, white, and blue silk as actor Tom Conti articulated the tagline, "We cover the world."

The following year, M&C Saatchi came out with "Dreams," a surreal commercial that focused on the hopes and dreams of 30 million people who fly BA every year. Sequences included a middle-aged couple splashing each other playfully in a lake, a woman watching lavish Chinese theater, a businessman struggling with a huge metal dollar sign, and a man being chased through the snow by faceless horsemen. Each reflected the dreams of BA passengers, later shown savoring the comforts of BA's business services. There was no spoken dialogue, only a voice-over at the end.

BA's general manager of marketing and communications, Derek Dear, said "Dreams" demonstrated three key objectives: BA's price competitiveness, its Club World relaunch, and the corporate change of gear from global to personal.

M&C Saatchi pumped out another lavish and emotional spot the following year. In "Tears of Joy" a montage of multicultural people joyfully cry at a wedding, a reunion, and the birth of a child. "The world is closer than you think," declared the voice-over as the by now familiar BA aria played in the background.

Other spots were more tactical. One showed a sleepy, suit-clad traveler literally floating out of his business club–class chair. Another accentuated price by showing a hospital patient rolling his bed into a deserted street and yelling, "Where is everybody?" They presumably have taken advantage of BA's low fares to Europe.

"Manhattan Landing" and "Face" helped give wings to British Air. The carrier, which in 1982 was losing 100 million pounds, by 1993 was the most successful international airline in the world and the most profitable. Load factors (that is, the percentage of seats filled) and profit margins grew and in most major markets it is rated more prestigious, more international, more "ahead of the field," and friendlier than its major competitors. The two spots became talked about (and spoofed); they've been hailed as the advertising world's equivalent of man walking on the moon.

QUALITY IS JOB #2

A flashy campaign avoids benefits and delivers glitz

A sporty compact Citroën Visa GTI is poised on the deck of an aircraft carrier, the Clemençeau, *while an enthusiast of the car bets that he can beat France's famous Super Etendard jet in a race.*

A pair of buffoon aviators, his pals, scoff and supply comic relief.

"Wow, that beat me," says one.

"How about taking a spin on the deck?" says another.

"With my GTI . . . sure thing," says a third.

"This guy's crackers!" says the first man.

"Get ready for the big splash," chimes in the second man.

As the announcer calls crewman No. 4 to the deck, we hear the revving of the car and jet engine. Then the car speeds down the flight deck of the aircraft carrier. As it races ahead, the driver gives the thumbs-up, but then as the jet takes off, the car somersaults off the edge and plummets into the ocean.

The first man laughs, "He really took a dive that time!" But seconds later, as royal marching music plays, a submarine surfaces with the Citroën perched on its foredeck.

"GTI: The wild one," says the announcer.

CITROËN

LE CLEMENÇEAU

ROUX SEGUELA CAYZAC GOUDARD, FRANCE, 1985

There was no promise in this commercial—no reason given to buy the car. But the spot, dubbed a "pub-spectacle" by the architect of Citroën advertising, Jacques Seguela, did something more important. It masked the car's aching vulnerability.

Throughout the 1980s, the agency's task "was to throw up a smokescreen while Citroën strove to modernize and extend its product offer," said Jean Luc Lenoir, head of the Euro RSCG division that handled the $118 million account. Years later Lenoir admitted that "in the absence of attractive car models, we tried to ensure that the brand image remained as attractive as possible."

Citroën was founded in 1919 but did not advertise for its first fifty years. The smallest of the big three French automobile brands, Citroën started running commercials in 1969—a year after the government began allowing regular TV commercials in France—because of growing heat from its competitors, according to one-time ad director Claude Planche. Before World War II Citroën was known for road handling and technological superiority: it was, for example, the first company to mass produce a front-wheel-drive automobile. But after the company's collapse in the wake of the first gas crunch in 1973—and its bailout by sister company Peugeot—Citroën was a shadow of its former self. Few new models were coming out, and those that did were considered unreliable. Its buyers were older, which also detracted from its chic image. Citroën's market share had dropped from 16.5 percent in 1979 to 13 percent by the end of the 1980s.

Short of a complete overhaul, the company needed some outlandish flashiness that didn't focus on specific benefits. Euro RSCG chairman Jacques Seguela said the spot is typically French in its bright, glossy, and just plain entertaining approach. The French are more disposed to appreciate good photography or a creative scenario; they are not ashamed to sit back and savor them. This flash put the company in a holding position while it reengineered itself.

By 1994, however, Citroën's products had caught up with its imaginative advertising and a new campaign was launched to focus on specific benefits. Lenoir said that by then emotion was not sufficient to drive a car sale. Prospects need to see solid product benefits, a promise that is "complete, programmatic, and practical," he said. With Citroën, the goal was to tell a story of modernity and technological superiority. With its benefit-specific "Discover what Citroën can do for you" advertising, after decades of decline, Citroën finally began to turn its sales around.

MANICHEAN UNITED

The moral of the story: just buy it

NIKE

GOOD VS. EVIL

WIEDEN & KENNEDY, NETHERLANDS, 1996

The spot opens on a Roman amphitheater in apocalyptic light. A cleft foot stamps in the ground; the lines of a soccer pitch are etched in flames. Dramatic music plays as an announcer declares in stentorian tones: ". . . and on that day, a dark warrior rose to the earth to destroy the beautiful game."

Suddenly, the arena is filled with a demonic, baying crowd. Horns sound and the crowd cheers as a team of monstrous devils line up against the world's best soccer players in their Nike garb. "Maybe they're friendly," Paolo Maldini says hopefully. The brutal opening action confirms otherwise. Appalling fouls by the forces of evil are ignored by the blind referee. There are many body slams and much deft maneuvering. Awesome play by Maldini, Patrick Kluivert, and Ronaldo leaves Eric Cantona facing the evil goalie, who has raised vast, black, batlike wings. The music grows increasingly intense with a drumbeat added and a chorus's chant. "Au revoir," says Cantona, the French star of England's Manchester United team. He boots the fiery ball through the chest of the eight-foot demonic centaur, who explodes on impact. Light flashes, then the Nike logo and sign: "Just Do It."

Since it was founded in 1972, Nike, has become synonymous with expensive, highly stylized, celebrity-packed advertising. This fresh, creative, technical tour de force fit right in. But when Wieden & Kennedy opened an office in Amsterdam to service Nike in February 1993, Adidas dominated the soccer market. Nike wasn't even in the same league.

Overseas, in a sport new to it, Nike started with a virtual clean sheet. "We couldn't assume that Europeans and Asians knew our stars that we'd put millions behind," said Joe McCarthy, Nike's one-time director of North American advertising. So the company did what it had done in other sports categories where it had established itself: it fired up the hero factory and put shoes on the feet of the star athletes in that category.

Directed by Tarsem, the visual extravaganza of "Good vs. Evil" grew out of the agency's previous soccer effort, "The Wall." The spot features a legion of Nike-sponsored soccer stars from around the world depicted as massive wall paintings who come to life and kick a ball around the globe. "The Wall" was so successful that Wieden & Kennedy decided to make another big statement about soccer, said David "Jelly" Helm, art director on the spot, who worked with copywriter Glenn Cole and creative directors Bob Moore and Michael Prieve. Moore wanted Nike to represent cultural diversity and figured an interesting way would be to re-create the bar scene from *Star Wars*. (Indeed, the characters look as if they'd been cast from that same scene.) The strategy was to show the competition (market leader Adidas) as so evil you wouldn't want to associate with it.

Helm said the spot looked a lot more expensive that it really was. The biggest production problem was getting all the players in one location—a second-century Roman coliseum in Tunisia. The spot was primarily live action: computer effects were only used to enhance what was already there.

Like "The Wall," "Good vs. Evil" exuded the energy, excitement, drama, nobility, and pathos of the sport. It celebrated the enduring grit, passion, and beauty of the players—and by extension, viewers who vicariously become part of that athletic moment. Like most Nike advertising, it was an appeal to what Nike founder Phil Knight calls "the idealized serious athlete who dwells in the imagination of millions of people." In stoking up viewers' personal fantasies, "Good vs. Evil" morally uplifted them. The shoes were associated with this aspirational urge and became a good deal more than footwear.

"The Wall" swept award shows but critics claimed it was more big budget than big idea. As for "Good vs. Evil," the spot was banned, however, by the Scandinavian advertising standards commission for "excessive violence" unsuitable for young audiences.

CHAPTER SIX

LESS IS MORE

Official Break of the Olympic Games.

It's easy to catch the consumer's eye with pyrotechnics, dramatic scenarios, and special effects. But to embed an idea in people's minds and change their perceptions about a product, all on a shoestring budget—that's brilliant advertising.

Clark's Shoes was able to implant, via a simple line drawing, the idea that its children's shoes fit superbly and its salespeople cared. Lego relied on the most basic stop-action animation to demonstrate the vast creativity and fun offered by its building blocks. MacGyver-like, Audi used a paper clip, a piece of string, a matchbox, and three matches to demonstrate an incredibly complex new design feature. McDonald's communicated the idea of a lifelong emotional attachment to its brand with an infant in her baby swing, rocking back and forth, smiling and scowling as she spies the Golden Arches and then loses sight of them. And Volkswagen padded a sidewalk lamppost to imply people would be so astonished by its unbelievable low prices that they'd walk smack into things.

In a no-frills, no-nonsense way, *The Guardian* showed the same scene from different angles to make us realize that only when you get the whole picture (as you do from this independent newspaper) can you fully understand what's happening. And Brazil's *Folha de Sao Paulo* juxtaposed a list of noteworthy accomplishments with a stark black-and-white photo that develops before our eyes into Adolf Hitler. Because "it's possible to tell a lot of lies telling only the truth," it's important that the newspaper you read gives you the whole picture.

SOFT PEDAL

A German ad, an American problem, a universal solution

A title card says (in German), "The Situation."

Cut to a paper clip lying inside a triangle of three matches in the shape of a highway danger sign. Fingers pick up the paper clip and model it into a steering wheel.

An announcer says (in German) "As a driver, you are most endangered by a head-on collision. The problem is the steering wheel mechanism, the most frequent cause of head injuries."

New title card: "The Idea."

Fingers tie one end of a piece of thread to the paper clip steering wheel and insert the other end through an open matchbox. The fingers slide the contraption into an ashtray, pushing the matchbox closed. As the front is pushed in, the "steering wheel" retracts.

The announcer says, "We guided steel cable from the engine block and connected it to the safety belts and steering wheel. In a head-on collision, the cables tighten the safety belts and pull the steering wheel out of the way."

Super: "The Result."

The announcer: "A new state-of-the-art safety system. One more reason to drive an Audi."

Super: "Advancement through technology."

Super: "Audi."

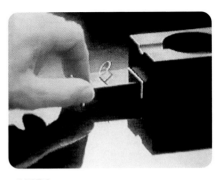

AUDI

PROCON-TEN

TEAM BBDO, GERMANY, 1987

When the Audi 100 was introduced in 1983, its unique technical advantages made it an incomparable breed apart, said Michael Hausberger, creative director of BBDO/Dusseldorf. Its most outstanding advantage was a safety system called procon-ten, but the technical details were complicated and difficult to explain. A team headed by creative director Eckart Rossler opted for stark simplicity—to not even show the car—to focus on this chief selling attribute.

"Our job was to translate this technical complexity into a simple but very convincing and impressive communication," said Hausberger. "We could have used a real crash scene to demonstrate how the cables tighten the safety belts and pull the steering wheel out of the way, but we wanted to convince people, not scare them," he said.

There was good reason to avoid scaring consumers. CBS's *60 Minutes* had run a segment in 1986 about purported incidences of sudden, uncontrollable acceleration in the Audi 5000, creating a worldwide publicity crisis for the company. Audi was besieged by more than one hundred product-liability lawsuits, seeking damages of more than $5 billion. Parking lots banned the 5000s and owners were gibed at for driving "the car that drives itself." Although a National Highway Traffic Safety Administration investigation would clear Audi in 1989 (it turned out that drivers were accidentally hitting the gas instead of the brake), the damage was done, said Richard Mugg who became head of Audi of America in 1988. Sales, which had topped 74,000 in the U.S. in 1985, plunged to just over 21,000 in 1989.

In the U.S., Audi dropped its 5000 line and reissued it under the 100 and 200 monikers. After a nine-month advertising blackout, it briefly ran an upbeat celebrity campaign to reassure owners, then sought to quell subliminal anxiety by softly promoting safety with its largest ad campaign since Audi had begun importing cars to the U.S. sixteen years before. "It's time we talked," newspaper ads boldly proclaimed. The company noted that all tests proved its safety and "apologized" for "letting the facts speak for themselves . . . Our silence not only offended our loyal customers but also prejudiced potential customers against us."

STYLE SENSIBILITY

A clear outline for a campaign based on old-fashioned values

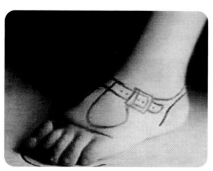

CLARK'S
BLUEPRINT

COLLETT DICKENSON PEARCE, U.K., 1977

"This little foot will get corns and bunions if a shoe's too tight across here," says an announcer, pointing to a tiny bare foot on which the simple outline of a shoe has been drawn. *"So Clark's makes a range that covers four different widths,"* he continues. *"And if a shoe only fits up to here, the foot can slide forward and stub the toes. So Clark's shoes always fit up to here."*

All the time, the announcer is drawing: over the foot, above the toes, around the foot, over the bridge, etc., until a complete sandal is drawn on the foot.

"And if the backs only come up this far, your child could develop claw toes trying to keep the shoe on. So all Clark's shoes carved the heel completely. And, of course, we always make sure there's up to three months' growing room in every pair. This is our blueprint—these are our shoes," he says as the drawn sandal dissolves into a brown, then blue, then tan leather shoe.

Super: "Clark's."

The beauty of this spot, created by Neil Godfrey and Tony Brigmore, was the impact achieved with such a small budget, said John Salmon, president of Collett Dickenson Pearce. People got the message: Clark's owns the franchise in well-tailored children's shoes and customer service. No one else is even in the same playground.

And the spot was flexible: the end of the commercial, where specific models were featured, could easily be updated as fashion dictated.

Clark's was founded in 1825 by brothers Cyrus and James Clark in the tiny English village of Street. Their first product, slippers called Brown Peters, stayed in production for one hundred years and helped build Clark's reputation for supple leather, expert stitching, wooden lasts, and loving craftsmanship. The company's ads, shop displays, and store personnel all stressed the shoes' features with no-nonsense cutaway diagrams. "Blueprint" furthered that approach and reinforced the brand's image.

Clark's ran "Blueprint" for a few years, but by the late 1970s, children were starting to make their own decisions about what to wear, and they wanted something glamorous, not stolid lace-ups. Clark's were worn by chalky teachers, Salmon said. They were out of step with mass-market fashion, the kind of shoes that were forced on you.

Since then, Clark's has taken pains to get hip while keeping hold of its core message of sensibility. It launched Commandos and Attackers—sensible and solid, but incorporating such features as animal-print patterns in their rubber soles and a compass in their composite heels. And more recent commercials demonstrate that, although Clark's has been making shoes since Queen Victoria was a girl, it also makes style-setters like the Desert Boot and is very much a company for the 1990s. (The Desert Boot was designed by Nathan Clark, the great-grandson of one of the company founders. Clark, who was posted to Cairo during World War II, had been inspired by British officers who wore handmade, crepe-soled suede boots bought from Egyptian street markets.)

In 1969, an ad for Clark's Desert Boots in *The New Yorker* featured a photo of a Desert Boot and a drawing of an "up-beat intellectual." The tagline read, "The off-beat casual for up-beat intellectuals." Neither the Desert Boot nor its target audience has changed much since then, but a recent ad, shot by David Bailey, pushes the fashion angle. Celebrities such as Oasis brothers Liam and Noel Gallagher, artist Damien Hirst, and actor Ralph Fiennes wear their original shoes, sandals, and Desert Boots.

TRUE LIES

A Brazilian newspaper brings failed leaders into sharp relief

FOLHA DE SÃO PAULO

HITLER

W/BRASIL, BRAZIL, 1987

The spot opens on a black dot. A slow pullback reveals that it is one element of a black-and-white photograph.

Voice-over: "This man took a destroyed nation, restored its economy and his people's pride." (A deep drumbeat.) "During the first four years of his government the number of unemployed fell from six million to 900,000." (Drum) "This man made the GNP gross 102 percent and doubled the per capita income." (Drum) "This man increased industrial profits from 175 million marks to 5 billion marks [drum] and reduced hyper-inflation to a maximum level of only 25 percent per year." (Drum) "This man loved music and paintings [the dots begin to reveal a face] and in his youth imagined he would pursue an artistic career."

The drum beats faster now as the camera pulls back to reveal Adolf Hitler.

Voice-over: "It's possible to tell a lot of lies telling only the truth. That's why it's important to be sure the newspaper you read gives you the whole truth. Folha de São Paulo. *Everyone buys it because no one can buy its opinions."*

Super: "Folha de São Paulo."

In 1984, a nationwide protest against Brazil's unpopular military rule, including a call for direct presidential elections, was led by the newspaper *Folha de São Paulo*, reasserting its commitment to freedom and to its readers.

"Hitler" vividly reinforced the paper's dedication and set it apart from its competitors. While much of the advertising in Brazil is colorful, sexy, celebratory, and fun, *Folha* used stark black-and-white minimalism with the texture of newspaper photos to cut through the clutter and mirror its solemn message.

Folha was already considered Brazil's most important newspaper then and it was advertising both a warning—lies can be told by telling the truth—and a covenant to the importance of freedom of the press, said Washington Olivetto, who, along with Gabriel Zellmeister, was the creative director on the campaign.

The commercial had extraordinary impact, according to Olivetto. And for very little money, *Folha* had an efficient, highly successful new approach that it has relied on since then.

In May 1991, for example, the paper ran an ad that showed the inconsistency between President Fernando Collor de Mello's campaign platform and his administration's first actions. (At the time, other newspapers were extolling the newly elected president.) The president had vouched, for example, that "all ministers will stay until the end of my administration," but most were gone within weeks of his election. "Although it's hard for the president to admit, he also makes mistakes like all human beings," said the same sober narrator. "To reveal these mistakes is not a crime. It is the duty of a newspaper that believes its readers have the right to know the truth." *Folha* repeated the spot in October 1992—after the president's impeachment—this time adding a reminder that the commercial had first been aired seventeen months before.

In 1997, to celebrate *Folha*'s seventy-fifth anniversary, W/Brasil ran a two minute and fifteen second commercial that narrated Brazilian presidential history (pointing out the leaders' toupees and inexplicable fatal strokes in a whimsical, breathless way). The spot "summarized our nation's turbulent political history with 100 percent true but incredible facts," Olivetto said. The point was to justify the commercial's end statement that *Folha de São Paulo* had been "trying to explain this country for seventy-five years."

NEWS VIEWS

A British paper argues for independence

This black-and-white commercial opens on a slow-motion scene as a young, rough-looking skinhead sprints down the sidewalk of a dull-looking street in an old industrial town. A car pulls up, slowing menacingly at the corner. A woman flinches on her doorstep as the punk runs past her.

The announcer, calmly and in a matter-of-fact way, says: "An event seen from one point of view gives one impression."

Viewers now see the same scene from a different angle. Now the tough-looking goon is dashing after an elderly businessman in a long coat and hat. He braces himself from what he anticipates will be the thug's attack by raising his briefcase to ward off a blow.

"Seen from another point of view, it gives quite a different impression," continues the voice-over while the camera cuts to a third shot from high up on a building across the street. Viewers see that directly above the oblivious older man, a large pallet of bricks is being hoisted up the side of a building and is swaying ominously. The punk sees it and races down the street to save the man's life by grabbing him to push him back against the wall—out of the path of the falling bricks as they rain down on the sidewalk.

THE GUARDIAN
POINTS OF VIEW

BOASE MASSIMI POLLITT, U.K., 1987

The voice-over continues: "But it's only when you get the whole picture you can fully understand what's going on."

The commercial fades to black. The words "The Guardian: The Whole Picture" appear in silence.

"Points of View" was created as part of a campaign to promote Manchester's *The Guardian* as an independent editorial voice. Most other major newspapers at the time were under the influence of entrepreneurial owners bent on convincing readers of their own views, thus affecting public attitudes and opinions and even the result of elections, said John Webster, the creative director of Boase Massimi Pollitt. *The Guardian*'s policy, he said, was to give writers of differing opinions the freedom to express them with little or no editorial censorship.

The film, shot in grainy black and white, looked more like a documentary than a commercial and demonstrated compellingly that, without perspective, nothing is certain. Except for a simple voice-over, the spot is silent, intensifying the drama.

"Points of View" was much admired and honored at the time, and there were many requests for copies of the ad. But perhaps the most interesting request came from a young South Londoner who phoned the agency asking to borrow a copy so he could use it in court to defend himself on a charge of assault.

KILLER KIPPER

Lego's abnormal play, plays well

LEGO

KIPPER

TBWA, U.K., 1980

To demonstrate a few ways Lego building sets can be used, the announcer starts out as a stop-motion animated Lego mouse standing outside his mouse hole when a Lego cat appears.

"You see, I was standing outside my mouse hole the other day, when all of a sudden along comes this cat," he says. To protect himself, he adapts a new persona. "So quick as a flash I turned into a Lego dog," he says as the Lego canine emits a timid "ruff, ruff."

"But the cat turned into a dragon," the newly transformed Lego creation continues with a roar. With this turn of events, things start to spiral out of control. "So I turned into a fire engine. How's that?" the creature adds with a degree of self-congratulation.

"And then . . . and then he turned into a submarine," the voice-over continues in a hilarious fish-tale buildup.

90

"So I became a submarine-eating Kipper." The creature transforms into Lego footwear to the chagrin of the toy narrator. "I said a Kipper, not a slipper.

"But he turned into an anti-Kipper ballistic missile," the high jinks continue, "so I turned into a missile cruncher . . . crunch . . . crunch . . . crunch . . . just in time to see him change into a very big elephant. So do you know what I did then? I turned back into a mouse and I gave him the fright of his life . . . just like that."

The elephant roars and keels over.

Super: "It's a new toy every day."

Lego is a variation of the Danish words *leg godt,* for "play well"— and, against the odds, this spot played very well indeed. At one time, the silly and imaginative "Kipper" appeared in the *Guinness Book of Records* as the most awarded commercial of all time.

The Lego company started out as a small carpenter's shop in 1916. By 1980, it had become Europe's largest toy manufacturer, largely by convincing schools and parents of the educational value of their toys. The company's advertising traditionally addressed the mother, playing to her joy in helping her child evolve, said Uli Wiesendanger, chairman of TBWA International.

"Kipper" went a giant step farther, Wiesendanger said. "It put the mother and child into the same persona. In this commercial, unseen, they play the game together."

This was a hard sell for the family-owned company, Wiesendanger said. "It didn't have young children or happy mothers cheering from the sidelines, which is what they thought they needed." And Lego had been so successful with their toys, the family that owned it figured, why rock the boat?

"Kipper" was essentially slipped through, Wiesendanger said. "It almost escaped their attention, and that's why it's so different from anything they've done before or since."

"Kipper" ran for only a few months and was then replaced by more conventional advertising. But even while the Danish company faces increased competition from upstart marketers of construction sets and the pull of computer games, it periodically has revived "Kipper" as Lego's icon commercial.

SWINGING UP BABY

McDonald's bid for the tiniest demographic

MCDONALD'S

SIGN

LEO BURNETT, USA, 1996

A darling infant is swinging in her baby swing to "Rock-a-Bye Baby." Forward and back she goes, letting out a happy smile when the chair swings up, but as it swings back she gives out a cry and makes a pouty face. Forward again, she lights up—only to swing back and sob. A reverse cut shows that the swing is directly facing a window. As the McDonald's theme music plays we see that as the swing comes forward, Baby can see blue skies filled with McDonald's golden arches. When the swing goes back, Baby can't see the sign anymore. A voice-over asks: "Have you had your break?"

Super: "Official break of the Olympic Games."

For more than a quarter century, McDonald's has followed the precept that, as society goes increasingly high tech, people need a high-touch antidote. Its advertising has consistently addressed the belief that people hunger for basic human values, to feel as if they are being addressed personally. McDonald's "isn't about slick ad slogans. Its job is to get the world comfortable with us, not call attention to itself," said Paul Shrage, McDonald's chief marketing officer. "It's all about humanity that establishes this friendly, homey turf as ours."

Perhaps for no other great service company has advertising played so key a role on such a scale. While McDonald's founder Ray Kroc brought predictability, it's the advertising that has brought the emotion.

"Sign" was designed to break through the creative competitiveness of Super Bowl advertising—not just stand out from fast food but from all advertising, said Cheryl Berman, Leo Burnett's chief creative officer. McDonald's had a reputation for producing Super Bowl winners, but other advertisers were catching up with witty creativity.

Most McDonald's advertising puts likeable characters in "honest" and realistic situations, speaking natural dialogue (not advertising copy) and captured with unexpected angles such as extreme close-ups or slow motion. More often than not, the camera flows with the action or creates action where none exists. Music is distinctive and mood-enhancing, often with lyrics that are to be sung instead of spoken. And there's a little magic moment that surprises you or chokes you up or makes you feel warm. The very palatable "Sign" had many of these ingredients.

The spot was conceived to communicate the emotional relationships people have with the brand—and that this lifelong relationship with McDonald's begins at a very young age. Creative director Bob Shallcross and director Jonathan Rodgers initially presented the idea on two slips of paper: one an open window with no Arches, the other with the Arches in plain view. The only sound would be that of a baby crying and then cooing.

Over the course of a day they filmed a baby in her swing, happy as can be, and then later on, catching her as her mood soured. In post-production they morphed scenes together of the happy baby seeing the sign and brightening, only to sadden when it vanished.

"Sign" aired only a handful of times and was the third-highest-rated commercial of the forty-one played on the Super Bowl. McDonald's did a Hong Kong version with a Chinese baby and Arby's created their own version: an ad showing a man on a porch swing doing the same thing in reaction to an Arby's sign. But great advertising (and $500 million a year spent on it) could not stanch McDonald's problems and the fact that too many restaurants are chasing too few stomachs. Its 1996 market share slipped to 41.9 percent while Burger King's rose to 19.2 percent, according to Technomic Inc.

HIGH IMPACT

Singapore raises a glass to discourage driving under the influence

The spot begins with a driver's-eye view of the road as a car races down a city street at night. To portray the effect of alcohol on the driver, a hand enters the screen and places first one empty glass and then several on the hood, between the viewer and the camera, distorting and blurring the driver's view bit by bit to the sounds of people chattering at a lively party. A final glass is added as suddenly, the car rounds a corner and the back of another vehicle appears. The car slams on its brakes, they screech, and the picture goes red. A voice announces (in Mandarin), "Each drink you have before driving impairs your judgment. Don't drink and drive," while the camera cuts to a red sign with the same message.

SINGAPORE TRAFFIC POLICE

GLASSES

SAATCHI & SAATCHI, SINGAPORE, 1992

In 1992, when Saatchi & Saatchi, Singapore won the assignment from the city-state's municipal traffic police to create a commercial to run around Christmas and again during the Chinese New Year, it proposed a morbid spot graphically showing the effects of drunk driving. Similar emotionally upsetting approaches had been effective in the past. But the Singapore traffic police nixed that notion because people had complained that gory ads spoiled their previous holidays. "Our challenge was to come up with a hard-hitting spot that didn't show dead bodies," said Francis Wee, art director for the commercial.

This Saatchi did with an engaging combination of music and mounting drama that brought to light the true dangers of drinking and driving (without specifically showing snarled fenders or bloody bodies).

93

The spot, conceived by creative director Linda Loke, copywriter Dean Turney, producer Anthony Lee, and directed by Larry Shin from Shooting Gallery in Hong Kong, must have worked: police statistics showed a 32 percent drop in arrests for drunk driving during the first year after the spot ran for its two months (of course, that only meant seventeen people versus twenty-five the year before). And they were compelling enough for Australian's primary road safety organization to adapt the spot and sponsor its airing Down Under. Belgium, South Africa, Canada, Hong Kong, and the United States also used the spot.

The Advertising Council, acting on behalf of the United States Department of Transportation, had created a similar spot in 1983 where a simple visual pun replaced the carnage. Two liquor glasses, shot in super slow motion by a camera designed to track missile launches, approach for a celebratory clink, only to shatter to the sound of screeching brakes. "When friends don't stop friends from drinking and driving, friends die," says a voice-over.

That anthem is repeated as two beer mugs also clink and break into shards. But the third time it happens, a hand intercedes—as the voice-over declares, "Friends don't let friends drive drunk." That spot, from Leber Katz Partners, also played around the world.

DANGEROUS POSTER

A knock-out ad about low, low prices

VOLKSWAGEN
LAMP POST

BMP/DDB, U.K., 1997

Two workers are busy on a city pavement making small talk. Using material from their van they affix white and red striped padding to a street lamp and affix a poster to the adjacent wall. "How many of these are there?" one man asks the other.

"Couple more I think," his colleague replies.

As they work the second man asks the other, "So you coming out tonight?"

His friend answers, "What do you think?"

His coworker chuckles. "Depends on whether she'll let you out."

Job done, they pack up, hoist their toolboxes, and start the engine. "Bet we catch all the traffic tonight," one says. The tires screech as they drive off. Viewers are somewhat confused, but see that the recently affixed poster is an advertisement for the Volkswagen Polo: "Polo, only £8145." A passerby strolls down the street and his head turns to stare at the ad. We are left with the certain knowledge that he will walk smack straight into the padded lamp post.

Super: VW logo, "Surprisingly ordinary prices."

With "Lamp Post," Volkswagen shifted gears to a proposition it had not before emphasized: low price. In 1994, as other car manufacturers had begun to catch up to VW on its quality perception, the German parent took control of its U.K. distributor and dealer network with ambitious plans to pump up sales. At that point, the deutsche mark was very strong—making Volkswagens, already perceived as expensive, seem even pricier and harder to justify. VW lowered its sticker prices, but research indicated that people weren't getting the message. "Consumers still believed that Volkswagens were way beyond their price bracket," said John Busk, account director at BMP/DDB. "The cars weren't making the shortlist" (the top three or so models considered by a given consumer).

Art directors and copywriters generally detest the assignment of promoting price or affordability. Andrew Fraser, who both wrote and art directed "Lamp Post," made a virtue of them in a believable and understated way that dramatized the surprising nature of VW prices. Its vérité style was in sharp contrast to the razzle-dazzle of most car advertising. Viewers, initially puzzled by what is easily taken for real footage, watched raptly, believing that they might have missed something.

"Lamp Post" was one commercial in a series that challenged consumers' perceptions head-on and, as required, communicated the new "affordability" of each of the VW models to their respective audiences. In another spot in the series, a woman gets queasy in the street discovering the almost unbelievable prices on a VW poster. In still another spot, a stiff-lipped Buckingham Palace guard does not flinch from all the tourists who try shenanigans to divert his attention. Only when a bus with the VW price tag drives by do we see a flicker of interest in his eyebrow. And in another, at a tennis match, all people's heads go back and forth watching the action and then stop. We don't see why until we spy the VW poster advertising price.

The distinctive and low cost "Lamp Post," directed by Paul Gay, ran on and off for a year. It helped push Volkswagen's U.K. sales to an all-time high in 1997 and changed people's perceptions. Having been regarded as 28 percent worse value for money than other cars in 1995, it shot up to 4 percent above the average in 1997 and its likelihood of being seriously considered went from 71 percent below its average in 1995 to 12 percent above the average in 1997.

CHAPTER SEVEN

LOVE IS ON THE AIR

Sex sells: it's been used to push everything from toothpaste to blue jeans to sleek sedans to condoms. Sometimes it's full of nuance and double entendres, as in Brooke Shields's come-hither, smirky "Nothing comes between me and my Calvins." Other times, it's more overt. In a Dunlopillo Mattress spot, items intertwine suggestively and, at the end, a train roars into a tunnel—reminding us that mattresses aren't just for sleeping.

But even risque advertisers largely hew to standard sexual tropes. Its teenage audience may be addicted to fads and change, but for decades Levi's has stuck to romance and rock to sell 501 jeans. It put its jeans on (and took them off of) perfectly physiqued, disenfranchised heroes who exude a raw sexuality that makes them palpably attractive to women in their orbit. Forget about the stomach, this is *the* way to a young man's heart (and wallet): our product will make you sexy.

But it's not just sex that sells. For many women, romance is even more seductive and erotically appealing—and turning it on its head, more winsome. Polaroid, with the sniping James Garner and Mariette Hartley, has toyed with Shakespeare's Beatrice and Benedict rapier-wit formula. Chanel's Egoiste (see page 46) gave the hyperattenuated *sturm-and-drang* sensibility a spin with its he-was-her-man-and-he-done-her-wrong commercial. That broke through the clutter by serving up the unexpected. So did Coty. It turned the usual boy-meets-girl formula upside down with a spot for its low-end perfume,

L'Aimant. In the ad, the air fairly crackles with sexual electricity as a woman and man lock eyes—before her true love arrives to playfully pull the rug out from under them and us.

On the other hand, Camay's unconventional couple—he, an aging, slightly paunchy shopkeeper, she, a matronly, staid, loyal customer—fall for each other (and new Camay) in a gentle spoof, making creamy lathering actually seem *less* lascivious. And in a particularly loopy spot, an unsuspecting, dorky soldier receives a Dear John audio in which his girlfriend croons that she's found another—his brother. On BASF audiotape "even the bad times sound good."

AUDIO INFIDELITY

A love song's beauty is in the ears of the beholder

A platoon is somewhere in a jungle when a helicopter flies overhead. Army trucks pull into the camera's view and a loudspeaker booms. The hard-bitten sergeant spits out mail call: "O'Riley! Pierce! Kowlasi! Crum! Gallagher!"

One dorky kid soldier receives a cassette. "It's from my girl, Shirley. We're gonna be married," says John as he pops the tape cassette into the player. Thrilled, he plays it out loud for his comrades to share.

"Dear John, oh how I hate to write," the song begins.

"Dear John, I must let you know tonight.

That my love for you is gone.

So I'm sending you this song.

Tonight I'm with another.

You'll like him, John, he's your brother.

So adieu to you forever, dear John."

Stunned, John lowers his head as the camera cuts away to a group shot and the slogan "Even the bad times sound good."

The camera quickly cuts back to the sergeant, who snaps, "Play it again, John."

BASF

DEAR JOHN

WHITAKER ADVERTISING, NEW ZEALAND, 1979

L ong before Maxell showed the power of its cassettes with the memorable image of the music fan being blown out of his chair or Memorex used Ella Fitzgerald to demonstrate its audiotape's superior reproduction, the German conglomerate BASF AG (Badische Anilin- & Soda-Fabrik) made a satiric play on the notion of fidelity—and Bogart's play-it-again-Sam scenario—with the notion that "even the bad times sound good."

BASF is one of the original players in the magnetic tape business, with products dating to 1932, but its advertising never made an explicit claim to technical superiority. Instead, it made a humorous pitch—with an implied claim of audio fidelity—to an audience that would lap up a sick joke.

Although BASF has since left the video and audio tape production business—and wants to shake the association so as to better concentrate on its core businesses of chemicals and pharmaceuticals—this commercial's effects are still felt. If the world continues to think of BASF as a tape company, it may well be because of ads like "Dear John."

OH, MISS BECKER!

A soap manufacturer works itself into a lather

CAMAY

SMALL STORE

LEO BURNETT, USA, 1969

The spot opens with a shopkeeper, Mr. Rogers, restocking his shelves with reformulated Camay soap.

"Out with the old and in with the new," the grocer announces. Miss Becker, a friend and loyal customer, glides by to ask for some. "Oh, Miss Becker, old Camay or new Camay?" the middle-aged and slightly paunchy grocer inquires.

When Miss Becker, a matronly lady in pearls, asks the difference, he explains that there is "twice as much lather in the new Camay, so much more lather, so much more cream." He rubs his hands together with the soap to test it out for her and then invites her to feel. He rubs some of the soap on her hands and they share some romantic epiphany as they gaze into each other's eyes.

"Oh!" she emits, weak-kneed as the wedding march plays in the background.

"Imagine all that lather putting all that cream on your skin, Miss Becker," the aproned Romeo continues as the pair work themselves into a lather, holding hands and looking sheepishly at each other.

"Oh, I feel it, I feel it," she breathes as romantic violins loudly swell.

"Albert," Miss Becker moans.

"Lucille," the smitten grocer sighs back.

And the announcer says, "New super-lathering Camay. Twice the lather, twice the cream. To believe it, you've got to feel it."

The super adds, "Super lathering."

It's hard to imagine in this age of high-tech niche soaps—antibacterials, moisturizers, hypoallergenics—that once, not all that long ago, there were but two basic soap segments: deodorant or complexion.

Camay was introduced by Procter & Gamble in 1926 and soon after carved out a front-running position among beauty bars. It was mild and gentle for the complexion and targeted to women in an era when they preferred white soaps. (Many imported soaps had colors added to mask impurities.) For years Camay was advertised as *the* soap for beautiful women, and it stayed at the front of the pack for years by selling sensuality, seduction, and irresistibility.

This gentle, romantic spoof, produced by Kaleidoscope Productions Inc., playfully continued that irresistibility theme. Other soaps, including Procter & Gamble siblings, had other pitches: Ivory had purity, Coast and Zest were body and soul rejuvenators, and Safeguard was the odor eliminator.

But as the soap aged, so did its users. What's irresistible to one age group is their father's Oldsmobile to another. And throughout the seventies, the women who bought Camay were lured away by many other soaps promising beauty, touting their bath oil, moisturizing cream, lanolin, or vitamin E emollients as a way to soften and condition skin. Camay lost ground to Dove and Caress and, in 1984, Procter & Gamble took it off the shelves for a year for a major makeover. It returned as a multiformula cleanser—pink soap in a pink wrapper promising "personal skin care for beautiful skin"—but the brand did not perk up, and Camay stopped advertising again in early 1986.

Four years later, with sales still dropping, Procter & Gamble again relaunched Camay with a new shape, new scent, and new positioning. It was now targeted to appeal to younger women, eighteen- to thirty-four-year-olds. Ads at the time showed the ethereal musings of three different women: classical-type Annie, natural woman Sophie, and exotic beauty Kate. Each represented one of the three new soap fragrances, flowery-soft and scented, fresh and pure, or "exotic, like orchids." Close-ups of flower petals were interspersed with shots of women soaping up in the shower, admiring flowers, and wearing dresses color-coordinated with the soap they represented. Camay marketers said the goal then was to represent emotions rather than lifestyle.

OBJECTS OF AFFECTION

A French company reminds us of the many uses for a mattress

A man and woman are in bed. As the romantic Serge Gainsbourg/Jane Birkin oldie "Je T'Aime (Moi Non Plus)" plays, the man rolls over and encircles the woman in his arms—a move imitated by the painting on the wall, which snuggles over to the companion framed nearby. The camera cuts away to the lace on one shoe reaching out to embrace the lace on the other. Two umbrellas entwine and one towel makes the moves on the other. The woman, smiling coyly, turns to face the man just as her shoe makes the move on its mate. The camera cuts away to the two hands of the clock: they also twist together. As the man rolls over onto the girl, his shoes mimic the missionary action. The commercial climaxes with the universal Freudian symbol of sexual penetration: a train roaring into a tunnel.

Voice-over and super (in French): "Dunlopillo, sleep as you love."

DUNLOPILLO

DORMEZ COMME VOUS AIMEZ

TBWA, FRANCE, 1986

f ever a commercial used sex to sell, Dunlopillo's ad for its mattresses is it. Indeed, the tagline, "Dormez comme vous aimez," carries a double meaning, said Uli Wiesendanger, chief of TBWA International. "It means both sleep like you like, that is, as it suits you best, and then to sleep like you make love," he said.

Traditionally, Dunlopillo had focused on its claim that its mattress was so well built that two people could move or sleep on it without disturbing each other. "Dormez Comme Vous Aimez" opened new territory to that "don't disturb the other" positioning. "It gently reminded people that mattresses are also the place where it is delightful to disturb someone else—where a lot of other things happen before or after sleeping," Wiesendanger said.

"Dormez Comme Vous Aimez" was an outgrowth of a long-running black-and-white campaign in France. Each of thirty different spots presented a captivating couple in bed—on their Dunlopillo mattresses. The overt sexuality helped lift awareness of Dunlopillo by 35 percent and worked particularly well with the young target audience, Wiesendanger said. Sales climbed 10 percent. Interest in the whole category rose. Dunlopillo benefited the most from the industry-wide surge in mattress sales.

But after two years, the company abandoned the campaign and opted for a rational-benefits pitch explaining why the mattress was so well built and how, when you awake, you feel rested. "The creative people had pushed the sexuality too far—objects were rolling around embracing—and the advertising lost its charm," said Wiesendanger.

PARLEZ-VOUS LE PARFUM?

A lesson in love and loss reverses the standard perfume pitch

COTY L'AIMANT

FRENCH LESSON

BOASE MASSIMI POLLITT, U.K., 1978

Super and voice-over: "A little French lesson."

Super: "La femme."

A woman wearing L'Aimant enters the bar. The voice-over translates le femme to "woman."

Super: "L'homme." The woman passes a man who is clearly attracted to her. The voice-over translates that as "man."

Super: "L'Aimant." The announcer "translates" L'Aimant as "le parfum." The man and woman catch—and hold—each other's eyes.

Super: "Les yeux." The announcer translates it as "eyes." The man and woman smile suggestively at each other.

Super: "La bouche" is translated as "mouth." The man leaves la chaisse, which, the language lesson continues to decode, is a chair, and walks toward her . . . just as the woman's husband—"le mari . . . oh, the husband" the super explains—joins her. The first man dejectedly returns to the bar, where he rejoins a "conversation" (the same word in both languages) that doesn't interest at all.

"Do you speak L'Aimant?" inquire the super and the voice-over.

Perhaps more than any other marketers, perfume makers know that sex sells, especially if it's sated. "French Lesson," however, playfully turned that formula upside down. Instead of allowing the prospective lovers to unite, the spot built up their hopes and passions—and then, in one deft and comic stroke, deflated them.

This was just one of many subtle twists in the campaign to reinvigorate the inexpensive fragrance aimed at office clerks, introduced by Coty in 1943. Most perfume advertising is high-tone imagery—"cold, detached, and snotty," said John Webster, art director of the spot. (Susan Trott wrote it; Hugh Hudson was director.) "French Lessons" instead offered an intriguing and involving story with a beginning, middle, and end.

In other ways, "French Lesson" zigged while its competitors zagged. Key rival Yardley was dallying with "prim English roses," and Max Factor and Goya were serving up "glossy cover girl stuff," Webster recalled. And while Chanel and other high-priced fragrances were presenting the French sensibility, no scent in L'Aimant's price league was doing so. "The English all think of the French as very sophisticated and romantic, having little dalliances," Webster said.

Indeed, for an extra air of authenticity, the agency hoped to film the commercial in the noted Parisian restaurant Prunier. Its proprietor, however, nixed the idea. Instead, BMP reproduced the restaurant brick by brick on a stage in London, flying over the props. Although hardly visible, elegant French food was on the plates. (Ironically, the lead actress was actually American.)

With all of these twists on the standard perfume pitch, the ad easily stood out from the pack, helping to make L'Aimant the company's best-selling fragrance. Young women were attracted by the advertising's wit and style and by the contrast of the very pedestrian words in the French lesson and the on-screen romance. And it didn't hurt that the perfume wearer was sought after by not one, but two men.

ORIGINAL BEEFCAKE

Rock and cowboys mean the real thing: authentic Americana

LEVI'S
CREEK

BARTLE BOGLE HEGARTY, U.K., 1994

An upright family traveling by horse-drawn, open-topped buggy pauses for a moment by the side of the road. While Father contemplates life and Mother reads, the two nubile daughters are allowed a few moments of liberation to explore a nearby creek. The sisters run playfully through a sun-dappled woodland, hair free from bonnets, when they're stopped in their tracks by the sight of our bare-torsoed hero bathing in the creek, a pair of trousers left on the bank. To the backdrop of the hard rock song "Inside," by Stiltskin, they experience their first sinful feelings on discovering this apparently naked young man in the water. Horrified, but unable to contain their curiosity, the girls scoop up the trousers to cover their eyes as the young hunk tantalizingly emerges from the water.

Alas, he is not in his birthday suit but in his Levi's 501 jeans. The pants on the riverbank—which the girls promptly drop—belong to a wizened old cowboy also swimming in the stream. The girls' eyes follow the nonplussed hero, watching him return to his horse and ride off into the distance.

Super: "In 1873 Levi's jeans only came shrink to fit. Levi's 501. The original jean."

Rarely do the characters in Levi's ads just wear the jeans: they interact with them. They put them on, take them off, tie them to cars, pawn them, freeze them—even swim in them. The jeans are active and rugged, just like the gods and goddesses who wear them.

This core message has changed little since Nick Kamen peeled off his pants to "I Heard It Through the Grapevine" in 1986 (see page 25). Over the years, Levi's came up with story after story (and classic song after classic song) that conferred a sense of freedom, masculine physical prowess, and sexual attractiveness on their jeans and, by extension, their prospective owners.

In one spot, as the Ronettes' "Be My Baby" plays, a hero tows a lovely young woman's disabled car using the only tool at hand, his trusty pair of Levi's 501s. In another spot, to the tune of B. B. King's "Ain't Nobody Home," a pawnbroker refuses a broke-but-handsome young man's watch and sunglasses, but accepts his 501s—much to the amusement of his girlfriend waiting outside. In another spot, a hunk removes his jeans from the fridge where he'd been keeping them cool in hot weather.

By 1992, however, suffering continued losses in market share from upstart designer labels and cheap knockoffs, Levi's began to focus more heavily on the authenticity component of its marketing approach. No one could compete with Levi's on *this* front—the company was founded in 1850—and "Creek" drove that point home while keeping in tune with its predecessors.

Shot in Pennsylvania using dramatic, monochromatic landscapes inspired by photographer Ansel Adams, the spot tells a (possibly apocryphal) story from the company's own archives. The hero, like his disenfranchised predecessors, exudes confidence, youthful rebellion, and authenticity. He wears his jeans as a badge of independence. And, most important, he looks great in nothing but a pair of Levi's.

RELIABLE ENGINEERING

Forget diamonds: a car is a girl's best friend

Dawn light glows in a fashionable London mews while Lindsay Anderson's somber hymnal "Everyone's Going Through Changes" plays.

A young lady emerges from the household and slams the door. She pulls her ring off and posts it through the letterbox, then storms down the street ripping off her pearls, slinging a bracelet past a cat, abandoning her fur coat over a parking meter. Poised over a grating into which she is about to dispose of her car keys, she has a change of heart as she considers what she'd be throwing away. Perked up enormously, she drives off in her VW.

Super: "If only everything in life was as reliable as a Volkswagen."

VOLKSWAGEN

CHANGES

BMP/DDB NEEDHAM, U.K., 1988

"Changes" was the second commercial in a series that represented a subtle strategic shift in Volkswagen's long-term strategy. Before that, the German automaker had dropped cars from great heights to demonstrate that they were tough. The new focus was on a different, emotional kind of reliability, said Michael Bray, managing director of worldwide accounts at BMP/DDB. "Instead of saying that the car is reliable, the new ads said that you can rely on them. It was a way to inject personality and warmth into a Germanic brand."

During the "falling car" era, the motto was "Very tough . . . very reliable." "Casino," the first commercial in the new series, ended instead with "Everybody needs something in life he can rely on," which evolved, in "Changes," to "If only everything in life was as reliable as a VW."

"Changes" was created "during the heyday of the feminist movement," recalled Howard Spivey, who produced all of the ten spots in the "if everything" campaign, which ran for six years. "Women were an important target for VW and, although the brief never asked the spot to specifically address them, showing this woman empowered and making these decisions was definitely a side bonus that attracted female purchasers."

Bray theorized that the appeal of "Changes" was the emotional proposition it presented: things in life go wrong, but people bounce back with touchstones of reliability and comfort to lean on.

"Changes," which was written by Barry Greenstead, art directed by Graham Featherstone, and directed by David Bailey, ran intermittently for a year (after which VW went back to dropping cars). Its previously unstar, Paula Hamilton—unknown at the time of the two-day shoot in London—became famous as the "Volkswagen Girl," despite the fact that she appeared in only one ad. The ad itself remained a part of the popular culture for years afterward.

People may have loved the campaign, but it didn't result in huge sales increases for Volkswagen. "Sales grew and value imagery was strong, but Volkswagens were essentially a high-priced premium import," Bray said, an issue VW went on to address quite effectively some years later (see page 94).

CHAPTER EIGHT

BABY, IT'S YOU

Ababy's smile, they say, is nature's lock on survival. Adults universally respond to tykes—which is why so many marketers "borrow interest" and use children in commercials. Like animals, they're notorious attention-getters, virtually guaranteeing that most viewers will at least *look* at the spots. But children can be more than just adorable props grabbing our attention; they can elicit profound emotions in us. When a Hallmark Cards minidrama offers up four cute but vulnerable preteen boys torn over whom they'll take to a school dance and how to ask her, we identify with their doubt and angst.

We identify with children as the purest part of ourselves—their very warmth and naturalness reduce our defenses. Aimed at the soft underbelly of doting adults, children in advertising are powerful messengers who, perhaps more than any other persuaders, are believable. Americans ate up adorable "Mikey," for example. Confident in the face of two scheming brothers who seemed to be getting the best of him, Mikey demonstrated that Life cereal was nutritious, good tasting—and the choice of clever underdogs who triumph.

Childlike innocence charms, but so does its deft subversion. Sometimes the technique is to present children as pint-sized adults, costumed physically or mentally to appear older than they really are. Waterman showed an adorable second-grade vixen, flirtatiously entrapping her guy—a smitten, bespectacled second-grade boy—and then dumping him once she's gotten what she wanted (the pen). A Danone yogurt spot in Spain showed kids cajoling their parents to eat with all sorts of games and promises—upending the traditional pattern of parents having to trick their kids to chow healthy foods. Apparel retailer Barney's, by presenting famous adults as precocious children, proved that children assuming the personalities of adults enchant—just as anthropomorphized animals do. Heinz baked beans in England added some cheek to the formula, and gave a dated brand a contemporary image, by offering a prim and haughty schoolgirl musing about growing up to be prime minister.

Children are a key ingredient in emotional home runs, but they can also be just plain funny, and work well in situations where adults just won't do. Shiseido, the Japanese soap company, erased its unapproachable image and reemerged as warm, family-centered, and everyday-ordinary by featuring a collection of sweet-faced boys—one of whom passes gas in a communal bath.

MEN OF DESTINY

The boy who would make the clothes that would make the man

Four New York luminaries as young boys are gathered together on the front steps of a brownstone, along with a little chap sporting a three-piece suit and glasses. He's Barney.

Mighty Casey Stengel of the Yankees asks: "What are ya gonna be when you grow up, Humphrey?"

Young Bogart replies, "I'm gonna be a big-time Hollywood actor, see."

All the boys snicker.

Bogart asks, "How 'bout you, Louie?"

Louis Armstrong says, "I'm gonna be a great horn player and singer someday."

The boys exclaim, "Ooh . . ."

Young Armstrong then asks, "How 'bout you, Fiorello?"

LaGuardia answers that he's "gonna be mayor of New York."

Casey expresses tolerant disbelief, "Naw . . ."

Louie: "How 'bout you, Casey?"

Casey: "I'm gonna be in the World Series."

All: "Na, na, you'll never make it."

Casey: "What are you gonna do, Barney?"

All: "Yeah, yeah, yeah, Barney . . ."

Barney: "You're all gonna need clothes."

Super: "Even then he knew. 7th Avenue at 17th Street, Barneys."

BARNEYS
MEN OF DESTINY

JACK BYRNE, USA, 1970

The men's clothier Barney Inc. ran into trouble in the late 1990s, but two decades before that its advertising reflected its wardrobe: sharp, natty, and very original. While other apparel makers and retailers trumpeted their clothes, Barneys implied a confident sense of style by its insouciant attitude and novel use of children. Its ad clearly identified the target audience as achievers.

The haberdashery was founded in 1923 when Barney Pressman hocked his wife's engagement ring to open a small store at Seventeenth Street and Seventh Avenue. He filled Barneys Boys Town with suits purchased at great discount at auctions and bankruptcy sales. Decades later, his son Fred expanded the company from a single store into a showcase for top European designers and added women's fashions.

"Men of Destiny" was the first TV commercial Barneys ever did. Written by Steve Gordon, who went on to write the 1981 movie *Arthur*, the commercial was art directed by Stan Kovics and directed by Steve Horn, who shot the spot in Park Slope, Brooklyn. "At the time, no one had shot on the streets in real neighborhoods," Horn said.

"The little boy who played Barney could not perform," recalled Horn. "We spent most of the day getting him to do his one line."

The commercial, in a thirty-second and one-minute format, ran for a year and was brought back locally. Barney's followed it with vignettes of the four lads growing up. They were not as popular as the simple children's takeoff on celebrities and were soon replaced by new-wave esoteric commercials. One featured a beautiful woman with a horse and a man driving a sports car chasing her.

But even the most interesting advertising could not shore up Barneys bottom line. In January 1996, the retailer sought Chapter 11 protection from creditors after failing to reach agreement with its partner, Tokyo-based Isetan Company, on how to repay $600 million used to prop up Barneys flagship stores, on Madison Avenue in New York City, in Chicago, and in Beverly Hills.

In June 1997, Barneys said it would shut four of its thirteen stores, including its founding site in downtown Manhattan, as part of a plan to save $10 million a year while it awaited a sale.

DAUGHTER KNOWS BEST

Children teach their parents well

DANONE

LEARN FROM YOUR CHILDREN

RILOVA CASADEVALL PEDRENO, SPAIN, 1986

The scene opens with a boy coaxing his bespectacled dad to eat. "C'mon, just taste a little bit," he wheedles (in Spanish).

Several vignettes show other tykes feeding their parents Danone yogurt. "I know you're gonna like it," one girl tells her dad, holding the food out to him.

Another boy whispers pleadingly to his mom, "It's good for you."

A third boy, imitating an airplane, "Mbmbmbm . . ." places the spoon in his daddy's mouth ". . . aaah!"

Another girl says, "One for teddy" as she feeds her stuffed bear "and one for you" as she turns to her mother.

Another girl mimics her mother's line: "Who's a clever girl, then?"

A fourth boy tries to reason with his parent, "It'll make your hair curly, Dad."

The last vignettes is of a little girl wiping her dad's lips.

Announcer: "Yoghurt Danone: Aprendre de tus hijos." (Learn from your children.)

Super: "Aprendre de tus hijos."

"Learn from Your Children" reversed the age-old pattern of parents having to play games with their kids to get them to eat things that are good for them. Instead, it put the kids in charge, making them authoritative yet innocent (therefore trustworthy) endorsers of a product with which they were intimately familiar—and positioning parents as oddly sweet children.

"Learn from Your Children" aimed to increase consumption among adults and reaffirm current consumers, said Luis Casadevall, who, along with Tito Mudoz, was the spot's creative director. "The goal was to position Danone's yogurt as a healthy and good way to take care of yourself, the theory being that if it's good for kids, it's good for you." The advertising was aimed at parents; children were a secondary target.

In addition to reversing roles, the spot reversed a decline in sales. In 1984, Danone yogurt sales had dropped 8 percent, and by 1985 they'd fallen another 4.4 percent. After the campaign in 1986, sales soared 9.9 percent and grew another 5.9 percent in 1987. Though the campaign was a hit, Danone stopped airing "Learn from Your Children" in 1990 because it was sponsor at the Olympic Games in Barcelona and all advertising of plain yogurt supported that event.

WANNA DANCE?

Hallmark's solution for the congenitally shy

The spot opens in the murk of a school library. At a table, four preteen boys discuss whom they'll be taking to the upcoming school dance and, more important, how they will do the difficult job of asking her to attend.

One of the boys, Dan, whispers, "Who are you taking to the dance?"
Tony tells him, "Patti Harney."
Another of the lads is amazed: "Oh, man, Patti Harney? She said yes and everything?"
Tony admits he's not that far along. "Well, no, I haven't really asked her yet, but I'm gonna."
Dan probes for details: "In person?"
"No way," responds a mortified Tony. "Probably just call her on the phone."
Another child decides to adopt the same approach. "Yeah, a phone call. I think that's what I'm gonna do."
Tony turns to Jerry. "So, who you going with, Jerry?"

HALLMARK
DANCE CARD

LEO BURNETT, USA, 1991

"Oh, well, see, there's this kid on my street; his name is Bob Shall-cross and, see, he plays hockey with the brother of Rachelle Tasker, and she has gym class with Manda Moore, and Manda Moore has a locker next to Cheryl Berman, and Cheryl Berman's like really good friends with Nancy Eaglin. So she's gonna ask her."

Tony is still confused: "Who?" he asks.

Jerry is amazed as his friend's thickness: "Cheryl's gonna ask Nancy for me," he says.

The same child who decided to phone now changes tacks: "Get a friend to ask for you. I think that's what I'm gonna do."

Jerry says, "Hey, how about you, Dan?"

Dan has another idea: "Well, I was thinking, what if you—uh, slipped a card into a girl's notebook?"

Jerry's curiosity is piqued: "What do you mean a card?"

"You know, a greeting card," Dan answers.

"Like a . . . Hallmark card?" wonders Tony.

"Exactly," says Dan.

The boys are aghast. "You mean you would put it in writing?" asks Jerry.

Dan is mystified. "Why not?" he replies.

"Man, what if she hates you?" asks Jerry. "She'd show it to everyone. It could even end up in the school newspaper."

Tony tops that: "Or in the girls' bathroom."

The fourth boy adds: "Or on the evening news."

"Evidence like that could ruin your reputation," Jerry says.

Dan protests, "I don't have a reputation."

But his friends rib him that he will now. As they laugh and slap hands the camera cuts to a nearby table showing that Dan has already acted on his thought. But then the cute recipient of it appears at his side: "Danny, putting this card in my notebook. That was really neat. I'd love to go to the dance with you."

Dan says, "Uh . . . OK."

The boys take sharp notice. "A card. I think that's what I'm going to do," says the impressionable lad.

Super: "Hallmark. When you care enough to send the very best."

In 1991, the company that Joyce C. Hall founded in 1910 continued to dominate the greeting card industry, as it had for decades. But jaded sensibilities and changing tastes meant that an increasing share of the nearly $7 billion greeting-card business was going to so-called "alternative" cards. Moreover, competitors were moving into nontraditional outlets, such as mass merchandisers, where Hallmark cards weren't sold. This dual threat forced Hallmark's marketers to reinforce its image as a vital relationship strengthener and drive home its brand image of quality and warmth.

Written and art directed by Burnett's David Linney and Jonathan Moore, respectively, and overseen by creative director Cheryl Berman, "Dance Card" was an emotional home run. The spot, with its straightforward storyline, is warm rather than syrupy, and evokes a smile. "It speaks to a truth we aim for in all Hallmark advertising—the yearning to express yourself and wanting some help to do that, which is exactly what the greeting card business is," said Brad Moore, former vice president of advertising for Hallmark Cards and now president of the Hallmark Hall of Fame Productions Inc. (Another element: it shows the recipient being surprised— "Out-of-the-blue packs more wallop and suggests that the advertising is real," Moore said.)

"Dance Card" was cast and directed by Joe Pytka and edited by Marty Bernstein. Over three days in Pytka's Los Angeles studio he shot hundreds of takes. "We ended up with two minutes from sixteen hours of wonderful footage," Moore said. When the Burnett team originally conceived the commercial, it was a more exaggerated story of boys ridiculing the lad who'd given a card. "They ribbed him about asking his mom or grandma, implying that cards are only for adults," recalled Moore. "We took that out because we didn't want to imply that cards are just for adults. On the set, we softened it and made it subtler," he said.

The spot got its first run on the fortieth anniversary of "The Hallmark Hall of Fame," a two-hour movie showcase that airs four times a year and features longer commercials produced especially for it. Moore said that although less than 20 percent of Hallmark's advertising runs on the show, it's what people associate with Hallmark. "It's our version of the Super Bowl, though with a much different audience." The spot has run sporadically since then to this day.

"Dance Card" is one of the three most popular commercials Hallmark has ever made, all of which define Hallmark as the flag bearer of old-school emotional connection. One, a 1990 spot also from Burnett, focused on the one hundredth birthday of a spunky grandma played by the now-deceased Fannie Peterson (Ma Pete) surrounded by her adoring (and sometimes irreverent) family and friends, one of whom confides that the matriarch is actually 101. The other spot, "Music Professor," created by Young & Rubicam in 1982, features a young piano student who surprises her curmudgeonly, emotionless professor by tucking a birthday card into his sheet music. "Thank you, Lisa," he mutters, barely able to contain his composure with a slight smile threatening at the corners of his mouth.

Hallmark does not track the short-term effect on sales of specific commercials, but Moore said that over time the campaign has helped define the company as an icon of high quality and good taste. "People think of Hallmark as one of the top ten companies when it's not even one of the top one hundred," Moore said. "That suggests our advertising has quite an impact. Hallmark has a reputation as one of the two or three most respected brands in America." A 1995 EquiTrend brand-quality survey put Hallmark in the top five best-quality brands nationwide.

LITTLE IRON LADY

Eat your beans and grow up to be... Margaret Thatcher?

HEINZ

MARGARET

YOUNG & RUBICAM, U.K., 19TK

The spot opens on a straight-backed schoolgirl at a kitchen table. Regal British music plays. Just as her mother enters, carrying a supper of baked beans on toast, the little girl asks with a certain prim pomposity, "I wonder . . . If I eat Heinz baked beans every day, do you think I could be . . . prime minister?"

Mom looks down proudly at her haughty daughter. "You might, Margaret," she replies, "you just might." Suddenly, with a look of dawning horror, she pulls the plate away.

Voice-over: "Millions of little Britons have grown up great knowing beanz meanz Heinz."

Super: "Beans meanz Heinz."

Heinz baked beans have been part of Britain's heritage since 1901, when Henry J. Heinz, the American son of German Lutheran immigrants, brought his beans to the U.K. Back then it was a family treat: a tin cost nine pence—more than $2 today.

The company ran "Beanz Meanz Heinz" TV advertising for years, making it one of the most successful slogans in England ever and pushing Heinz to the top of the bean heap. But when supermarkets began selling private-label beans (that were in fact Heinz's own, packaged under the store's name) at half the price, millions of Britons tried them and found them quite palatable. Heinz ran very rational advertising—animated films that ended with the thought "the extra penny you spend on Heinz baked beans is a penny wisely spent" to try to justify its premium price. But Heinz felt it didn't need to be sold rationally. It was enough that consumers believed they were the best beans and always had been, said Patrick Collister, who wrote several of the "Beanz Meanz Heinz" spots.

Heinz was so nervous with the high-road course that it took eleven months—and thirty different scripts—to get the campaign approved. They did finally approve the concept, however, and a series was born. The com-

mercials, art directed by Anthony Stileman, featured famous British personalities as little kids sitting at a table (with Heinz beans, of course) and, in a
series of cuts, getting older until they became their famous, familiar selves
(still eating beans). Pop star Cilla Black and cricketer Ian Botham were
among the celebrities chosen because they were beloved by families. In each
spot, repartee at the end established that Mum was still in charge.

Those spots did it with wit and cheekiness, but the takeoff on prime
minister Margaret Thatcher had real wick in it. Director Simon Cheek
(aptly named) found the precocious little girl only the evening before the
shoot. The wholly undeferential spot was written with the expectation that
Margaret Thatcher would not participate, although she was invited to.
Y&R's chairman, John Banks, somehow managed to persuade 10 Downing
Street to approve the script.

The Thatcher spot ran for six months, during which time Heinz's share
rocketed and an old brand got a more modern, contemporary face. It also
generated free publicity that promoted the Heinz brand and its other foods
as well. The commercial was parodied by several comedy shows. In one, a
young Neil Kinnock, then leader of the opposition to Mrs. Thatcher's Tory
government, asks, "If I eat enough baked beans, do you think I could become prime minister?" His mom tells him not to "talk daft . . . Not a
chance in hell"—and, indeed, his three attempts at the office all ended in
failure.

BIG CRUNCH

A child sacrifices all for a bag of chips

Super: "The Laura Scudder's Pledge."

*Voice-over: "Now again: The Laura Scudder's Noise Abatement
League Pledge . . . I will not roller-skate in the hall."*

*A chubby little boy, before being allowed to snack on his chips, raises
two fingers to swear that he won't "roller-skate in the hall."*

*"I will not crack my knuckles," the voice-over continues in the oath.
The boy, looking pained, promises, "I will not crack my knuckles."*

The voice-over continues with the vows:

"I will not drop my combat boots on the floor."

*The boy earnestly agrees: "I will not drop my combat boots on the
floor."*

*"I will not dribble my basketball down the stairway," intones the an-
nouncer. The boy repeats the basketball edict.*

**LAURA SCUDDER'S
PLEDGE**

DOYLE DANE BERNBACH, USA, 1963

"I will not practice Little League cheers before eleven A.M. *on Sunday morning," continues the demanding announcer.*

"I will not . . . ," the boy falters.

"Practice . . . ," goads the announcer.

The boy, prodded into compliance, completes the oath: ". . . practice Little League cheers before eleven A.M. *on Sunday morning."*

"I will not encourage dogs to bark or cats to yowl," the announcer perseveres.

Either from mischief or weariness the boy twists the oath: "I will not encourage cats to bark," he says.

No slouch, the announcer corrects him, and the boy says the oath correctly.

"I will not kick tin cans," persists the announcer.

The boy agrees.

"I will not slurp my soup."

Again, he complies. Finally, we see the impetus for his agreeing to be as quiet as a mouse around the house.

". . . and this I do willingly to compensate for the noise I make when eating Laura Scudder's potato chips. The noisiest chips in the world."

Upon finishing his oath, the tyke eats a Laura Scudder potato chip: the crunching noise is very nearly deafening.

Super: "Laura Scudder's potato chips."

Several years ago, research by the Washington State Apple Board turned up a key finding: the major element of an apple's appeal was its crunch. The Laura Scudder's team at Doyle Dane Bernbach, copywriter Ron Rosenfeld and art director Len Sirowitz, could have told them that years before. To demonstrate their potato chip's crispness, they literally made a lot of noise on TV: each bite was made to sound like an explosive blast.

Potato chips are fun food, so potato chip advertising can't take itself too seriously. This spot had to be—and was—as light and entertaining as consumers' feelings about potato chips, all while driving home the key pitch—Laura Scudder's chips are crunchier than the rest.

Thus: an adorable menace willingly agrees to be angelic if he can only keep eating those chips. This appeals to moms, the real audience for a convenience-food spot, on two levels. It shows that Laura Scudder's chips are so appealing to children that they will do anything to get them—even give up roller-skating in the hallway. This is a strong endorsement, as anyone who has dealt with a young boy will attest. More subtly, however, the spot positions potato chips—junk food—as a positive part of child rearing. Chips, especially crunchy chips, are a way to reward good children. The big crunch is a treat, and if your children are very good, they've earned it.

Doyle Dane followed up "Pledge" with other spots presenting Laura Scudder's as the noisiest potato chip in the land, taking the big crunch to new levels of extremity. In one, a man bites into a chip and his image on the screen completely shatters.

AIR TIME

The effective use of flatulence in product positioning

The commercial opens with the camera panning from left to right to focus on the very serious faces of eighteen little Japanese boys. Under marching music interrupted by clashing cymbals the boys march to the bath. Once immersed in the water, the boys' faces still bear the stern look—until the last boy recognizes the olive soap and his mood changes, along with the music, to a happy, playful melody. After soaping, the boys return to the water to warm up. Suddenly, all move away from one boy when they see air bubbles popping at the surface of the water, the clear result of mischievous flatulence on his part. The song halts abruptly. The last shot is of the boy, a sheepish look on his face and a washcloth on his head, alone in the tub.

SHISEIDO

TURKISH MARCH

SHISEIDO DIRECT, JAPAN, 1968

For many years, Shiseido soap had an image of luxury, elegance, and grace. The soap sold well during gift-giving seasons, but Shiseido worried that it didn't sell well enough at other times. "Turkish March," conceived by Hideyuki Kaneko and directed by Toshiomi Yaguchi, was launched to give Shiseido a warm, family image—to make it a democratic, everyday item with a less pricey and exclusive image.

The goal, according to planner Yoshinori Nakano, was to get ordinary consumers to buy the soap and use it more often. Featuring boys as soap users was one way to make the cleanser less tony and exclusive; using humor—especially this essentially adolescent kind built around the very pedestrian and low-brow occurrence featured here—was another. The music in this sixty-second spot set the mood for fun and, combined with the unexpected flatulence, created an enjoyable, memorable spot.

Midlevel management at Shiseido wanted to kill the commercial. It was a radical departure from previous advertising and potentially embarrassing for a company which, in 1970, manufactured some 1,800 products, generating more than $2 billion in annual sales. (Shiseido was the biggest manufacturer of cosmetics in its home country and the third largest in the world, behind America's Avon and France's L'Oreal.) But the

117

president and board laughed out loud when they saw it, and so the debate was over.

Soaps were the gifts of choice then, and soap companies spent lavishly on promoting their products as convenient and intimate. After Shiseido broadcast its commercial, many other companies adopted its strategy and used children to suggest everyday versus special occasion usage. Some even used a communal bath setting.

"Turkish March" boosted sales and attracted a lot of publicity, which dramatically increased brand recognition. The company subsequently came out with an "Olive" deodorant. But the commercial itself ran for only a season. In an apparent shift in marketing philosophy, Shiseido introduced a new high-prestige (high-profit-margin) soap and came out with a traditional commercial to promote it.

PENULTIMATE HEARTBREAK

One boy's sorrowful story of love and penmanship

WATERMAN

LE GRADUATE

BENTON & BOWLES, FRANCE, 1977

The scene opens in a classroom of second graders taking a math test. As dramatic piano-and-string music plays, an adorable little girl leans over to a bespectacled boy, who assumes she wants to copy his test answers. She eyes him coyly, twirls her curly hair, and blushes appropriately until, smitten, he offers her his paper. She makes it clear that she is interested in his Waterman pen instead. He gives her the pen and puts his arm around her. The girl, having gotten what she set out for, shrugs him off and goes back to her test with her new pen. A voice-over declares, "Waterman Graduate."

Super: "Waterman."

Oh, false promise, hopes dashed. It may have wounded the rejected suitor for life and honed his later misogyny, but the zag into the unexpected in this charming tale surely grabbed viewers. In 1977, Waterman Pen turned to then fledgling agency Benton & Bowles/Paris for help in launching a new pen named Graduate. Andre Matzneff (who also produced and art directed the spot) presented four handwritten lines to the client summarizing the plot. This product-as-hero commercial revolved around a craving for the new pen that was so pervasive that the young and adorable flirt was willing to go all out for it. Allowing the coquettish tease to partner with the boy would have been predictable and considerably less interesting, says Claude Marcus, who was managing director of the agency at the time. It also would have distracted from the object of the quest. For surely this is a holy grail story, although the seeker is an unlikely and unsympathetic heroine.

"Without even a reel—director Catherine Lebfevre had only shot two commercials for Colgate before—and without formal approval, we went off and shot," recalled Matzneff.

The boy and girl were unknowns and the commercial was made for a very small amount of money. Waterman had a minuscule TV budget, recalled Marcus. They ran it briefly during back-to-school and Christmas seasons but once the commercial did its job—launching the pen—Waterman cancelled the quirky love story.

CHAPTER NINE

ANIMAL MAGNETISM

Advertising has gone to the dogs . . . not to mention cats, cows, alligators, penguins, elephants, rhinos, bears, and other creatures. You'd expect Morris or the Meow Mix felines crooning for cat food, but animals have made tracks for all sorts of other products.

Advertising was something of a Noah's Ark long before Qantas's koala bear (who claimed to hate the airline) winged its way into tourists' hearts, an angry ape demonstrated the indestructibility of American Tourister luggage, and Merrill Lynch went bullish on America. The goofy, bug-eyed Chihuahua who blurts out the catchphrase "*Yo quiero* Taco Bell" is a direct descendant of RCA's little fox terrier, Nipper, Borden's Elsie the Cow, Exxon's tiger, Smokey the Bear, and party pooch Spuds MacKenzie.

Often marketers use animals when there's nothing new to say about their products and all they need to do is get viewers' attention (Budweiser's Clydesdales, ants, and frogs and Pepsi's flying geese and dancing bears). Other times they function as metaphors, powerful symbols of virility, honesty, goodness, strength, naturalness, whatever. A spot for Southland Corporation's 7-Eleven stores features sheep bleating "latte" to denigrate those flocking to trendy coffee shops.

Sometimes animals can deliver a specific message in a way that cuts through clutter—and lets people absorb messages that would be ridiculous if said outright. Warner Lambert Company's alligator warned what skin can turn into without its Lubriderm cream.

Ambipur's blindfolded cat couldn't smell the fish after the air freshener had worked its magic. The Yellow Pages used an ostrich to symbolize the personality type who never consults its pages.

Animals are fun to watch and, because of their innocence, we feel for them and trust them, especially when they're humanized. In a commercial for HBO, the first to ever win an Emmy, chimpanzees being studied by scientist Jane Goodall utter familiar lines from famous films they'd seen on her TV. And TV España's forlorn and lovable pooch, who packs up and leaves home—and his glued-to-the-set master—charmingly showed the down side of too much television.

Working with animals, even trained ones, requires ingenuity: ad makers snip that if a shoot involves animals, double its cost. To get the stag in the Hartford Insurance Group commercials to nose a tricycle off the sidewalk, his trainer hid cookies, apples, and corn in the right spots. To get a bulldog, black cat, and teeny mouse to nuzzle before a fire, the Chamber of Coal Traders used lighting tricks, discreetly hidden prawns, and paper cups to conceal the "natural enemies" from one another. The Merrill Lynch team resorted to howling, firing shotguns in the air, even hovering helicopters to prompt a stampede.

On the other hand, with animals you don't have to worry about multiculturalism, political correctness, a sordid past or the possibility of an equally distasteful future of, say, posing nude or punching an umpire.

SMELLS FISHY

A room deodorizer passes the blindfolded-cat test

To the left sits a cat in a blindfold, to the right, a dish with a fresh whole fish on it. In the middle stands a package of Ambipur air freshener. The cat sits still, facing straight ahead.

Voice-over (in Spanish): "With an Ambipur air freshener, it smells of flowers. But without Ambipur . . ."

A hand removes the product and the cat instantly gets a scent of the fish and is down on his haunches sniffing around feverishly in the right direction. The blindfold slips back from over the feline's eyes.

Voice-over: "Ambipur air freshener by Cruz Verde."

There's the sound of a gavel hitting a desk.

Voice-over: "Proven effectiveness."

AMBIPUR

CAT AND FISH

RILOVA CASADEVALL PEDRENO, SPAIN, 1983

Ambipur, owned by the Sara Lee Corporation, had been in the market for a few years when Rilova Casadevall Pedreno won the account. (Saatchi & Saatchi bought the agency in 1986.) Virtually every air freshener then on the market was being sold for the appeal of its lemony, piney, or otherwise delightful fragrance. Ambipur took a different tack. Its raison d'être and advertising claim was that it was the most efficient way to eliminate bad smells. This was always done through clear and simple demonstration: use Ambipur and there's no bad smell; take it away and the bad smell is obvious.

The spot's real masterstroke, however, was in using a cat—known for a heightened olfactory sense—as the subject of that demonstration. This deftly avoided the real reason for the room deodorizer—foulness. An ad focused on diaper bins and toilet bowls would have a hard time competing with the alpine imagery of the typical air freshener spot. Instead, a cat allowed Ambipur to make its odor-free claim concretely (if Ambipur works for a scent-sensitive cat, it will certainly work around the diaper bin) and at the same time shroud the unsavoriness its product must conceal.

GOOD BOY!

A pint of beer is a dog's best friend

**JOHN SMITH'S
DOG TRICKS**

BOASE MASSIMI POLLITT, U.K., 1981

"Dog Tricks" starred the John Smith duo, Stan and Arkwright, at the bar with pints of John Smith's Yorkshire Bitter. Stan notes that Arkwright has a new dog, and tries to coax it to do some tricks.

"Like your new dog, Arkwright," he says. "Here boy! Up! Up! Down! Sit! Heel!"

The dog does not respond.

"Doesn't do much, does he?" asks Stan.

Arkwright shows him otherwise, with the right inducement, of course.

"Fancy a drop of John Smith's?" the owner asks his pooch.

Upon hearing this offer, the dog goes into an incredible assortment of tricks as circus music plays. He stands on his head, juggles, and balances a bar stool on his nose.

"He just needs the right motivation," Arkwright comments.

Voice-over and super: "A tough act to follow. John Smith's Yorkshire Bitter."

The John Smith Brewery was founded in 1758 and taken over by Courage in 1970. Within a decade, it accounted for about half the company's total sales. Competition in the bitters market, the single largest sector in the whole beer market, is fierce, and when sales of John Smith's started to fall despite a static market the company looked for reasons—and solutions. There was no change in the product, the pricing was in line with competition, and there were no production or distribution problems. But the venerable Yorkshire heritage that had been its main selling point was being adopted by other bitters, leaving consumers confused.

Courage decided it needed new advertising to shore up its commitment to loyalists, reattract lapsed drinkers, and, most important, interest the under-thirty set. They're the biggest beer consumers and tend to drink what's popular among their peers. A brewery adage is that young people "drink with their eyes," meaning they buy a brand for what it says about them, not how it tastes. In blind taste tests, in fact, they often choose a brew they had rejected with the blinds off.

Research convinced Courage that John Smith's did not have a strong point of difference or distinct personality. As a mainstream brand, it essentially had to be all things to all men. The execution needed to be "masculine, sociable, working class, assertive, and contemporary in style," said John Webster, who was both art director and copywriter on the spot. "We wanted consumers to believe that drinkers of the brand weren't boys but admirable drinking men who knew their beer."

124

That laid the groundwork for "Dog Tricks." The pooch's strange and outrageous behavior shows the lengths to which folks (and dogs) will go to get a pint of John Smith's. And it drives home the working-class image with a light touch.

Director Ian McMillan said that in the end the commercial was a simple split-screen job. The actors had to do a complete take to fit within thirty seconds while imagining the dog carrying on between them. "We spent the rest of that day and the next shooting all the cuts of the dog to fill the center of the panel." McMillan said that the company mistakenly sent the film to the lab on two different nights. As a result, they never could get the color of the middle panel the same all the way through.

Another highlight: the dog auditions. "I must have seen nearly two hundred dogs including circus acts," McMillan recalled. "But there was only one who made me laugh just to look at it."

DUMBO'S REVENGE

A moment of selfishness creates a lasting memory

The spot opens with scratchy, sepia footage of a young, curly-haired kid in an argyle vest watching a circus parade while eating a Nestlé's Rolo candy. When a baby elephant marches by, the kid mischievously shouts, "Hey, Dumbo," and pretends to offer it his last candy. But as little Dumbo reaches for it with his trunk, the brat snickers and teasingly snatches the sweet away to gobble it himself.

The next shot, in full color, is present day. A man wearing the same vest and again watching a circus parade while eating the same chocolate and caramel confection is obviously the selfish boy grown up. And so has the baby elephant grown up, and never forgotten. He takes his great big trunk and bashes his one-time tormentor around the chops before roaring—and grabbing the Rolos.

Announcer and title cards deliver the pitch: "Think twice what you do with your last Rolo."

NESTLÉ

ELEPHANT

AMMIRATI PURIS LINTAS, NETHERLANDS, 1996

Rolo had been sold worldwide for years but in some markets the chocolate and caramel concoction had begun to lose its magic. It had not been advertised for more than seven years and its market share was slowly and steadily declining. Though still bought by loyal, mostly older consumers, it wasn't cool enough to attract new users.

Nestlé conducted qualitative research asking people what they thought

125

of Rolo, and discovered that many regarded the brand as dull, tired, and uninteresting.

Working with the Ammirati Puris Lintas team of creative director and copywriter Diederick Koopal, and art director Marcel Frenschf, Nestle marketers determined that the brand should not go the music-and-cynicism lifestyle route of its target audience (teens and young adults). Rather it should be daring enough to stand for something else—and careful enough not to alienate older current users.

The team looked for something that would set Rolo apart from other chocolate caramel candies. They hit upon the idea that a roll of Rolos is ideally suited to be shared, while a candy bar, which comes in one piece, is more often eaten alone.

The agency set about producing a campaign revolving around the hardship of sharing something you love—especially if it's your last one. Humor, they decided, was the ideal way to express this pain. But they needed more: for the message to break through, they needed a surprise to associate with that notion of sharing. Which they found in portraying the consequences when the wrong choice is made.

The resulting ad was relevant, original, and solidly linked the surprise to the product itself. And "because it was virtually wordless, it could transcend cultural borders," said Helayne Spivak, then creative director of Ammirati worldwide. The spot ran in the Netherlands, United Kingdom, Germany, Australia, and New Zealand.

In another spot, "Cinema," a young man in a movie theater makes a too hasty decision to use his last Rolo to seduce the pleasant-looking young woman next to him. But then he's caught short when the bare-midriffed blond beauty of his dreams sits next to him on the other side. He then tries to wrestle the half-eaten Rolo right out of the first girl's mouth, intending to present it to the new charmer.

Nestlé's objective was to boost Rolo's brand image, drive awareness, attract new users, and to get Rolo, in marketing parlance, back into the "evoked set," that is, up for purchase consideration. They had hoped to raise sales 10 percent. In one year the brand grew an astonishing 89 percent, despite a 5 percent decline in the overall candy category.

And "Elephant" delighted viewers—the British and Dutch ranked it their favorite commercial of the year and it won the Grand Prix at the Cannes International Advertising Festival. A subsequent promotion in which cards were distributed in movies and restaurants for participants to win one of the amusingly outdated argyle vests prompted one of the highest responses in promotion history.

FURRY FOES

A fire in the hearth melts hearts

The spot opens on a cozy fire roaring in a fireplace while the Shirelles sing "Will You Still Love Me Tomorrow?" The door of a room opens. In waddles a bulldog, who settles down in front of the fire, panting blissfully. The camera cuts back to the door as a fluffy black cat enters, crosses the room, and plops down next to the big dog, leans over, and gives him a sweet little kiss. The camera returns to the door again as a tiny white mouse scurries in. He takes his place right beside the cat. She leans down and gives the mouse a little kiss too.

Super: "Now you know what people see in a real fire."

SOLID FUEL ADVISORY BOARD

FURRY FRIENDS

SAATCHI & SAATCHI, U.K., 1989

The (now defunct) Chamber of Coal Traders in the U.K. wanted to implant the idea that a real coal fire was well worth the effort among people with open but unused fireplaces. The challenge was how to overcome the perception that a lovely fire in the hearth was not worth the time, mess, and effort involved in getting it lit.

Before this the chamber had run a campaign based on poems—how fire inspires musing—and a widely acclaimed play on the old story "The Sorcerer's Apprentice" in which toys come to life and dance by the fire. Adrian Kelmsley, the art director at Saatchi & Saatchi, along with writer Charles Hendley, creative director James Lowther, and agency producer Suzy Rodgers conceived the idea (without research) that, to make the hearth—instead of the TV—the center of the home, they should show "natural enemies" from the animal kingdom feeling quite comfortable, and amiable, in front of it.

Not surprisingly, that posed some problems. One director proposed getting around it by using split screens to composite independently filmed animals. Another advised going with people dressed as animals. Tony Kaye, who was then just breaking in as a director, said he'd shoot it for real—and vowed to keep shooting until he got it. Amazingly, the footage used came largely from the third take, although he went on to capture dozens more.

To cast two dogs and two cats, the team saw some forty different creatures of each species. They then had two pairs of trained dogs and cats live together for a few weeks to get used to each other. Getting the mice, who are untrainable, "was a bit of a free-for-all," admitted Kelmsley. At one point they tried a rat, "but it just made a mess," he said.

One problem required an ingenious solution. Kelmsley said that he hadn't realized before "that bulldogs don't want to sit near fire because they have respiratory problems." The solution: in a commercial to film the benefits of a real fire, the fire wasn't real, it was actually trick lighting.

Initially, the cat refused to sit—or to follow the mouse urine trail set for it. To get the finicky feline to go to the dog, Kaye placed a prawn behind Rover's ear. It worked. To picture the cat approaching the fire, as if running toward a shaft of light from an open door, the team got him to run away by scaring him with a light from behind.

A paper cup was put over the mouse next to the cat. When Kaye was ready to roll, the cup was removed and the mouse and cat were startled and sniffed at each other. By the third time, the cat went for the mouse and the crew intervened to save the rodent. By the fifth take, Tabby was bored with the game.

The animals kissing actually happened in postproduction. During the taping they were sniffing; the tape was edited to reverse so the cat's head went backward and forward to appear as if it were smooching with the mouse.

The original plan called for the footage to be laid over Frank Sinatra's "Strangers in the Night." But Kelmsley had second thoughts because of the high usage fee and Saatchi co-chief Charles Saatchi feared it would over-whelm the film. During the editing process Kelmsley heard a Shirelles song, got a copy, and laid thirty seconds of furry friends behind it. The agency talked the Shirelles' agent into a lower fee, positioning the commercial as a public service spot to help old people from getting hypothermia.

The spot ran for three months in 1988 beginning in November, when most people are susceptible to lighting a real fire, and was so well liked that it was reprised the next year. Kelmsley said that after, there was pressure to do another dog, cat, and mouse spot. "But I didn't think I could top this, so I did something completely different built around the natural enemies feel-ing quite comfortable in front of a fire theme."

That something was inspired by an article about a four-year-old boy from Borneo bathing with his pet rock python. Enlisting Kaye again, the agency flew the boy and his family to the U.K.—where the snake was inad-vertently left on the tarmac and nearly died before eight burly handlers car-ried it into the Penta Hotel for a warm bath. That follow-up spot of a child and python sharing a hot tub, however, was withdrawn after a mere two weeks because of protests from ophidiophobic viewers who would go into a panic whenever they saw the snake.

The furry friends ad created high awareness and viewers did take away the message that a real fire is cozy and worth the effort of making it. But the increase in coal sales wasn't significant. According to Kelmsley, however, there was a subsequent big increase in the purchase of bulldogs. "Sadly," he added, "it did more for the sale of fake fires than real coal ones."

A year later, the chamber produced another cat, dog, and mouse spot and then stopped advertising. They never went back.

LEAVING HOME

A desperate dog deserts his couch potato master

TV ESPAÑA

LEAVING HOME

CONTRAPUNTO, SPAIN, 1989

The scene opens on a sad and lovable old sheepdog fetching a suitcase from the closet. He lays it on the floor and opens it with his nose as sentimental music plays in the background. The forlorn pooch packs his dish, his brush, his bone, and, finally, his leash. He pauses on a photo of himself and his young master and gives it a farewell pat before closing the suitcase and picking it up. The dog casts a last sad look at his boy, glued to the TV, as he leaves.

Voice-over (in Spanish): "If your best friend leaves home, it may be because you're watching too much television. Learn to watch television sensibly."

Super: "TVE para todos los públicos."

While most network television advertising is fare or program specific—"tune-in" marketing designed to increase viewership, drive up ratings, and allow the network to command higher advertising rates—some is also designed simply to brand the network.

This spot got a double hit as both a brand identifier and a public service. What better way to brand TV España, the Spanish equivalent to the BBC, as extraordinarily captivating than to show its sometimes unhappy effects on those you love. In contrast to most television advertising—which orders people to watch shows—TV España's fresh message urged socially responsible restraint. It was a brave step for a TV company that depended on audience numbers to justify advertising prices.

"Leaving Home" put TV España on the side of the angels—like liquor companies' designated driver campaigns and Philip Morris's $100 million campaign to urge teens not to smoke. It also generated enormous free media coverage.

The specific charm of "Leaving Home," of course, is the use of the pet to mimic human behavior and the extraordinary panache with which that mimicry was executed. The commercial was so popular that for the next year or so, dog star Pippin—or his look-alikes—turned up in dozens of commercials. In one, he finally returned home, drawn by a new brand of dog food.

CHAPTER TEN

REAL CHARACTERS

In 1936 B.T. (Before TV) General Mills gave birth to Betty Crocker, a no-nonsense home economics authority. She stood for all that was good about the brand, and though she had no existence in the real world, she nonetheless came to resonate with consumers. And, like Aunt Jemima and the Pillsbury Doughboy, she has changed over the years to reflect the times.

Many marketers create characters to give their messages character. These creations also add warmth. Madge the Manicurist starred in Palmolive's slice-of-life series for fourteen years; two decades of Mr. Whipple warning us not to squeeze the Charmin made it America's best-selling toilet tissue. Michelin had the "Tire Man" and McDonald's has Ronald.

Real celebrities are often used to symbolize the most relevant strategic idea in a category. American Express enlisted dozens of almost recognizable celebrities wielding the widely accepted card to get them both recognition—and the goods. And Coca-Cola brought a smile to even the then world's toughest guy: Mean Joe Greene. Some celebrities function as a security blanket of familiarity and a "tiebreaker" in a sea of similar products. When haughty John Houseman harrumphed that Smith Barney earned money the old-fashioned way, he imbued the brokerage with credibility based on little more than the quality of his voice and his starring role in *The Paper Chase*.

While only 16 percent of viewers could remember the name of a product in an average commercial, Starch Research found that adding a star could double that identification. But using real stars is risky. They cost, they fade, and they can overpower the message and spread themselves too thin. They can also threaten a brand's values. In 1991, Squibb dropped Billie Jean King as endorser for its Theragran-M vitamins just as her "galimony" suit broke. Anita Byrant's right-wing politics cost her orange juice sponsors. And Ace Hardware found itself in a vise when Suzanne Somers bared it all.

INMATE RELIEF

Nothing new to say? Get three hundred prisoners to shout it!

George Raft plays an inmate in a prison mess hall. As three hundred tough men sit down and begin eating, the amplified noise—and the bad food—disgust Raft. He throws down his fork, looks around for a means of expression, and picks up his tin cup. With an air of contempt he bangs the cup on the table, inciting the entire group to join in, thunderously pounding the tables and demanding "Al-ka-Selt-zer, Al-ka-Selt-zer, Al-ka-Selt-zer . . ."

Super: "Alka-Seltzer, Miles Laboratories Inc."

ALKA-SELTZER

PRISON

JACK TINKER & PARTNERS, USA, 1970

The idea for "Prison" came from the scene in *White Heat* in which James Cagney yells for his mother, recalled Charlie Ewell, who wrote the spot. "Humor ingratiated Alka-Seltzer with consumers and bought it a competitive edge when it really hadn't any," he added.

Indeed, gut-busting-funny commercials had been Alka-Seltzer's ticket to success through the 1960s, even as it jumped from ad agency to agency. "Prison" ran around the same time as "Spicy Meatballs" (see page 175) and other episodes of gastronomical distress: the hapless diner harangued to "try it—you'll like it," the culinarily aggressive bride who serves her groom an almost fatal dumpling, and rumpled Ralph, the stupefied glutton who can't believe he ate the whole thing.

Those glory days for Alka-Seltzer came to a sudden end in 1972 when the Food and Drug Administration, spurred by Ralph Nader, undertook a major regulatory review of over-the-counter drugs. Alka-Seltzer came in for negative publicity about its effects on the stomach and Miles stopped promoting it for upset stomachs alone.

Miles cut back on advertising and tried different campaigns, including some with celebrities. Sammy Davis Jr. crooned for the brand and Kim Basinger (making a transition from cover girl to actress) joined a then unknown Morgan Freeman as part of a singing bowling team. Nothing clicked until the Wells Rich Greene agency came up with "Plop, plop, fizz, fizz, oh, what it relief it is" in 1976. That ran for three years, and was then replaced by more fizzlers.

Despite America's willingness to overindulge on Alka-Seltzer advertising, the fact is, they just weren't overeating and overindulging in general the way they used to. And while that spelled relief to millions of heads and stomachs, it spelled only trouble for Alka-Seltzer. What's more, when the company introduced Alka-Seltzer Plus, it cannibalized the brand, implying that regular Alka-Seltzer wasn't strong enough.

The well-known aid for gluttons, bingers, and all-purpose overdoers had become synonymous with a hangover cure in the public's mind, and therefore almost obsolete in temperate times that shirked the executive lunch launched with a few martinis. Its message was more apropos to the permissive, pill-popping sixties and seventies than to the all-things-in-moderation 1980s, said Michael Sennott, senior vice president at McCann-Erickson. And people had stopped identifying with the schlumpy characters in Alka-Seltzer ads, he said. Interview subjects invariably drew Alka-Seltzer users as potbellied and tieless, while sketching other antacid users as well groomed.

McCann sought to motivate consumers to reach for the familiar blue-and-white packet by presenting Alka-Seltzer as an upbeat remedy for the symptoms of stress that come with success (the anxious upset stomach and thumping headache)—giving it more universal appeal. It replaced the ridiculous with the sublime: in one almost surrealistic spot, two tablets bob in slow motion in a water cooler, looking more like sculpture than medicine as an Erik Satie melody plays and a soothing voice salutes those climbing the corporate ladder.

JUST FOLKS

Synthetic booze sells down-home values with pseudo-hayseeds

BARTLES & JAYMES
YUPPIES

HAL RINEY & PARTNERS, USA, 1986

Two down-home hayseeds are sitting on a country porch. The loquacious one of the pair, straight-faced Frank Bartles, opens the spot: "Hello. We were interested to learn from our most recent research that one of the groups that liked Bartles & Jaymes best are the yuppies. Well, if some of our customers have chosen to be yuppies as their calling, it is okay with Ed and me."

Stone-faced Ed Jaymes, who doesn't say a word, reinforces Frank's point with an incomprehensible chart filled with "research."

"I believe that it is entirely their own business, even though I would personally prefer not to shave my head and stand around in airports," Frank continues. "So please continue to enjoy the Bartles & Jaymes Premium wine cooler even if you are a yuppie or whatever your race or creed. And thank you for your support."

"Frank Bartles" was, in fact, an Oregon hog farmer named David Rufkaur. His sidekick, the fictitious "Ed Jaymes," was in real life Dick Maug, a Santa Rosa, California, building contractor and an old fraternity brother and fishing buddy of Hal Riney, the architect and creator of the ad series. Together, these hayseeds manqués, who you might imagine were brewing cases of the cooler in their bathtub, made what may have been the first soap opera beverage advertising and gave nationwide recognition to Ernest and Julio Gallo Winery's Bartles & Jaymes wine cooler. In its heyday, Gallo sold ten thousand cases of the stuff a week and Bartles & Jaymes was the hottest name in the booze world.

Their aw-shucks style was as deliberate as their names—and the omission of Gallo's own name from any packaging or advertising (to duck any possible prejudice against it). Riney, who was then managing director of Ogilvy & Mather, San Francisco, wanted a name that would set the new cooler apart from the competition and he wanted initials that went well together and could easily be shouted at a crowded bar. Riney thumbed through the San Francisco telephone directory. Bartles had the right tone. The agency couldn't clear Jameson and the more basic "James" didn't sound exactly right. Riney made it the more distinctive Jaymes.

The O&M team evaluated more than nine hundred would-be rubes before casting Maug and Rufkaur. Riney rewrote each script of the short-lived, droll, and relatively inexpensive series on the set, often up to the final take. In one two-day film session with director Joe Pytka, sixteen commercials were produced.

The first of them debuted in October 1985. The Mutt and Jeff home-spun entrepreneurs, one chubby and chatty, the other skinny and silent, sat on the wooden porch stoop while Frank haltingly introduced Bartles & Jaymes Premium wine cooler. "Hello there. My name is Fred Bartles and this is Ed Jaymes. You know, it occurred to Ed the other day that between his fruit orchard and my premium wine vineyard, we could make a truly superior premium-grade wine cooler. It sounded good to me. So Ed took out a second on his house, wrote to Harvard for an MBA, and now we're preparing to enter the wine cooler business. We'll try to keep you posted on how it's going, and thank you very much for your support."

In another spot, Frank says that buying Bartles & Jaymes would be a "personal favor to Ed because he took that second on his house and soon he's got a big balloon payment coming up." (The colloquial dialogue apparently convinced some viewers these guys were for real: some wrote offering Ed help to pay down his debt.)

In still another spot, Frank noted that people may not have realized how good Bartles & Jaymes is with a meal. "So Ed engaged in a scientific program to determine which foods go well with Bartles & Jaymes coolers. So far Ed has found only two foods which don't: kohlrabi . . . and candy corn. All other foods are fine."

In an early spot, beefy Frank asked viewers to suggest names for the sweet and low-cal wine: in a sequel he thanked them but announced that they were sticking with Bartles & Jaymes. "If you don't like it, please don't tell us because we've already printed up our labels." Then he suggested that viewers could "call it Bartles and skip the Jaymes altogether. Ed says that it's okay with him."

The Bartles & Jaymes spots are the quintessential work of their creator: a masterful blend of sentiment and spoof, emotionally charged and understated, strong on mood and with believable characters not often seen in TV commercials. Riney says that most purchase decisions are made for emotional, not rational reasons and the underlying premise of this advertising—and most of his work—is that soft-sell understatement and dry humor work better than overstatement.

The Bartles & Jaymes series violated several cardinal rules of advertising: to be simple, repetitive, and not assume too much. These ads assumed a sophisticated viewer who could get subtle jokes and tongue-in-cheek humility. Not that Bartles & Jaymes ever let you forget the cooler they were hawking. The message was clear but not obvious. Ogilvy vice chairman James Benson said viewers might be mesmerized by the visual tone and not notice the strong sell in the words.

It would be hard not to notice the digs to the lifestyle of the target audience—and to advertising in general. In one spot Ed is seated reading a book—*Riney on Advertising*. In another spot, the duo are conducting "consumer research" in Los Angeles. "We're at the corner of Hollywood and Vine to get the average person's reaction to Ed's new Bartles & Jaymes Premium wine cooler," says Frank, as punk rockers, motorcycle hoodlums, leather freaks, and a man carrying an English bulldog in his arms stream by. "But we're still waiting for an average person."

Within a year, the campaign had made Bartles & Jaymes the best-selling cooler in the hottest wine category. By 1984 a category that hadn't existed three years earlier had sales of $330 million. A year later they topped $700 million—a tenth of the total $7 billion wine business, growing faster than any beverage, even diet soda, largely by appealing to young women. By 1985 there were 125 cooler brands along with Bartles and Jaymes, including New York Canandaigua Winery's Sun Country, Seagram's Cooler, and the original California Cooler.

In 1992, seven years after their B&J series began and some 230 Bartles & Jaymes commercials later, the public had cooled to the duo—and coolers. Gallo pulled the plug on Rufkahr and Maug, who went on to star in an ad for *Golf Illustrated* magazine. On April 23, 1996, Rufkahr, then sixty-one, died of a heart attack.

THANKS, MEAN JOE!

Coke's tearjerker is a touchdown in cynical times

As wounded Pittsburgh Steelers' glowering defensive lineman limps down the stadium tunnel toward the locker room, a shy, moon-faced fan, startled at finding himself so near to his hero, tries to commiserate and buck up an idol who is clearly angry with himself.

"Mr. Greene? . . . Mr. Greene?"

The Steeler is hard as nails. "Yeah . . ." he relents.

"Ya . . . ya need any help?"

"Naw," snarls the curmudgeon.

"I just want you to know, I think you're the best ever," the boy tells him.

"Yeah, sure," Greene mutters.

"Want my Coke?" the boy asks as a last resort, holding out a bottle of Coke to him. "It's okay. You can have it."

Greene demurs, but the boy again insists, "Really, you can have it."

Greene sighs, "Okay, thanks." He lifts the bottle and chugs it down. The music swells and the lyrics proclaim, "A Coke and a smile, makes me feel good, makes me feel nice."

The boy has played his last card and is deflated. "See ya 'round," he says, turning to leave. The lyrics continue, "That's the way it should be and I'd like to see the whole world smiling at me."

The Coke, or the boy's generosity, has restored Greene's humanity: "Hey, kid . . . catch!" The hulking lineman throws the lad his jersey and flashes a dazzling grin.

"Coca-Cola adds life, have a Coke and a smile," continue the lyrics.

Boy: "Wow! Thanks Mean Joe!"

Super: "Have a Coke and a smile. Coke adds life."

COCA-COLA

MEAN JOE GREENE

MCCANN-ERICKSON WORLDWIDE, USA, 1979

Just as Marlboro owned macho cowboys, Coca-Cola thought it could own "the world of smiling Americans," said Bill Van Loan, then vice president of marketing operations at the soft drink giant. Unlike Pepsi advertising, which invited people "to join some mythical group, Coke spots featured product as hero, causing the smile," he said.

America ranked "Mean Joe" as the most popular commercial of its time, just as it had "I'd Like to Teach the World to Sing" years earlier. Van Loan said the seemingly realistic, honest exchange between two people was saved from being melodramatic or overly sentimental because it didn't over-promise. The advertising recognized that Coke is only a soft drink—the pause that refreshes. It won't change the world or heal Mean Joe's injury, but it can—and did—restore his spirit and smile. And the transition from "Mean Joe" to "Nice Joe" also brought a smile to potential consumers.

137

(The client originally wanted Dallas Cowboy quarterback Roger Staubach; Roger Mosconi, who art directed the spot, insisted on Greene as more dramatic and emotional.)

Director Lee Lacy shot "Mean Joe" at a high school in New Rochelle, New York, rather than a pro stadium, to emphasize Greene's 260-pound muscularity. The shoot took three days because the boy, ten-year-old Tommy Oken, was so awed by Greene that he kept missing his lines. On the last day, Greene had to gulp eighteen 16-ounce Cokes.

Penny Hawkey, who wrote the spot, said she wanted to do something different from the happy jingles and well-scrubbed folks working up a thirst that had characterized most Coca-Cola advertising. She thinks the unironic emotional spot wouldn't work in more cynical times.

It sure worked then. The top brass at Coke hadn't expected to get it on the air so soon, but after presenting it to its bottlers, they demanded it be aired immediately and Coke poured it on. The sixty-second spot aired in seven other countries, with Brazil and Thailand reshooting it with local soccer stars in the starring role. George Wallach produced a TV movie, *The Steeler and the Pittsburgh Kid,* for NBC on what happens after. The boy (played by Henry Thomas) feared that the loss of Greene's jersey would sap his strength the way the loss of Samson's hair neutralized him, so he set out on an adventure to return it. Coke was never mentioned in the movie, which supposedly was shot in less time than it took to film the commercial.

Soon after, rival Pepsi came out with a hip spoof aimed at making "Mean Joe" seem mawkish. Basketball giant Shaquille O'Neal asks a seemingly gullible boy for his soda, but the boy won't part with his Pepsi.

Two years after "Mean Joe" first aired, a new management team canceled the "Coke and a Smile" campaign, calling it pleasant but ineffective in the face of the Pepsi Challenge. During its tenure, Coke's market share held steady while Pepsi's climbed. In supermarkets, where customers had a choice, Pepsi had begun to outsell Coke.

UH HUH

Ray Charles sings the praises of Pepsi

The commercial starts with casual shots of Ray Charles rehearsing: "You know when it's right.

"You know when you feel it, baby.

"You hold it. You hear it. You taste it. It's right.

"Diet Pepsi."

The scene shifts to a glitzy performance with Ray at a grand piano in a lavish setting with palms, a glass staircase, and the Raylettes (in retro black wigs and hip-hugging, gold-sequinned outfits) sashaying and lip-synching around their leader as he joyously belts out the Diet Pepsi anthem. A platoon of showgirls in satin shorts and halters perform a rocking routine on the staircase.

Ray and girls: "Uh huh . . . uh huh."

Ray Charles: "You got the right one, baby."

Ray and girls: "Diet Pepsi."

Ray Charles: "If it's irresistibly sippable, uncontestably tastable, and intimately wonderful, you got the right one, baby."

Girls: "Uh huh."

Chorus: "You got the right one, baby."

Ray Charles: "You know when it's right. You know when you taste it!"

Super: "You got the right one, baby, Uh Huh. Diet Pepsi."

DIET PEPSI

UH HUH

BBDO, USA, 1990

The first in a trilogy of musical productions around the "You Got the Right One, Baby" theme debuted on Super Bowl XXV. But it almost didn't happen. The Gulf War was raging and arch-rival Coca-Cola, sensing America's grave mood, killed its lighthearted spots for Diet Coke. At the eleventh hour Pepsi canceled a heavily promoted call-in contest but decided to go ahead with soulful Ray Charles warbling the soda's new jingle.

Viewers interpreted Coke's patriotic replacement ads as party-pooping moralizing, an exploitative climb onto a pro-war bandwagon. But they savored the jazzy ads from the perennial second-place cola contender. The spot—and subsequent nine more in the series—went a long way to establish Pepsi's position as "the choice of a new generation." By portraying Diet Pepsi as the real thing, this series cut into Coke's marketing theme. Reportedly, the phrase "uh huh" was banned at Coke's Atlanta headquarters.

Diet Pepsi had been changing its somewhat limp advertising slogans frequently. "The right one" was conceived in 1989, but William Katz, now BBDO president and then head of the Pepsi account, said it "felt a bit stilted and marketingese." Creative director Alfred Merrin and jingle writer Peter Cofield tried to tailor "the right one" to Charles's jivey delivery and threw in "baby." They had two syllables left over for the Raylettes: Merrin said they played with the idea of doo-woo but ultimately went to uh huh, "a two syllable grunt that embodies affirmativeness."

Within a week, the spot had achieved cult status as people latched onto the new jingle. The "uh huh" catchphrase popped up on the top-rated *Cosby Show* and George Bush used it in a famous debate to deride Michael Dukakis. Pepsi began selling out its proffered assortment of T-shirts, hats, jackets, nightshirts, and boxer shorts emblazoned with the "You got the right one" jingle and even tried to make April "National Uh Huh Month." And the company filled supermarkets with life-sized cutouts of Charles and the Raylettes and let customers record their own version of the jingle at promotional karaoke booths.

Ironically, Coca-Cola had used Ray Charles as its endorser in 1969. Twenty-one years—and a reported $3 million in endorsement fees—later, the blind singer appeared in a commercial for Diet Pepsi in which the cans are switched and Charles catches on because of the taste.

In surveys, consumers ranked "Uh Huh" as their favorite commercial and initially closed the "forced choice" gap with Diet Coke, which had traditionally led it 70 to 30. In 1991 Coke's lead had dropped from 52 to 48 percent. Pepsi contends that the Charles spots exceeded their objectives, that they drove volume increases twice as large as the overall category, increased volume share across all channels, and created unprecedented levels of brand advertising awareness.

But by 1992 consumers were again buying the soda that was on sale. Shares retreated to pretty much the same as before "uh huh" was ever uttered. *Beverage Digest* publisher Jesse Meyers explained at the time that soda is a distribution business; it's all price promotions.

NOTHIN' BUT NET

Jordan and Bird square off in a battle for the burger

MCDONALD'S
SHOWDOWN COMBO

LEO BURNETT, USA, 1993

A super announces "The Showdown. McDonald's" as basketball super-star Larry Bird dribbles in a deserted gymnasium and asks Michael Jordan, "What's in the bag?" After Jordan tells him that lunch is a Big Mac and fries, Bird asks to play for it. "First one to miss watches the winner eat," says Jordan.

As funky upbeat music plays, the shots start out easy enough but soon escalate: "off the floor, off the scoreboard, off the backboard, no rim." As the balls swoosh through the net and the players move around the stadium to attempt the seeming impossible, Jordan raises the ante: "Over the second rafter, off the floor, nothin' but net . . ." then "through the window, off the wall, nothin' but net." The last scene shows the two atop the John Hancock Building with the goal now set at hitting the ball "off the expressway, over the river, off the billboard, through the window, off the wall . . . nothin' but net . . ."

Super: "McDonald's. What you want is what you get."

. . . and, The ball goes in, nothin' but net.

In Super Bowl 1992, McDonald's "Perfect Season," its touching ninety-second ode to peewee football teams across the country, tugged at our hearts. The mud-covered kids with their errant throws and confused plays were more interested in a grasshopper and an outing to McDonald's than in their coaches' motivational speeches. And their dads—arms outstretched, posing as goalposts—were the real heroes, for whom a good day wasn't determined by who won but by being with their sons.

But that spot reinforced McDonald's support of youth and commemorated its recently formed partnership with the NFL, wedding emotion to a macho sport, and showing why people came together, said Burnett's chief creative officer, Cheryl Berman. The warm fuzzy paean to boys' football, voiced by Richard Dreyfuss and directed by Steve Horn, had so much humanity and viewer empathy in it that Steven Spielberg called art director Bob Shallcross and copywriter Jim Ferguson to write a movie (*Little Giants*) based on the commercial's theme.

The next year, McDonald's turned its attention to the NBA and decided to showcase its long-term relationship with that sport and its premier players. McDonald's had signed Jordan; Burnett suggested adding Bird. Although "Showdown" is on a grand scale compared with the grassroots "Perfect Season," one is a natural outgrowth of the other, Berman said. "They're both very personal, entertaining, and humorous, brimming with humanity, and they both felt like what happens in them could really happen."

Well, almost. The Bird-Jordan taunting rings true and the winner-takes-all game seems like something Michael Jordan and Larry Bird could have come up with. And that they were arguing over a Big Mac was also believable. The contest itself, while not believable, *was* playfully handled and universally understood. Director Joe Pytka shot "Showdown" in Phoenix, then matted Chicago's Hancock Building in and used other special effects to simulate those far-flung baskets.

"Rather than distracting from the product story, the icons of Michael Jordan and Larry Bird actually helped trigger the crave," Berman said. "It's wink and a smile advertising."

"Showdown" premiered in the 1993 Super Bowl and scored the highest "ad meter" rating ever received. According to Berman, Jordan said it's the favorite commercial he's ever been in, because in addition to endearing people to the brand, it also endeared them to *him*. Factoring in talent costs, it was also one of the most expensive commercials ever produced, reportedly costing more than $2 million. But its appeal was widespread. McDonald's in Israel adopted it as the first commercial it ever ran.

"Showdown" ran for a little more than a year, until the talent contracts expired. It has been reprised for occasional airings since. Although it's hard to credit advertising alone when it runs concurrently with promotions, McDonald's reported a $500 million boost in sales, up 3.8 percent, in 1993. "Nothin' but net" became part of the American lexicon, and "Showdown" became the basis for one of the most successful NBA promotions ever.

BO KNOWS DIDDLEY

Or: Why God is a Bo Jackson fan

NIKE

BO KNOWS

WIEDEN & KENNEDY, USA, 1989

The words "Cross training by Bo Jackson" appear against a black background followed by "Music by Bo Diddley" as heavy drums and electric guitar jam to Bo Diddley's 1955 hit "I'm a Man."

In cameos, well-known athletes sound off about Bo Jackson's versatility, intercut with shots of Diddley and his band.

"Bo knows baseball," testifies Los Angeles Dodgers star Kirk Gibson.

"Bo knows football," adds the Los Angeles Rams' Jim Everett.

"Bo knows basketball, too," confirms Michael Jordan as he stuffs the ball.

John McEnroe looks dubious. "Bo knows tennis?" he asks quizzically.

Track star Mary Decker weighs in with "Bo knows running."

Even Bo has his limits as hockey star Wayne Gretzky attests when he skates up to the camera, shakes his head, and says, "Naw."

The bodybuilders at Muscle Beach acknowledge that Bo knows weights.

Finally we see Bo Jackson in spandex workout pants laughingly hacking at the guitar beside the Diddley band, loudly and off key.

Bo Diddley tells him, "Bo, you don't know Diddley!"

Super: "Just do it."

Super: "Nike."

142

In the remarkable dual-sport athlete Bo Jackson, Wieden & Kennedy's legendary copywriter Jim Riswold saw a way to fashion a new mythology. Riswold initially harnessed Bo to Nike's new air-cushioned shoes in a commercial in which the Oakland Raiders running back/Kansas City Royals outfielder furiously pedals a bike, then mischievously asks, "Now when is that 'Tour de Force' thing?" Then director Joe Pytka (who also shot "Bo Knows") served up a Bolympics Bo-nanza starring a total of fourteen Bo Jacksons at once. Bo appears in basketball gear, tennis togs, as a hockey, cricket, and soccer player, surfer, weight lifter, auto racer, golfer, caddy, and jockey. The Bos notice one another and compliment each other's shoes; Sonny Bono walks on, claiming he thought it was another "Bo-nos" commercial.

At a local bar, wrestling with ideas for another sequel, Riswold muttered, "Bo." Patrons peppered him with Rorschach responses: Beau Brummell . . . Bo Derek . . . and, finally, Bo Diddley, the Mississippi-born singer and guitarist. Riswold knew that was the one, and later that night mapped out the "You don't know Diddley" theme and cast of athletic testifiers.

Jackson, who stuttered badly, didn't utter a single line: endorsements from the other athletes and the one-time king of cool said enough to establish him as marketing manna—warm *and* cool and physically powerful and the second most famous athlete in the world after Michael Jordan.

When Nike employees previewed the spot at a giant sales meeting, more than one thousand of the reps jumped to their feet, roaring approval. Without testing it, Nike scrapped all running shoe advertising, put the money behind "Bo Knows," and doubled its intended media budget.

Nike threw the dice again: on the day of the baseball all-star game, it ran a full page ad in *USA Today* announcing the stars who'd be joining Bo at the top of the fourth inning of the game—even though spots in sporting events often get shuffled. Luck was with Nike that night. The spots ran as planned and—miraculously—followed a home run Bo slammed his first time at bat that night. Watching in the stands, Riswold reasoned that "God is a Bo Jackson fan."

Nike didn't air "Bo Knows" again for three weeks, but the public saw a lot of it anyway: news and talk shows and *Entertainment Tonight* gave it what Nike estimated as close to $20 million in free exposure. A *New Yorker* cartoon even claimed that "Bo knows fiction."

Within months of the debut of "Bo Knows," Nike had captured 80 percent of the new cross-training market. The category, whose sales stood around $40 million when John McEnroe alone pitched them, topped $400 million. Six months later, a new spot showed the younger, far more muscled Bo playing guitar and the older Bo conceding that he did know Diddley after all.

But the tongue-in-cheek commercials played better than Bo did on the field—and within a year they stopped running. (Reebok was similarly let down when seeming Olympic shoe-ins "Dan and Dave" bombed.)

The effect of the Bo spots, however, lingered for years before bloated inventories and an anti-swoosh backlash put a cramp in Nike's legs. Scott Bedbury, former Nike ad director, said " 'Bo Knows' helped reassert Nike as the leader for jocks, displace Reebok as number one, and broadened Nike's point of access across many sports with humor and inspirational storytelling."

DUST UP

A cleaning lady polishes Pliz's pitch for market share

PLIZ
MADAME CHIFFON

DOYLE DANE BERNBACH, FRANCE, 1981

A crotchety-looking cleaning lady sprays Pliz polish on a boardroom table. She wraps herself in a duster, takes a running start, and launches herself into a fifteen-yard slide down the length of the table to produce a brilliant shine, a shine that lasts. A voice-over announces (in French), "Of course, Pliz does wonders for removing dust. But that's not all . . ." dramatic music builds up ". . . with Pliz, the dust stays on the cleaning cloth. And furniture stays brighter longer."

Woman: "And that's good, because I can't do this every day."
Voice-over and super: "Pliz takes the dust."

Consumer research indicates that, among all household tasks, removing dust is one of the most hated. "Unlike cooking, where you receive compliments, dusting is something no one notices when it's done, but they do notice the dust if it isn't," said Nicole Lanoix, account director on "Madame Chiffon."

The DDB team of copywriter Anne Jambert and art director Christian Vince took the idea of a Sisyphean task—the dust just keeps coming back—and marrying it to Pliz polish's product benefit. Because with Pliz, more dust stays on the rag and so the chore needn't be done as often.

To reinforce Pliz's leadership (it's called Pledge in the U.S.), the creative team decided to use a product demonstration—the only way to convince, said Lanoix—but one that was exaggerated and funny (to neutralize the boring task) and very different from rival advertising (to generate interest and create an impact).

The actress, Marie Pierre Casey had been a relative unknown, cast because she looked grouchy, scowling, and stubborn—exactly the type who would be credible snarling that she would not do this every day. In fact she had to do the difficult slide several times, damaging both herself and the camera on *different* takes. "Madame Chiffon" made her famous. Subsequently she did comic sketches on TV and ran a one-woman show.

The payoff line, "I can't do this every day," became part of the common lingo in France. The commercial also paid off for Pliz. Sales grew heartily since the commercial aired, Lanoix said.

"Madame Chiffon" ran for two years, after which time Pliz began running more basic, more serious slice-of-life commercials. "They changed so frequently that finally the brand lost its personal touch and identity," said Lanoix. Soon after, Johnson Wax realigned all Johnson products at another advertising agency.

CHAPTER ELEVEN

COMPARATIVELY SPEAKING

American viewers well know Visa's combative ". . . and they don't take American Express" advertising. Some marketers estimate that a third of all advertising in the U.S. consists of hard-hitting comparisons with other brands. Research suggests consumers recall the messages and sponsors better in comparative ads than in noncomparative ones, and that people are more likely to intend to purchase the more aggressive brand.

But great competitive ads rarely use side-by-side comparisons or graphic illustrations—or even the competitor's name. Overt aggression can backfire; sometimes more subtle strategies are required. Southern Airways draped its bellicosity with mirth. "Orgy" compared a bacchanalian feast with what looked like steerage on the world's most brutal slave ship to pitch its socialistic, one-size-fits-all class of service—and to demean those airlines with tiered service. And the then third-place burger player Wendy's, on a relatively puny budget, hilariously laid down the gauntlet with its feisty "Where's the Beef?" commercial in 1983. Without referring directly to the Golden Arches (or, as the commercial would have it, the "Home of the Big Bun"), Clara Peller nonetheless made it perfectly, charmingly, and unforgettably clear that McDonald's offered a lot less beef on a lot more bun.

Pepsi, on the other hand, has delivered its barbs with both soft lobs and sharp strikes. Its taste tests, which ran from 1975 through 1984, were hardly subtle, but the archaeology professor of the future who can identify such relics of our time as a split-level ranch house, a baseball, and a guitar, but is stumped by the dirt-encrusted, icon-shaped Coke bottle, irreverently and indirectly belittled Coke and portrayed Pepsi as the choice of tomorrow.

But comparative ads have their critics. In some countries comparative advertising is frowned upon, if not illegal. In Brazil, for example, regulations are so strict that comparative advertising is virtually nonexistent. "Where's the beef?" would be an illegal question in some European countries. All five major Tokyo channels refused to run rapper/Pepsi spokesman M.C. Hammer's derision of the "Feelings" crowd and their soft drink. To get that spot on the air in the U.K., Pepsi had to replace the Coke can with that of an anonymous cola.

And while viewers do find competitive ads persuasive, they consider the source—and overall find them less credible than noncomparative ads. What's more, people tend to like comparative ads less than noncomparative ads, especially in countries where comparative ads are not widely used. Unless, that is, they're served up with wit and sizzle.

MEALS ON WINGS

The way to a flyer's heart is through his stomach

The spot opens as two catering company salesmen show a microscopic hamburger to the purchasing agent of, according to the super, "another airline."

Music plays as a voice-over sets the background, "These days a lot of airlines are cutting corners on their meals."

The first salesman says, "This little beauty we like to call banquet on a bun. Right, Bob?"

Bob dourly repeats, "Banquet on a bun."

The fat purchasing agent says, "I like it."

The lead salesman motions his lieutenant: "Set it down, Bob." (A drum noise sounds as it hits the table.) He continues, "Now with this, you can serve a whole planeload for just pennies."

The fat purchasing agent says, "I like it."

He also likes the other seedy offerings:

"Plastic parsley—you can use it over and over," says the lead salesman.

"I like it," repeats the purchasing agent.

"Pygmy chickens, you can get 105 in one shoe box. . . ." continues the salesman.

It's up to the announcer to set things straight: "At Alaska Airlines we spend a little more on our meals and you can taste the difference."

ALASKA AIRLINES MEALS

CHIAT/DAY/LIVINGSTON & COMPANY, USA, 1985

Not all competitive ads need be side-by-side graphic illustrations, as this hilarious romp from Alaska Airlines proves. The story goes that in the summer of 1979, on a competitor's breakfast flight from Seattle to Los Angeles, John Kelly, then vice president of marketing at Alaska Airlines (and now president), hungered for an omelet breakfast—and got a doughnut instead. Kelly was disgusted. His airline served hot meals on every breakfast, lunch, and dinner flight.

His irritation sparked a nineteen-spot campaign that propelled awareness of his airline sky-high. The now defunct Seattle agency Livingston & Company had proposed three campaigns to Kelly to replace Alaska Airlines' conventional "come fly with us" style spots. One was to focus on Alaska's rugged, frontier hospitality. Kelly was nonplussed. Another was to present the regional carrier that covers the West and Alaska as the ideal choice for the independent-thinking business traveler. He nixed that as well.

Then agency chief Roger Livingston came up with the combative idea of illustrating how most conventional airlines weren't taking care of their passengers—they were cutting back on service and food and jamming in more seats—while Alaska was catering to them, serving real cream and butter, and almonds instead of peanuts. Why not point out the atrocious personal service of some of its rivals? he suggested. The collective effect of these small individual advantages, he theorized, would leave viewers believing that any airline so in touch with how its passenger feel must be a good one. The commercials wouldn't promise pheasant under glass, he said, but people would "hear" better overall quality. (Indeed, research later showed that, although no commercial ever alluded to cleanest plates, people guessed it was Alaska that had them.)

It was Kelly, spurred by his breakfast caper, who proposed turning the idea into a parody and turning its filming over to director Joe Sedelmaier, a budding funnyman who went on to create "Where's the Beef?" for Wendy's and other comedy gems. Sedelmaier brought humor to the storyboards, transforming would-be emotional spots into laughable larks.

One of them started with the notion of a young boy warmly reminiscing about his first flight and became an ad in which a 1920 Ford Tri-Motor plane bounces nauseatingly, the passengers squirming in their tiny seats, and a stewardess lurching in the aisle. Cut to modern times . . . and there's no change: the camera shows the same scene on a cramped modern plane. Finally, the camera shows life aboard roomy and calm Alaska Air, where relaxed passengers are savoring a meal. In another spot, slack-jawed passengers stare at a video screen as a stewardess shows them an appetizing bowl of fruit and bids them "*Bon appétit!*" But their tiny paper bags contain nothing resembling fruit.

"Joe assembled a cast of odd-looking, unpolished, and unprofessional characters, put them in unreal situations, and told them to stop acting on the set," recalled Dave Palmer, vice president of marketing. The star of one spot was a retired high school principal, who Sedelmaier hooked when he wasn't even looking to act. "He had people read lines we'd never talked about and they ended up in the spot: like when a stewardess says 'munchie time,' or '*bon appétit*.' We were careful never to portray our competitors as dark villains in a mean-spirited or harsh way," Palmer said.

Palmer said the campaign strongly positioned Alaska "as an airline with a different sense of self and attitude; we were fun. We told people that we know it's hell out there and that we can laugh at it with them and empathize with them. They believed we cared and understood."

They also believed Alaska was much bigger than its actual size, and, in fact, the ads helped build bookings and revenue. Three years after the campaign began, Alaska's passenger load had mushroomed from 1.3 million to 2.5 million, and passenger revenue from $151.2 million to $314.2 million. And, a possibly apocryphal story goes, United Airlines subsequently changed its West Coast food service after passengers held up boxed meals and chanted, "This is it?" a line from an Alaska spot.

"As a small airline going against formidable competitors spending fifteen to twenty times what we were spending [on advertising], we needed to do something to stand out and were willing to take a risk," Palmer said.

The campaign ran for twelve years before Alaska retired it. "The industry had changed dramatically," Palmer said. "Travelers were looking for airlines to go everywhere they wanted to go because of frequent flyer miles and although we're a dominant player on the West Coast, in the grand scheme we're small." Then too, Palmer said, Alaska had stopped serving lavish foods.

LYRIC TRANSLATION

The song says more about the tape than the tape says about the song

A cool-looking dude, dreads shoved under a knit cap, is standing in front of a motley van grooving to the ska classic "Israelites," by Desmond Dekker. As he bobs his head to the beat, he flips a series of cards on which appear the lyrics he thinks he hears:

"Get up in the mornin'/sleeping for bread, sir.
Sold out to every monk/and beef-head.
Oh Oh/Me ears are alight
Why find my kids/They buck up and a-leave me
Darling Cheese head/I was yards too greasy
Oh Oh/My ears are alight."

His final card: "I think that's what he says, but I need to hear it on a Maxell."

MAXELL

ISRAELITES

HOWELL HENRY CHALDECOTT LURY, U.K., 1990

High-performance audiotapes are essentially parity products with little to distinguish them from one another outside their own advertising. Most of that aims to be youthful and full of attitude. In "Israelites," however, the selling point *is* superior reproduction, but it's pitched in an ultrasoft way. No evidence is given for Maxell's claim to superiority. Instead, the ad's own ineluctable hipness is transferred to the product and those who use it, the hoped-for subconscious logic being that Maxell can actually solve the dramatized problem that arises from rival tape because it is so in tune with its consumers' lifestyles. The commercial, in itself, becomes the brand benefit.

It's not just the quirky character (unknown Larrington Walker) or his off-the-wall translation that makes us grin. And it's not just that many of us recognize that the spot was inspired by the 1965 Bob Dylan "video" for his song "Subterranean Homesick Blues," in which he himself holds the (correct) lyrics on placards. (Though such cultural touchstones do allow Maxell consumers to feel they are among the elect.) It's also the jolt we get from the realization that this situation, created by even the most innocuous pop music, is an almost universal problem. We're all in a fog trying to figure out the words to our favorite songs. Maxell gets it.

"Israelites" wasn't the only hilarious spot for Maxell audiotape. A similar one, also revolving around garbled lyrics, shows a scruffy young man who reveals hand-lettered charts misinterpreting lyrics from the Skids' new-wave hit "Into the Valley." Steve Lowe, who worked on the spots with art director Tim Ashton and writer Narash Ramchandani, says that these commercials allowed viewers to laugh at other cultures and/or themselves without being malicious. Lowe recruited one of his cue card holders off a London street corner. The other one had laid the carpet in his London apartment.

Graham Bednash, account director at Howell Henry Chaldecott Lury, said that the budget was meager but that the commercials garnered immense publicity for the brand and helped push Maxell from fifth place to second. It also resulted in increased shelf facings in all key outlets and a market share increase from 11 percent to 14 percent in three months.

WEIGHTY READING

A book club takes a swat at magazine readers

NORWEGIAN BOOK CLUB

TRAIN 1

DRAMSRUD & WERNER, NORWAY, 1982

Two men are in a train compartment, one reading a magazine, the other a book. As the train chugs along, a fly starts to buzz around the compartment. The man reading the magazine flails after it several times, hitting the window, but always missing. The man reading the book, however, without even looking up, raises his book and snaps it shut, then casually flicks the fly out and continues reading as accordion music plays.

Super: "Get wise. Read books."

The Norwegian Book Club was—and still is—the dominant book club in Norway, with a market share of 60 percent. In 1982, after twenty years in business, it had approximately 350,000 members, more than 80 percent of whom had joined through direct marketing. But that was essentially a closed channel with little opportunity for brand building in the open market. So, to expand the brand against the total market, Norwegian Book Club undertook a more conventional approach: commercials.

The advertising, modeled after a 1930 U.S. campaign "Give Me a Man Who Reads," had two aims: to attract new members and to encourage existing members to maintain their membership for a longer time, said book club marketing manager Terje Kolstad. Both groups had a limited amount of time to read, and many were devoting that time to—horrors!—magazines. The ads would have to drive home the message that magazines are for flighty people who can't concentrate on larger issues. Read a book, on the other hand, and you will reach zenlike equilibrium.

"Train 1" was created by Norwegian art director Johan Gulbransson at the Dramsrud & Werner ad agency and produced by Rolf Soleman at Jarowsky Film. It was filmed in Stockholm, Sweden, in March 1981 and was the first of three spots showing the same pair in different situations with the same humorous melody, the same absence of conversation, and just the logo at the end. Each commercial cost around $60,000 to produce. That series was followed by print ads urging readers to "Catch a fly yourself; be a member."

Though "Train 1" was originally produced as a cinema commercial, it ended up running a year on television. Recognition of the book club rose from 53 to 75 percent and membership climbed to 624,000—a hefty percentage of Norway's 4.5 million population. The book club still runs the ad from time to time, and did so as recently as autumn 1997. "Although it's fifteen years old, it still makes sense as a brand builder," Kolstad said. A timeless classic.

DIG IT!

Pepsi argues that Coke is the choice of a (very) old generation

In the far future, an archeology professor takes his class through an old dig that, he explains, used to be a split-level ranch house. On their expedition, the students refresh themselves, drinking from cans of Pepsi. As synthesized music plays eerily, the professor intones, "This, class, is perhaps the greatest discovery of our time, a dwelling called the split-level ranch. Marvelous!"

A girl student picks up a baseball. "What's this, Professor?" she inquires.

The professor replies, "A spherical object they used to hurl at each other with great velocity as others looked on."

A boy unearths a guitar and asks the professor, "What's this?"

"Oh!" says the sage, delightedly offering an explanation as he swivels his hips. "This device produced excruciatingly loud noises to which they would gyrate in pain."

PEPSI

ARCHEOLOGY

BBDO, USA, 1985

After removing the dirt and corrosion of another relic—an old Coke bottle—another girl queries: "Professor, what is it?"

Stumped, Mr. Erudite crunches his face in puzzlement.

"Odd," he allows.

Space-age sounds punctuate the confusion. The girl again inquires, "What is it?"

Bewildered, the professor admits: "I have no idea."

The announcer and super deliver the punch line: "Pepsi, the choice of a new generation."

Pepsi and Coke have long been fierce combatants in an ice-cold cola war. The weapon of choice has been advertising; the reward, the lion's share of a $54 billion industry that accounts for more than a quarter of all beverages consumed by Americans—including water. "Archeology" was one of the most effective gambits in that war.

It was classic Pepsi advertising: irreverent, nonformulaic, and totally unpredictable, said Phil Dusenberry, vice chairman of BBDO and creative director on the spot. It was written by Ted Sann, now co–chief executive of BBDO, art directed by Harvey Hoffenberg, and filmed by Joe Pytka. Alan Pottasch, senior vice president for creative services at Pepsi, oversaw the BBDO team. The goal for this and other Pepsi ads at the time was to create mini-movies, "little shows—entertaining and compelling enough to keep viewers' riveted on the screen," Dusenberry said. Despite its sharp barb, "Archeology's" not-so-subtle knocking of the competition comes off as soft sell. "Hard, loud, sharp, and pushy are simply not Pepsi," says Dusenberry.

The team decided that Pepsi's taste tests, which ran from 1975 through 1984, had become too subjective for anything other than promotions. They were also too far afield from Pepsi's advertising mission "to touch, tickle, dazzle and delight," while selling a promise more than a product—a promise of fun and youth and joy and laughter and good times, Dusenberry said. Assuming that one's soda is a good indication of one's personality and style, "Archeology" focused more on the people who'd be drinking it than on product attributes such as taste or calories.

Leaving archrival Coca-Cola the warm, sentimental terrain of nostalgia, Pepsi relied on humor to win customers. "It's hard to walk away in the middle of a joke," mused Dusenberry.

Like virtually all other Pepsi advertising, the sixty-second "Archeology" didn't stint on production values. Many Pepsi spots cost more than $1 million to make; an oft-repeated joke around Pepsi headquarters was that the soda company gave BBDO an unlimited budget but somehow the agency managed to exceed it.

The commercial was shot on a stage in California over three days with computer-generated special effects (the spaceship) added later. The original production featured upbeat, brassy music with comedic overtones. Dusen-berry heard it and overnight called in the New York music house Elias Brothers for a more leading edge, new-age track.

Earlier Pepsi advertising aimed to make Pepsi classy. In the 1950s there was "Say Pepsi, Please" and "Be Sociable, Look Smart" with the soda served from champagne coolers as debonair men in tuxedos toasted women in cocktail dresses. Pepsi had been considered downstairs to Coke's upstairs, and the advertising was crafted to drag it out of the kitchen into the living room.

But after BBDO won the account in April 1960, it aimed for a different lifestyle—young people who wanted to distinguish themselves from their parents and who weren't looking to be effete but to "be alive," to live life to its fullest. The 1965 campaign, "You're in the Pepsi Generation," replaced cocktail attire with surfing gear and other high-energy play clothes.

In 1984, BBDO launched "The choice of a new generation," which it calls the world's first lifestyle campaign. It exalted the product-user rather than the product and made America look at commercials with their feelings.

Pepsi soon realized that "the Pepsi Generation" was more than an advertising slogan. It became an expression of optimism, a reflection of what people wanted to be, to feel, to live. "We hitchhiked onto an evolution in music, social freedom, and the optimistic attitudes of thirty million baby boomers," Ted Sann said. Since 1964, all Pepsi advertising has flowed from the idea of a massive, younger market with its own attitudes, styles, and soft drink. Many commercials relied on music, which BBDO calls "the shortest distance between making the Pepsi sale and the average teen."

"Archeology" made friends, opened minds, and closed sales. Pepsi says the commercial helped drive its volume to at least twice the rate of Coca-Cola's through 1985 and that it pressured Coca-Cola into changing its formula and ultimately introducing New Coke. Ironically, three years before, when the advertising idea was initially presented, Pepsi turned it down flat. The following year, Pepsi again rejected it. BBDO persisted and in the third year, Pepsi relented.

NO CLASS

An appeal to the tired, the poor, and the coach-class masses

SOUTHERN AIRWAYS ORGY

MCDONALD & LITTLE, USA, 1974

A bacchanalian feast is going on punctuated by raucous laughter and champagne corks popping. A passenger enters the first-class cabin clutching his ticket in hand; the stewardess directs him to the "second cabin, please." Here, instead of the royal treatment, he opens the curtain to dreary slow music and people in rags sitting on the floor amid all their worldly possessions. In what looks like steerage on the world's most brutal slave ship, he is offered a bowl of gruel.

An announcer explains, "Southern Airways believes that no man should be subjected to the indignity of being labeled or treated like a second-class citizen. Which is why when you get on a Southern jet, you'll find no curtains separate the peasants from the nobility. No one takes the leg room from you and gives it to someone else. On Southern, there is only one class of service, and it isn't second."

The camera cuts to a modern Southern jet, where there is only one class and everybody gets champagne and plenty of leg room.

Stewardess: "Hi, Mr. Gill. Sit anywhere you like."

Super: "Nobody's second class on Southern."

The agency has gone out of business and the regional carrier it glorified has long been grounded, but the jolt of empathetic recognition viewers get from "Orgy" is as sharp today as it was a quarter century ago.

The agency took the fact that Southern had one single class of service and mined it, turning it into a positive through the use of humor and the slogan "Nobody's Second Class on Southern," said Bob Culpepper, who supervised the commercial.

Culpepper said the agency knew it had created a great campaign when the creative team saw the look of horror on the face of the "ultraconservative" chairman of Southern. Perhaps he didn't get the humor of the deadpan visual style that's been described as equal parts Edward Hopper and Bugs Bunny. It was vintage Joe Sedelmaier—and indeed, it launched the director who later went on to serve up "Where's the Beef?" and "Russian Fashion Show" for Wendy's and "Fast Talking Man" for Federal Express.

"Most commercials create a false problem and then solve it," Sedelmaier said, "but anyone who has ever flown coach can identify with the poor schlemiel here—an ordinary person trapped in a grotesque caricature of daily life gone haywire."

To emphasize the ad's "schlemiel appeal," the director cast quirky passengers who were more "lived-in" than professional models (see also Alaska Airlines' "Meals," page 149). And the humor is both subtle and encom-

156

passing. It doesn't hit you over the head, insult your intelligence, or revolve around a punch line, Sedelmaier said. "Here it's the telling of the joke that's funny. We feel for this guy who finds himself in an absurd situation and we, like he, try like hell to maintain our dignity."

WHERE'S THE CHOICE!?

Cold War propaganda from a scrappy burger contender

A single fleshy model keeps strutting down the runway in identical drab brown smocks. First the "dayvear," then the "eveningvear" (accessorized with a lovely flashlight), and finally the "beachvear" (holding a beach ball)—all to demonstrate "variety" as it is practiced by the other burger chains. A thickly accented commentator redundantly describes the outfits (with subtitles), driving home the point that having no choice is no fun.

WENDY'S

RUSSIAN FASHION SHOW

DANCER FITZGERALD SAMPLE, USA, 1985

Wendy's chairman, Dave Thomas, said he founded the company because he was "tired of going into fast service restaurants where the pickle was bigger than the hamburger. I wanted to know where the beef was." With just $8 million to spend on media—less than a tenth of what rivals McDonald's and Burger King were shelling out—Wendy's created a national anthem with "Where's the Beef?" The commercial implanted a slogan in people's minds and communicated clearly and directly a key sales message—that those who demand quality and search for it will find it at Wendy's. The catchphrase seared its way into the American vernacular, becoming a national password, an instant way to say *relief*. Preschoolers and sports teams taunted each other with the question. The slogan was emblazoned on T-shirts. Johnny Carson used the line in his monologues and Walter Mondale to advance his presidential candidacy over rival Gary Hart. Even a competitor's marquee paid homage by blaring: "The beef is here."

Two years after Clara Peller uttered those immortal words, Freeman and Sedelmaier struck again with "Russian Fashion Show." Linda Packer, Wendy's director of marketing, said the chain made its point about freedom of choice by taking the stereotype of Soviet society to a ridiculous extreme. The implication, absurd as it was, was that Wendy's, with its many menu choices, is all-American. Its rivals wore the dark hats.

The commercial, called the best Cold War spoof since *Dr. Strangelove*, first aired during the week of the Reagan/Gorbachev Geneva conference. Viewers flooded the company's Ohio headquarters with complaints that it could jeopardize the peace process. ("People don't really take commercials like these seriously," director Joe Sedelmaier said. "They recognize it's all in the spirit of fun."

The commercial was inspired by the classic movie *Ninotchka,* in which Greta Garbo was supposedly amazed by the freedom of choice Americans enjoyed as contrasted with the limited choice Russians have. The model in the spot, which cost $250,000 to make, was actually a man, Howard Fishler, whom Sedelmaier had used to play a woman once before in an Alaska Airlines spot. They shaved Fishler's eyebrows off and put a wig and glasses on him. (Originally, Sedelmaier sought three models but on the day of the shoot he decided to use one and have "her" wear the same thing each time.)

"Russian Fashion Show" was shot at the South Shore Country Club in Chicago, its great Byzantine columns creating the aura of an old tsar's palace. Russian lettering on the banner around the promenade actually said, "Keeping your teeth clean at all times is important."

Sedelmaier said his only complaint was that it took Wendy's so long to run the spot, which was completed long before there was even any talk of a summit meeting. (The delay occurred because Wendy's changed the product. It ran in test markets originally with the accent being on a whole menu of choice. Then the foodery switched it to a choice of toppings.)

The original plan didn't call for subtitles, but in editing Freeman and Sedelmaier decided that the commentator's thick accent made some remarks hard to understand. They added subtitles that say exactly what viewers hear in the same language—there's no translation.

Ultimately, Wendy's went a more traditional route, using chain founder and chairman Dave Thomas as spokesperson, framing him in humorous situations. To date, Bates USA, Wendy's current ad agency, has run more than five hundred commercials featuring Thomas. Once ridiculed as a showcase for a steer in half sleeves, the spots with Thomas have cut through because of their genuineness and honesty and resulted in record-setting gains.

CHAPTER TWELVE

DEFT ...AND DAFT

Beside making us laugh, parody may be one of the last ways to get a marketer's message through to jaded, distrustful viewers. Parody tells consumers that the company dishing it out understands their cynical attitude about advertising—and woos them to their side. It works especially well with alienated teens, who don't respond to "sweet." And it offers surprise, something increasingly hard to accomplish for viewers who've seen it all. As one marketer has said, parody is humor that's not just daft, but deft.

For it to work, what's being parodied must be well known, be it a social phenomenon or another ad. The Xerox monk who leaves his austere monastery to go to a modern duplicating shop for the five hundred copies requested by his monsignor spoofs the notion of miracle-making. Diesel Jeans used black humor to parody social issues of the day, including homosexuality, gun control, and the eroding ozone layer. But its principal targets were other fashion advertisers, who implied that the right clothes will change your life.

Many commercials clamber on the backs of other ads to make their point. By ridiculing Folger's secret substitutions for brewed coffee, Regina gave its vacuum cleaner a jolly image. (At a famous restaurant outside Chicago, they secretly replaced the coffee with sand and ground-up clam shells to see what happens. What happened is people choked and sprayed the floor with sand and clam shells for Regina's Electrikbroom to clean up.) Boston Market seized the angst of Calvin Klein commercials to serve up anorexic models on a windswept beach agonizing over how to "fill this empty void of emptiness." The solution? "Eat something."

Perhaps the most famous of them all are the Energizer Battery spots featuring the irrepressible bunny. Spoofing commercial after commercial, the energetic hare marched right out of his spot and onto the sets of several others, including ersatz chic coffee (Tres Café), decongestant (Nasaltine with fast-acting Muconol), wine (Chateau Marmoset), Soap (Alarm!), pork rinds (J. D. Pigskins), and a female cop show (*H.I.P.S.*). Parody entertains and attracts attention—but it also delivers a message in particularly beguiling ways. The escapades of toy rabbit E.B. demonstrated that Energizer batteries last so long that a single commercial couldn't contain them.

Parody may pack punch but it's also risky business. Legendary adman Hal Riney warns that marketers who make fun of themselves gamble that people will take their ads—and claims—less seriously. A bigger risk, of course, is that people will completely miss the gag—and the pitch.

A still bigger risk is that they'll alienate customers. Xerox secured permission from the Catholic Church for their gentle spoof of monastery life, but complaints that their ads were offensive and trivializing poured in nonetheless. And parody can be counterproductive. Young & Rubicam creative director John Ferrell cautioned that it makes advertising the subject of the commercial when all eyes should be on the product and its benefits. Making a viewer laugh never guarantees she'll buy.

GOD, QUEEN, AND CURRANT

A British soda spokesman fizzes over with patriotism

A Tango spokesman introduces himself as Ray Gardner then waves a leter from French exchange student Sebastian Lloyd, who tried the new soft drink, Black Currant Tango, and didn't love it. "Well, Sebastian," Gardner says, "all I can say is sorry." His apology seems sincere. "We've done all we can to try to provide satisfaction to all Tango drinkers even if you're only visiting our great nation. Ah, it's not easy."

Then as dramatic patriotic music plays, Ray grows irritated and marches out of his office. "You're an exchange student, aren't you, Sebastian? All hair gel and fancy loafers." Marching through the parking lot and into open fields, his diatribe goes vitriolic. "What are your credentials, Sebastian? What drives you? When did you last get up at four in the morning for something you believe in passionately? We don't need you, ya hear? You're one dissenting voice in a billion, Johnny French."

As his pique picks up steam, so does the army of coworkers following him—and as he marches along he sheds his clothes. "Yes! Black Currant Tango is a change for the taste buds," Gardner rants. "Yes, it's feisty! Yes! It's got guts! But so have we, Sebastian. Look at us!"

The flag-waving crowd cheers and chants as Ray, now in boxing shorts in a purple ring on the white cliffs of Dover, issues his final challenge while a squadron of RAF carriers hovers overhead. "Come on then, Sebastian. Come on! Right here! Right now! You and me! Come on, France! Europe! The world! I'll take you all on! I'm Ray Gardner! I drink Black Currant Tango! Come and get me!"

BLACK CURRANT TANGO

ST. GEORGE

HOWELL HENRY CHALDECOTT LURY, U.K., 1997

In 1997, Tango was the best-selling carbonated fruit drink in England. It had risen from being an insignificant player to the number-three carbonated soft drink of any kind in the U.K. (after Coke and Pepsi), largely on the strength of its weirdly provocative and funny advertising.

The granddaddy of them all, the original Orange Tango "Slap" commercial, produced in 1991, broke the mold of typical "lifestyle" soft drinks advertising of the late eighties. It featured a twenty-something guy drinking a can of Tango with friends on a street corner. All seems normal until we hear two soccer commentators who appear to be "viewing" the scene. They rewind the film, and this time, as the guy takes a gulp, a fat man painted orange runs in and slaps him on both sides of his face. The commentators explain that this demonstrates the "bite and buzz of real oranges" in Tango.

The "St. George" spot that launched Black Currant Tango was designed to demonstrate the soda's distinct taste sensation, just as previous advertis-

161

ing "touted the 'hit' of oranges, the 'seduction' of apples, and the 'euphoria' of lemons," said Chas Bayfield, who along with Jim Bolton wrote the spot. The advertising aimed to speak to young Britons from fifteen to thirty-five and to put pressure on Coke and Pepsi. That's why it was ninety seconds long, an epic only the big two would ever contemplate, he said.

The spunky commercial, in which a mild affront sets a man off on an aggressive harangue about the French lack of taste, was blatantly patriotic rather than just plain British, he said.

The continuous-action march into different locations, shot from a circling helicopter, required director Colin Gregg to move seamlessly from one visual style to another—a process hampered by unpredictable weather. The spot was shot over three days. Day two was plagued by fog, which didn't lift enough for the chopper to take off for twelve hours. On the last day, in mid April, when Ray marches outside, it snowed. Ray was finally nailed taking off his trousers perfectly after twenty-three takes.

Tango stopped running "St. George" a few months later, once the Black Currant flavor was launched.

THE SUDS OF WAR

One beer's long battle for the hearts and minds of Britain's youth

CARLING BLACK LABEL
DAM BUSTERS

WCRS, U.K., 1989

As Eric Coates's rousing march from the 1954 war epic The Dam Busters *swells, an RAF Wellington bomber makes an approach over a strategic Norwegian reservoir. The German sentry on the dam drops his sandwich and scurries down the ladder to bravely block the first bouncing bomb. Five bombs are dropped on the next run over the dark water. But the brilliantly athletic sentry has removed his coat and uses it to make five acrobatic soccer-goalie saves.*

The camera cuts to the bomber cockpit, where the members of the flight crew exchange looks and the squadron leader says the beer brand's long-running catchphrase, "I bet he drinks Carling Black Label."

This sixty-second parody of the classic World War II epic, *The Dam Busters*, was part of a forty-four-commercial campaign begun in 1983 for Bass's Carling Black Label lager, the company's biggest brand.

In 1965, Carling was the first draft lager in England and Wales. By 1971, it outsold all other lagers. But its growth was not unbroken. From 1979 to 1982, the beer's advertising featured quaffers testifying that they "got it right by drinking Carling." But they got it wrong with young folks. That advertising reinforced the perception that Carling was for older drinkers, said John Carter, WCRS director of planning. And volume sales slipped almost 8 percent.

The agency revised its goal: make younger drinkers feel that this robust, chunky-tasting lager was not their father's drink. "Lager drinkers in the eighties thought themselves a little wittier, a little more sussed than their ale-drinking counterparts, whom they associated with their dad's generation," Carter said. WCRS aimed to make Carling an everyday part of young drinkers' lives by presenting it as the drink of those a little bit cleverer than everyone else. Humor had to be irreverent and "deft, not just daft," he said. "Certainly the lads want a belly laugh, but if it's too simplistic, there's nothing to admire in either the drinker or the brand."

In one of the resulting comedies, a window washer is cleaning the outside of a plane during a flight. One passenger considers that so heroic he suggests that the window washer must drink Carling Black Label. His seat-mate rejects the notion: "Nah . . . he's missed a bit." Dozens of other irreverent commercials followed, including "Dam Busters."

Copywriter Kes Gray teamed with art direct Jonathan Greenhalgh and director Roger Woodburn using Carling cast regulars Mark Arden and Steve Frost to parody the 1954 war film. They sent the script to the Dam Busters Squadron and War Widows Association for approval before shooting. Crew members praised it as funny, but complaints that it was tasteless and offensive and that it trivialized World War II poured in anyway. (That the spot ran during the early days of the Gulf War perhaps fueled criticism.)

During "Dam Busters" first two years on the air, Carling Black Label volume sales grew 10 percent and market share increased from 14 to 15 percent. In the dozen years that it ran, the campaign helped the brew's volume sales soar 48 percent while the beer market as a whole remained flat. And it outperformed its sector of the market, standard lagers, by 40 percent.

NIHILIST CHIC

Diesel deconstructs the promise of style

It's 5 A.M. reveille at a boot camp in the Alps. After morning exercises, a burly sergeant instructs the youths on mouth-to-mouth resuscitation. One scout volunteers, assuming he'll get to practice on the gorgeous blond model in the training poster, but instead finds, after coming forward, that the subject is a yellow-toothed, craggy-faced mountain man. He bends

DIESEL

5 A.M., MONO VILLAGE

PARADISET DDB, STOCKHOLM, 1997

*over to blow air into the man's lungs, which induces a dream of fields of
flowers and a beautiful Nordic maiden and riding off onto happy trails
on white horses. The spot ends with the scout and mountain man heading
out into the sunset hand in hand.*

Super: "For successful living: Diesel. Jeans and workwear."

Diesel's funny, edgy ad stories put the hip Italian jeansmaker on the
map. Its high-profile, bizarre commercials appeal to young people worldwide by irreverently turning socially acceptable stereotypes on their heads with tongue firmly in cheek. Johan Lindeberg, Diesel's
marketing director, said the advertising has created a counterculture personality for the $80 dungarees and helped make them the second-best-
selling jeans behind Levi's in many European countries.

Founded in 1979 as the epitome of urban chic, Diesel has steered a
course apart from the product-oriented jeans campaigns and sex-and-youth
approach of its rivals. It has spoofed such issues as homosexuality, gun control, the eroding ozone layer, and the fashion-industry concept that the right
clothes will change a person's life.

Diesel's ad director Maurizio Marchiore said the company knew it had
to distinguish itself and thought surprising, humorous irony was an effective
way to do it. In an early ad, models aim guns at the viewer, while a voice
proclaims, "How to teach your children to love and care." In another, head-
lined "How to smoke 145 cigarettes a day," a talking skull asks, "Man, who
needs two lungs anyway?" These ads were not about selling jeans but
"about making our mark and establishing our image as a company," Marchiore said. "Consumers don't buy jeans, they buy the image, what sur-
rounds the jeans." People who think an ad is cool think the company is
cool—and that buying their products makes *them* cool.

"The concept was completely new and innovative and in sharp contrast
to most jeansmakers promise that if you bought their gear you'd become
smarter, better-looking, richer, able to get the girls, and fantastic," said Joakim
Jonason, founder of Paradiset. Since 1991, the "Diesel for Successful Living"
series has included one hundred ads and twenty commercials; Jonason has
been art director on all. Linus Karlssom was the writer and Ulf Johansson the
director on "5 A.M., Mono Village" and its sibling parody, "Little Rock."

In "Little Rock," a handsome guy in impeccable Diesel jeans kisses his
wife and baby good-bye before dueling with a grubby, despicable man who
kicks dogs—and shoots our hero dead. It's typical Diesel black humor. Another sixty-second spot showed a World War I British soldier so pleased
with the Diesel jeans he's received from home that he parades around in
them—saved from laughing German snipers by a fellow soldier who takes a
bullet and dies protecting him. Another spot featured several pigs daintily
sitting down to the Christmas table to eat . . . a roasted pig, served by a girl.

Experts warn that shock tactics, Benetton style, often obscure the product and can turn off as many people as they turn on. (For a decade Benetton has draped its clothes around thought-provoking, eye-catching social issue ads, but admits it doesn't know if they work.) Diesel founder Renzo Rosso, however, believed good advertising meant taking risks. He told his agency: "You are more in danger of boring us than shocking us."

Many viewers nonetheless decried the campaign as tasteless and offensive, but it was ultimately a success. "I can't say exactly what the advertising has meant for the company, but since the campaign started, Diesel is five times bigger than it was," said Jonason. In 1985 sales hovered around $9 million; last year Diesel sold $350 million worth of jeans, sweats, T-shirts, and related garb. Jonason said that the oddball scenarios intended to jolt the viewer with the unexpected endings were aired without benefit of research. "It was advertising from the heart."

STILL GOING

This battery bunny's got legs

The scene opens on a competition of battery-operated toys as an announcer says, "Don't be fooled by commercials where one battery company's toy outlasts the others'." An ultracool mechanical bunny, shades on, head cocked back, has been banging on a big brass drum; the banging gets louder as the voice-over continues. "The fact is, Energizer was never invited to their play-offs. Because nothing outlasts the Energizer. They keep going and going." The indefatigable bunny marches off—right out of the commercial and into the studio.

"Stop the bunny, please," the director yells.

But the bunny is unstoppable, tramping onto a set where a commercial for Tres Café coffee is being filmed. A woman murmurs, "I love the sound of rain." Her friend responds, "And I love the taste of your fresh-brewed coffee." The first woman replies, "Oh, thanks, but it's not fresh brewed. It's new . . ."

The bunny strides into another commercial shoot in which a little girl invites her daddy to smell flowers. "Oh, my sinuses." Daddy recoils as the lab-coated doctor delivers the clichéd pitch for a fake decongestant. "When sinus trouble strikes, reach for Nasaltine. Only Nasaltine has fast-acting Muconol. Watch as . . ."

That scene fades as the drum-beating hare "keeps going and going"

ENERGIZER BUNNY

TBWA CHIAT/DAY, USA, 1989

*into a wine commercial where a snooty expert intones, "The painting,
Renoir. The vase, Ming. And the wine, Chateau Marmoset." Seeing the
bunny, the startled actor knocks over the glasses, breaking them, as the
announcer concludes, "Nothing outlasts the Energizer. They keep going
and going."*

Forget about the fuzzy pink ears. This campaign's got legs. The average TV commercial wears out in three years; Eveready's irresistible bunny has kept going and going for three times that long, drumming his long-lasting message home in more than one hundred spots and separating Energizer from the battery pack.

Since the pink pitchman burst out of his first commercial and tramped off screen in October 1989, the strategy has remained the same: convince consumers that Energizers are long-lasting, said Keith Schopp, spokesman for Ralston-Purina Group's Eveready Battery Company. "The bunny is a metaphor for long-lasting and perseverance."

In parodies and spoofs the toy rabbit E.B. drummed his way through mock ads for such invented products as Alarm! soap, Chug-a-Cherry soda, Airedale air freshener, and J. D. Pigskins pork rinds, through a female cop show called *H.I.P.S* and a movie called *Dance With Your Feet,* and even gone head-to-head with Wile E. Coyote and Darth Vader.

A spoof of late-night TV advertising prompted twenty thousand viewers to try to order an $18.95 four-record set of Olga Monteiro and the Magic Harp. "Some people didn't realize the commercial was a fake," said Dick Sittig, who was creative director at Chiat/Day in 1990. (Initially, the hare ran into commercials for other Ralston products—Purina Cat Chow, Hostess Twinkies, and Chex cereal—ostensibly to get Ralston double exposure, but viewers were confused and those were killed.)

The bunny never interrupted a favorite commercial—only the kind of advertising people hated. "He became a hero for shutting those ads up," said Steve Rabowsky, creative director of TBWA Chiat/Day's Venice, California, office. "The ads told skeptical consumers, 'Hey, we're on your side.' "

Man-made ad mascots aren't new: the Jolly Green Giant debuted in 1926. Pillsbury's dimply Doughboy has grown into dimply manhood and Charlie has been Star-Kist's animated spokestuna for decades. But the relentless rabbit has moved beyond potent spokescreature to cultural icon. He's been featured in cartoons, conversations, and political campaigns as a symbol of persistence, although his popularity has grated on some. David Letterman attacked him with a baseball bat.

"This isn't parody for entertainment's sake or simply an attention-getting device," said Sittig. "The bunny demonstrates the Energizer battery's long-lasting quality—in fact, that it lasts soooo long one commercial can't contain it."

It was actually Doyle Dane Bernbach that created Energizer's first up-beat bunny spot, but that agency insisted the hare was a one-shot commercial, not a campaign. Eveready moved the account to Chiat/Day, which strove to make the commercials the bunny interrupted be believable. "The more believable the commercial, the better the interruption worked," said Chiat president Bob Kuperman.

Ironically, it was rival Duracell that first used the pink bunny, back in 1975, to outdrum a room full of percussionist bunnies. Five years after Duracell dropped its bunny advertising in the U.S., Eveready picked it up. (To combat the bunny, Duracell unearthed and since recalled the "Puttermans." A mean-spirited battery-powered clan, the Puttermans laugh raucously as victims of second-rate batteries keel over.)

The bunny replaced jarring and abrasive Jacko, a 245-pound Australian rugby star who bombastically power-slammed his way through doors. Jacko was a big hit in Australia, where Eveready's share rose from 35 to 51 percent, but he fizzled in the U.S.

The bunny scored. Eveready claims unaided awareness of its battery went up sixteen points and correct brand identification 51 percent. More than nine in ten Americans have a positive view of him, said Rabowsky. "That's crucial for impulse and dour-faced purchases like batteries."

But the hugely popular campaign hasn't helped Eveready overtake Duracell, which accounts for almost half of all batteries sold in the U.S., compared with Ralston's 38 percent—figures that haven't changed in years.

NIXON/NOXIN

Beepers call on a new market, but careful reading that message!

A TV game show's contestant is ushered into the booth where he could win the prize of prizes—cars, holidays, appliances, cash, and, it seems, a beautiful, bikini-clad playmate.

The smarmy host mans the microphone (in Swedish): "And now, ladies and gentlemen, the final question. If one of you contestants gives the right answer, he's going to walk away with all of this." The crowd cheers.

Tension is high as the host reads from his questionnaire card: "Now the final question: Which American president was forced to resign because of his involvement in the so-called 'Watergate scandal?' "

We see the crafty contestant slip a Minicall receiver out of his cuff. The camera cuts to his family at home, preparing to send back the an-

SWEDISH TELEVERKET

NOXIN

HLR DRUMFABRIKEN/BBDO, SWEDEN, 1993

swer. When they hear the question and immediately know the answer, they excitedly whoop it up and one cautions, "Easy, write it . . ."

A gong sounds and the host declares: "We'll have to have your answer now."

The Minicall beeps and the contestant, now duly informed of the answer, blurts out, "Noxin!"—he's holding the answer upside down!

"Noxin?" asks the perplexed host.

"Noxin?" asks the unbelieving family.

"Noxin?" laughs the host as the crowd claps and there's the sound of a check being torn up.

"Close . . . very close! But not right," says the jubilant host. "We'll have to bring in the next contestant."

Voice-over and super: "Minicall. Used correctly it solves a lot of communication problems."

Cell phones may be as common as pierced ears now, but from 1990 to 1992, sales of beepers in Europe had stagnated. Advertising focused almost exclusively on business use and the category had a dull image. Marketers had not considered the potential of the consumer market, said Ole Soderblom, creative director and copywriter on the commercial. The challenge, he said, was to reposition the category "from boring and stressful to fun, from constraint to freedom, and from only business to the consumer market."

To expand its usage occasions and bring about a full-scale attitude shift regarding pagers, the team decided to show a situation removed from the expected business use and demonstrate with levity and humor how the system works. What fresher way to draw viewers in than with a zesty tale in which the cheater gets his comeuppance? And how rare it is for the bad guy to be the protagonist, demonstrating how the product works! This was an attention-getter that had the clutter-cutting advantages of a good parody and the selling power of a clear product demonstration.

"Noxin" was part of the campaign that launched Swedish Telephone Company's Minicall theme: how to get reached without getting disturbed. Awareness of the product in Sweden's largest cities rose 30 percent to 90 percent, and Televerket Minicall pager sales increased 500 percent, according to Anders Bergmark, account director at HLR. The marketing concept was exported to Europe and South America.

MIRACULOUS!

A faux monk from Brooklyn warms Xerox's image

Working by candlelight in an austere monastery with spiraling arched columns, a chubby Franciscan monk painstakingly hand-letters and illuminates a manuscript while a Gregorian chant plays in the background. With a glimmer of smug pride, the monk carefully carries his parchment treasure through glum corridors.

Announcer: "Ever since people started recording information, there's been a need to duplicate it."

The monk presents the sheets to his superior, who murmurs approvingly, "Very nice work, Brother Dominic, very nice." Brother Dominic thanks him, but then Father Superior drops the bombshell: "Now, I would like five hundred more sets."

Brother Dominic is dumbfounded. But by the next scene, he has regained his composure. He takes a city bus to his local duplicating shop, where the owner greets him, "Brother Dominic, how are you?"

Brother Dominic looks at him: "Could you do a big job for me?"

Announcer: "Xerox has developed an amazing machine that is unlike anything we've ever made. Xerox 9200 Duplicating System. It automatically feeds and cycles originals; has a computerized programmer that coordinates that entire system; can duplicate, reduce, and assemble a virtually limitless number of complete sets. And does it all at the incredible rate of two pages per second. The Xerox 9200 Duplicating System."

Mission accomplished, the monk returns with his copies to the astonishment of his superior: "There are your sets, Father."

Father: "Huh?"

Dominic: "The five hundred sets you asked for."

The startled father looks heavenward and piously proclaims, "It's a miracle."

Super: "Xerox."

XEROX

MONKS

NEEDHAM HARPER STEERS, USA, 1975

Before 1975, copiers weren't all that much faster than copying by hand: Xerox's original 914 could reproduce seven documents a minute, and IBM and Kodak were just beginning to sell machines that produced thirty to forty copies per minute. Then Xerox's 9200 copier came along, able to make 120 copies a minute—and sort and collate them into booklets. At $25,000 a machine, however, the audience for the 9200 was very limited.

Initially, Allen Kay, creative director on the Xerox account, and now chairman of Korey, Kay & Partners, advised Xerox not to do a commercial but rather to send a letter to the thirty or so people in the country who'd care about this complicated technology. Xerox pressed for advertising for the

9200, however, wanting the world, employees, and Wall Street to know about the machine's high-tech capabilities. And it had to be humorous because the Xerox team felt humor implied intelligence, warmth, and innovation.

Kay decided that as long as they insisted on advertising it had to be as grand as the quantum leap the technology demonstrated. "This had to be much, much larger than life; it had to live up to the future of the machine," Kay said.

Kay rejected an early idea for a spot about bookies reproducing their tout sheets. Although that conveyed the idea that the 9200 makes tons of copies, it didn't fit with Xerox's image. Similarly he dismissed a technical approach and office setting (too dull) and football play books for coaches and scripts for authors (unoriginal). A Guttenberg Bible idea wasn't simple enough either. Kay mused about an Egyptian writing on papyrus and having to reproduce the blueprints for everyone working on the pyramid. That too landed on the scrap heap: insufficient charm.

Then, eureka!—the idea of a monk and manuscript and calligraphy hit him, and although it was 4:00 A.M., Kay phoned his partner, Lois Korey, to describe his vision. The next day Kay teamed with copywriter Steven Penchina (now at Penchina Selkowitz) to flesh out the script. Pechina came up with the "It's a miracle" line at the end.

The client loved the idea but worried that using a religious person in its advertising, something not done before, might be seen as blasphemous. The company consulted with religious advisers, even sending the storyboard to Cardinal Cook of the archdiocese of New York to make certain it was acceptable to the Catholic Church. The archdiocese warmed to the project and even suggested locations to scout. Director Neil Tardio of Lovinger Tardio Melsky decided on, ironically, an Episcopal church in Harlem, New York.

Tardio and the Xerox team considered more than sixty people to play Brother Dominic before Brooklyn-born Jack Eagle, then a fifty-year-old, five-foot-four-inch, 210-pound former big-band trumpet player and Jewish Catskills stand-up comedian came in. The agency team was struck by his warm, pleasant semi-ethereal look, an angelic expression, and that he was so huggable.

The abbot was originally going to wear a white robe to contrast with Brother Dominic's brown one. A sharp-eyed Franciscan on the set warned that only the pope wears white.

The Xerox team ultimately loved the spot, but at first there was some resistance. "At the time we launched the 9200 copier, corporate pushed for image, not specific product advertising," says Karl Fleischmann, then marketing communications manager. But after the spot's first broadcast in a ninety-second version during the Wimbledon Tennis Tournament on June 25, 1975, it got an instant response and captured everybody's imagination, he said. A sixty-second version was also produced. "We got so many letters saying it was terrific that it became a groundswell to do more and the monk became an eight-commercial campaign which ran through 1982," Fleischmann said. He added that the original Brother Dominic spot ran only fifty-six times.

The agency worried that using the little, lovable magical monk would dilute its effectiveness, and that with a considered, expensive purchase—which, unlike a tube of toothpaste, you don't just throw away—it might not gloss Xerox's reputation.

But Fleischmann insisted on spin-offs and sequels. "Son of Monk" a year later introduced the 9400 model, which copies on both sides of the paper at once. And "Gone to Vespers" showed the machine was so easy to use that even the abbot could work it.

At a time when Kodak, IBM, and a host of Japanese competitors were doing nuts-and-bolts advertising, Brother Dominic made Xerox a leader and a friendly, cuddly company, Fleischmann said. "He gave a warm glow to a high-tech photocopier and softened the image of a large company and the copying industry overall, and affected hiring and Wall Street." He also made sales calls. Kay recalls that for one account that Xerox couldn't crack, Eagle, in monk's robes, walked into the chairman's office and the prospect became a Xerox client.

In May 1976 the chubby, friendly monk made his first trade show appearance at the In-Plant Printing Management Show in Dallas. Local newspapers celebrated Brother Dominic, giving the sense he was blessing the equipment in a feature story. In subsequent trade shows Xerox had Brother Dom posters with the words "It's a miracle." Customers wandered over specifically to see the monk or the "miracle machine." Research showed the monk was associated with not just the 9000 series copiers but with all of Xerox.

Eagle still appears at trade shows, product demonstrations, and seminars today but never touches a copying machine, an act Xerox considers to be unmonkly. Through the years Xerox has distributed Brother Dominic T-shirts, posters, and coffee mugs. Eagle claims that consumers thought he was real. Once, he said, he was summoned to Lake Placid for the Olympics when there was no snow—and when he left there was five inches. And after he was called upon to bless the Houston Rockets, the NBA team, which had never before beaten the Los Angeles Lakers, finally did.

CHAPTER THIRTEEN

KILLER COMEDY

By one estimate, a third of all TV commercials are funny—or aim to be. Humor warms people up and relaxes them. It creates connection, opens a window to get a message in, and makes people feel good about a brand—and inclined to spend money on it. If you share a smile with someone, the theory in adland goes, you've made a friend.

Some say Wendy's famous "Where's the Beef?" spot in 1984 made the airwaves safe for jocularity by showing how funny could pay off in a big way. But waggish advertising was used long before that. In 1973, Vittel mineral water's ingenuous Dame Pipi figured out a way to drum up tips as a washroom attendant—while making a very serious case that Vittel mineral water is a diuretic. In the 1960s, Alka-Seltzer built a brand name on the back of funny commercials, most memorably with the stupefied glutton who couldn't believe he ate the whole thing. And Volkswagen left the classic car-on-winding-road scenario to others and opted instead for witty, self-deprecating, theater-of-the-absurd advertising that made us chuckle—and remember that VW was synonymous with economy.

And humor lets advertisers get away with messages that might otherwise just be annoying. It was unfailing jocularity that kept smokers watching as their comrades grappled with the disadvantages of the new, longer Benson & Hedges 100's. Few probably noticed that these spots, which seemed to belittle the product, were more

hard sell than droll, repeating again and again the cigarette's "longer than king size" selling proposition.

Some marketers think their product is far too important to joke about. For years, financial services companies believed that, "if it's your money, it's not funny," and insurers thought death and injury too serious to jest about. Both have joined the laugh track in recent times. Centraal Beheer insurance's Rastafarian in "Hedgehog," for example, accidentally drips a white line down the middle of a highway to the edge of a cliff—to illustrate one of life's unexpected reasons to "just call us."

Going for the guffaw can be perilous. If a gag fails, it can turn viewers off. And what's funny to one person isn't to millions of others. A copywriter once noted that there's not one funny line in the two most influential books ever written: the Bible and the Sears catalog.

Then there's the story of the Bert and Harry Piel beer ads, which were so funny they killed the very suds that they were selling: people rushed to sample the beer, then, disenchanted with the taste, never bought it again.

MAMA MIA!

Alka-Selter's ad about an ad that adds to the indigestion of its star

The spot opens on a man in a TV commercial eating spaghetti and meatballs and repeatedly failing to say his line properly. "Mama Mia! That's some specy," Jack says. The director cuts and corrects his pronunciation. And on to take twenty-eight . . .

"Up, Tony—and action," the director calls, but this time Jack muffs the accent. "Meesy, micey, ballsy, balls," he mutters, spaghetti dangling from his mouth. The scene moves on to take fifty-nine. Jack, full to bursting by now, has another go at it, and the voice-over delivers the sell: "Sometimes you eat more than you should. And when it's spicy besides, mama mia, do you need Alka-Seltzer. Alka Seltzer can help unstuff you, relieve the acid indigestion, and help make you your old self again."

Back on the set, Jack has said the line flawlessly and is exuding relief when, alas, the oven door falls open and the disgusted director tells the crew to break for lunch. Close on Jack's anguished face.

ALKA-SELTZER
SPICY MEATBALLS

DOYLE DANE BERNBACH, USA, 1969

Storyboard

Miles Labs concocted the first—and only—product combining aspirin and an antacid in 1929. It became associated with relieving hangovers and, in 1933, when Prohibition ended, sales spurted. They grew through the 1940s and 1950s when Speedy, the three-dimensional animated figure and precursor of the Pillsbury Doughboy, charmed TV audiences with "Relief is just . . . a swallow away." Rather than scolding, the unthreatening Speedy character seemed to wink, "Oh, boy, you've done it again." His successor in the early 1960s was an animated talking stomach. A cartoon man sat in one chair while his irate little (though bloated) food chamber sat in another and took him to task for all his pepperoni binges.

Concurrently, Alka-Seltzer aired what it figures is one of its most remembered commercials ever: the stomach montage. The camera panned a universe of assorted abdomens. Just before the end a voice intoned, "No matter what shape your stomach is in, when it gets out of shape, take Alka-Seltzer." (A second stomach ad featured the man and his stomach arguing about food. The man likes spicy; his stomach does not. The narrator settles the snit by recommending Alka-Seltzer for any food preference.)

The late 1960s were Alka Seltzer's heyday. Americans guffawed as a waiter urged a hapless diner to "Try it—you'll like it." They laughed when a tiny bride fed her hubby a dumpling almost her weight, then planned additional culinary aggressions while the groom surreptitiously gulped Alka-Seltzer. That study in gastronomical distress, "Groom's First Meal," was conceived when adman Marvin Honig's fiancée decided to impress him with her cooking skills. And viewers so enjoyed the stupefied glutton Ralph's lament, "I can't believe I ate the whole thing"—and his wife's retort to her glassy-eyed, rumpled spouse, "No, Ralph, I ate it"—that they made it part of the vernacular.

Another highlight: "Spicy Meatball," with its requisite hilarious situation and absurd characters. "The assignment called for a commercial on overeating, but that's tough to do without making someone appear a glutton," recalls Evan Stark, who wrote the spot. "In a brainstorming session with [art director] Roy Grace we decided on a commercial within a commercial approach."

In the eleventh hour the team had to change the product's name from Mama Mia spicy meatballs to Magadini's spicy meatballs because the agency's legal department discovered that six companies in the U.S. were marketing Mama Mia products. The agency chose Magadini from its company phone book and paid $1 to the account executive for rights to his name. The actual commercial, directed by Howard Zieff, required 175 takes, which meant actor Jack Somach bit into 175 meatballs before the day was over. He refused the team's invitation to lunch and dinner.

Despite its brilliance and popularity, the most famous commercial about making a commercial didn't work. People thought it was for spaghetti sauce and Alka-Seltzer sales slumped.

CAR REPAIR

For a Rebel on the rocks, parallel parking is the least of challenges

AMC
DRIVING SCHOOL

WELLS RICH GREENE, USA, 1968

A nervous driving instructor feigning calmness directs the driver-trainee: "All right, now, let's see if we can find first." (Grinding gears) "No, that's not it."

The driver-in-training laughs nervously. The passenger-coach encourages her, "Believe me, it's in there somewhere." Squealing tires and brake noises. The camera pans to the car's license plate to reveal that she's a student driver.

Voice-over: "No matter how rough you treat a Rebel, it's awfully hard to hurt it. A survey of professional driving schools shows that they use more of our cars than any other kind."

A male student driver navigating erratically inquires, "How am I doing?"

The instructor gratefully assures him, "A lot better than yesterday."

The instructor then directs a female student. "Turn right."

"I can't do it while you're watching me," she tells him.

"Okay," says the instructor agreeably. "Turn left." Instead she careens onto the sidewalk and there's a cacophony of squeals, fender-bender crash noises, and beeping horns.

Next the instructor is seated beside a catatonic man.

Instructor: "How does it feel the first time out in traffic, Mr. Moss? . . . Mr. Moss? . . . Mr. Moss?" He waves a hand before the paralyzed occupant of the driver's seat to the sounds of cars crashing.

As the car trundles along, the instructor now warns a Barbie-like driver to "look out for that truck."

"What truck?" she asks blithely.

"Behind the bus," the instructor bleats.

"What bus?" Barbie bleats as tires squeal.

Voice-over: "Rebel has held its own against some of the worst drivers in the world."

Man: "Sh-sh-should I turn the windshield wiper on?" he asks as water from a fire hydrant he's knocked over cascades over the window.

Voice-over: "At this point, it looks like the Rebels are going to outlast the teachers."

Super: "American Motors Rebel."

In this spot, director Howard Zieff, who later went on to movie fame with *The Main Event* and *Private Benjamin,* used humor to highlight the car's key product benefit: durability. But funny as the vignettes were, the commercial itself was no laughing matter. It was waging a desperate fight for the very life of American Motors.

"AMC was a dying company on the verge of bankruptcy," said Charles Moss, chairman of Dragotti Moss and formerly creative director at Wells Rich Greene on this account. "An article in *Life* magazine at the time asked if Mary Wells [the agency's charismatic founder and then leader] could save American Motors. The goal of this advertising was to keep the company alive for a short time, until new cars could come on stream."

Certainly the old ones were being left behind on the highway. "Mustang took the stuffing out of our Javelin, and our Ambassadors were being driven off the road by Lincolns," said Moss. And the Rebel was so detested that a contest at the time offering a tube of Gleem, a carton of Burma Shave, a packet of Personna Razors, and a Rebel elicited responses from participants to "keep the Rebel," he said.

The plan was to "call attention to superior features and, oh-by-the-way, slip in that we're much less money," Moss said. The cars were less expensive but American Motors executives didn't want to advertise that, because they believed it cheapened the car, he said.

The second goal of the advertising was to make American Motors look young and frisky and take it off its creaky hinges. "Its image was that of the builder of Aunt Martha fuddy-duddy-type cars, but in the late 1960s, at the peak of America's love affair with the auto, AMC wanted jazzy. So we had to present this dowdy car in a youthful, hip way," Moss recalled.

WRG spent two weeks crawling around the cars to discover competitive advantages. The Rebel's very stolid feel led credence to the implied durability claim. "In truth," said Moss, "the Rebel was the dog of the line. It hadn't changed styling in years. But the fact was, more Rebel cars than any other kind were used in driving schools—because they were so cheap. But that fact could be harnessed to support our durability claim."

The agency got started on the account on July 4 and had to have finished commercials running in mid-September—a very short time for casting and dramatics and dialogue. Before this, AMC had taken a totally rational approach, showing the Rebel's benefits, such as factory rust-proofing. The advertising bombed, Moss said, "so we went for a jazzier treatment that cracked stereotypes, was a bit aspirational, and never put down the user. Its sense of humor dispelled AMC's old-fogy image; people found it heartwarming," he said.

American Motors had such faith in the agency—or was so frantic—that WRG shot "Driving School" without a storyboard, Moss said. "The client doubted it would be funny, but we told them to just trust us, that it would be. They sprang for eighty thousand dollars on our say-so," he recalled.

They also sprang for a commercial showing the Rebel taking a bone-jarring, nine-hundred-mile trek over rocks and chuckholes through the Baja peninsula of Mexico. A Mexican actor questioned whether the car could make it, referring to the Rebel as "a hunk of tin."

AMC approved both spots with great trepidation. William Pickett, vice president of sales at the time, admitted that "Mary Wells has been traumatic for our dealers, used to advertising that shows a pretty car with a pretty girl beside a limpid pool." And John Secrest, vice president of finance at the time, noted then that "for many of us who grew up in the automobile business," the new advertising "approach sometimes jolts our nerve endings with its boldness."

Secrest said management eventually approved the advertising because the goal was to point out AMC's differences and "make an impact with the 1968 line." The recall of those ads, he said, ran more than double the recall of all automobile advertising. A year before, the recall rating was well below the average, he said.

After a year of advertising the Rebel, WRG moved on to talk up other models like the Gremlin and Pacer. As for the Rebel, there was a brief resurgence in its sales, but in 1971, AMC reworked the model, stretching its stubby wheelbase and sloping its nose and reintroduced it as the Matador. Four years later, AMC was sold to Chrysler.

GREAT LENGTHS

A careful explanation of the downside of more-for-your-money

One man gets his elongated cigarette caught between elevator doors in the first of a succession of quick cuts showing hapless smokers adjusting to the longer length of their Benson & Hedges 100s. Another crushes his smoke on his car window when he turns his head to follow a passing female. Another lights his in the middle. Still another inadvertently sets his newspaper on fire.

The announcer introduces new Benson & Hedges 100s with a humorous disclaimer: "Oh, the disadvantages of the new Benson & Hedges 100s. They're a lot longer than king-sized, and that takes some getting used to."

B&H's bossa nova theme song swells as the announcer continues: "Benson & Hedges 100's are the new longer filter cigarettes. Three puffs longer, four puffs longer, maybe five puffs longer than king-sized. Once you get the hang of them."

Super: "Benson & Hedges 100s. Regular or menthol."

BENSON & HEDGES

OH, THE DISADVANTAGES

WELLS RICH GREENE, USA, 1966

Critics have called this series of amusing vignettes advertising's equivalent to *Rowan and Martin's Laugh-In.* What it really was, was innovative marketing that stood convention on its ear. Wells Rich Greene took what might have been a product gimmick or passing fad and turned it into a hot and growing product category by dispelling the rule against selling negatively.

Rather than ignore the many disadvantages of smoking extra-long cigarettes, "Disadvantages" presented them with charm and unfailing good humor.

In different spots in the series, a violinist gets his cigarette caught in his bow, and a mountain climber's elongated smoke burns part of the rope holding him up. Interestingly, however, Dick Rich, the one-time middle partner of Wells Rich Greene, contended that the campaign wasn't funny at all; it was really a very hard sell. It said again and again that Benson & Hedges 100s are longer than king size.

Directed by Howard Zieff, "Disadvantages" debuted on a Saturday during the TV show *Mission: Impossible.* Rich called it an overnight sensation, "one of the two most successful cigarette introductions in history: the other being Salem." The swinging bossa nova score, orchestrated by *Man of La Mancha* composer Mitch Leigh, became a Top 40 hit. The ad helped shine Benson & Hedges's image while broadening its appeal beyond the increasingly tenuous upscale market, consumers who were the most zealous about giving up smoking. And the brand quickly moved up to third place.

The campaign was ultimately forced off the air, however, by the Federal Trade Commission, which banned cigarette advertising from television. It limped along in print but, unlike Marlboro, needed TV. Once the advertising stopped, the brand began to slip.

Benson & Hedges advertising didn't attract as much attention until almost two decades later when it ran the cryptic "For People Who Like to Smoke" campaign. In one of the enigmatic spreads, a man wearing only his pajama bottoms has wandered into a festive brunch where a group of women and one man are socializing at a table. There is no hint as to who he is or why he has appeared dressed like that. Marcia Grace, executive vice president–creative director at Wells Rich Greene at the time, said the ads were vague but the message was not. They said that "smoking is a personal choice and you can feel okay about it," she said.

Psychologist Carol Moog has noted that the key to this advertising is "the complete acceptability of the people, the complete comfort these people have as smokers. Benson & Hedges has created an image of a company that accepts you," increasingly important as prejudice against smokers has intensified. Health concerns were handled more subtly—with clean, white-walled rooms and props of fruit and herbal tea and orange juice.

The pajama-bottomed man made an impression but not a sales difference, said Ken Olshan, a former chairman of the agency. The ad didn't translate well into billboards, an increasingly important medium for cigarette advertising.

NAKED LUNCH

Lacking differences in fare or routes, one airline says, "Fly the funny skies."

BRAATHENS SAFE
NAKED LUNCH

LEO BURNETT, NORWAY, 1993

An amorous husband quietly lets himself into his apartment, coming home to surprise his wife with a midday romantic rendezvous. In the hall, he pulls off his tie and shrugs out of his jacket. Crossing the dining room he strips off his shirt, then removes his trousers, and yes, even his underpants. Wearing only socks he peers through the keyhole into the living room. A keyhole shot shows his wife in profile. He sticks a rose in his teeth and, bursting open the door, leaps in. Alas, his wife is not alone. She is having tea with an older couple—her parents, also in for a surprise visit. No one knows quite where to look.

Title Card (in Norwegian): "Warning: we're flying in your in-laws at half price. Braathens SAFE."

When "Naked Lunch" was created in 1993, there was little to differentiate Braathens SAFE, Norway's national airline, from rival SAS, which had been recognized as "the businessmen's airline." Both airlines went to the most important cities in Norway and the pricing was set by the government. The ostensible goal of the ad was to announce a new discount fare for seniors, said Oisten Borge, ad manager at Burnett. But at the same time, the advertising was intended to give the airline a personality that would distinguish it from its rival and make people prefer it, all other things being equal. Burnett decided to position Braathens as the friendly, familiar airline with a sense of humor.

The commercial did more than amuse viewers: it sold tickets—all that were available before the end of the senior discount promotion period. At the same time, Borge said, Braathen's overall market share grew 5 percent within three years. That was a considerable achievement considering that destination, timetable, and frequency are the principal factors that people consider when choosing which airline to fly. Partly propelled by this commercial and its tongue-in-cheek attitude, the fifty-year-old Braathens became the most popular airline in Norway.

The spot is typical of Braathens's humorous approach. In another commercial, a farmer who stutters slightly when he's nervous is in a field next to a spotted cow and stuck on the name of a new destination to which Braathens flies. "Mal-mal-mal-mal . . ." he sputters, until the cow completes the name, adding, "mooooo." The new destination, Malmoo, is therefore embedded in viewers' minds. When the client initially saw the storyboards he panned it, thinking the farmer's stuttering would offend viewers. Burnett produced it anyway, hoping the client would reconsider when he saw the concept on film, which is precisely what happened.

CALL US

An insurance company's vivid illustration of life's unforeseen hazards

CENTRAAL BEHEER

HEDGEHOG

DDB NEEDHAM, NETHERLANDS, 1995

A Rastafarian is driving a little car along a mountain road grooving to the music in his head. He sees a hedgehog crossing and swerves wildly, finishing up on the very edge of the cliff. Very, very carefully he puts the car in reverse and edges back to safety. He drives on happily. But viewers see the white line that his vehicle has been painting along the middle of the road has followed his swerve: it leads over the abyss.

"Just call us," announces the super. Then the spot cuts to the logo and telephone number for Centraal Beheer insurance.

The "Just Call Us" campaign began in 1986 to show the unexpected things that life pitches our way, and how being prepared is the only safeguard. Its aim was to bring humor to the solemn category of insurance and convert those amused into customers.

Before this TV series, Centraal Beheer had run print ads touting its car insurance as the cheapest and best available because it required no middleman, said Paul Meier, creative director at DDB Amsterdam at the time. "We initially added the 'Just call us' theme to print," he said. It subsequently moved from posters to television.

The first TV commercial featured a Formula 1 racing car making a hasty wheel change during a pit stop. But before the mechanic can install the last wheel, the car has peeled away. "Just call us," announced the tag line, as viewers understood the dire implication.

Another spot, made especially for the cinema, showed a girl in a big loft undressing. The camera catches her from the back; the moment she turns around and the audience can see her breasts, the film breaks. "Just call us," intoned the voice-over.

Other, similarly time-sensitive spots followed. In one commercial created in 1994, a young sailor in an Asian port visits a tattoo parlor. The tattoo designer takes a phone call while at work and botches the job disastrously—"Just call us."

In a spot that broke a year later, two men arrive at the airfield at their prearranged times and take off together in a glider. Soon after, two more men arrive: their instructors—"Just call us."

Every year the agency has produced three to five new commercials in the series and the campaign is still going strong more than ten years after it first burst upon the scene. From the start, the campaign attracted attention—almost 100 percent of target prospects are aware of the slogan. And it motivated insurance prospects to call. Meier said that sales have climbed 800 percent since the campaign began. And Centraal Beheer continues among the ten most sympathetic brands in the Netherlands—the sole insurance company on the list.

CIGAR BREAK

A mild smoke skirts ad laws and soothes the soul

A somewhat disheveled man attempts to fix his thinning hair in a photo booth and poses for his photo. There's a long delay. The distinctive, soothing Hamlet cigar theme begins to play. He bends forward to investigate the cause of the delay, and the flash goes off just as the lank hair he's wound over his pate falls forward onto his face. The man repositions his hair and poses for the next shot. He experiments with different facial expressions, smiling, grimacing, and just as the picture is taken, the stool collapses. A match is struck, the Hamlet music starts up again. The hapless fellow remains on the floor, choosing to savor his mild cigar.

Voice-over: "Happiness is a cigar called Hamlet. The mild cigar."

HAMLET
PHOTOBOOTH
COLLETT DICKENSON PEARCE, U.K., 1987

"Photobooth" began as a TV sketch for a comedy show. Philip Differ and Rowan Dean, copywriters at the Collett Dickenson Pearce ad agency, saw the skit and decided it would make a wonderful ad. They hired the same actor, Gregor Fischer, and gave the writer of the sketch a credit.

The cigar brand itself was created in the wake of the U.S. surgeon general's report on smoking, said John Salmon, president of Collett. Even though cigarettes were banned from TV, cigars were exonerated. Three other cigar brands were introduced simultaneously. "Photobooth" was designed to play up the product's mildness, in contrast to its earlier positioning as strong and flavorful. Gentle, soothing music encouraged the notion that a Hamlet was a stress antidote.

"Photobooth" was one of eighty commercials in the "Happiness is a cigar called Hamlet" campaign. This sixty-second spot was directed by Graham Rose, art directed by Garry Horner, and produced by John Hackney, and was created on a very low budget. Viewers responded to the humorous twist on the slice-of-life scenario and to the engaging character.

And they bought Hamlets. For more than two decades the brand has accounted for around half the cigars sold in England, sometimes slipping as a new product makes inroads, but always bouncing back.

The series ran for twenty-eight years—"a triumph of repetition without monotony," said Salmon. It was finally banned five years ago because British commercial TV transmitters' areas overlapped part of France and Scandinavia, and in the Continental common market all tobacco advertising was banned from TV.

Collett Dickenson Pearce subsequently resorted to posters and print ads. And it still uses radio to keep the musical theme going.

PIZZA WAR

The little guy launches a new patrol in an unrelenting battle for customers

LITTLE CAESARS

TRAINING CAMP

CLIFF FREEMAN & PARTNERS, USA, 1994

Somewhere in the Gobi Desert is a remote training camp in which young men are intensely and rigorously trained to deliver pizzas. They are taught how to knock on doors, ring bells, and carry stacks of pizzas while kicking the delivery car door shut with one foot. They learn other arcane skills: how to endure sprinkler systems and dodge barking dogs while picking up speed and efficiency. The reason for this training camp? The spot ends on a sea of hands holding up car keys and a super declares: "Little Caesars introduces delivery."

If pizza wars were based solely on ad appeal, Little Caesars would have won ages ago. Its wacky ads from Cliff Freeman & Partners grabbed viewers' attention, entertained them, delivered a memorable message, and created a strong brand personality.

Art directed by Matt Vescovo, written by Steve Dildarian, and directed by David Kellogg, "Training Camp" was one of one hundred hilarious spots Freeman cooked up for Little Caesars in its eleven-year run. The first commercial showed a goofball pizza employee fashioning an origami pterodactyl out of a pizza box. In other cheesy spots, strands of mozzarella, long as bungee cords, stretch and stretch until—*blammo!* a pizza explosion. In a 1996 side-splitter, an old gent wheeled down a hospital corridor to get his tonsils out grabs a pizza slice as he passes a nurse's desk. The stretchy cheese rockets him out of the operating room, scatters doctors and nurses, and lands him in an expectant mother's lap in the maternity ward. In another, mozzarella (made of rubber) is so stringy that a giggling baby and her high chair are slingshotted out of the living room to the front yard, where her surprised grandparents catch her.

To show how "crazy, crazy" it is to charge only $7.98 for two pizzas, bread, and sodas, a Pee Wee Herman type character conducted "canine nuptials." The dogs, in antique ivory gown and top hat, soon find themselves at the canine shrink. Another spot featured two male orangutans who prefer two of everything: bananas, female orangutans, and pizzas.

Other spots associated pizza with fun. A dog dances in a conga line; a scientist with a Scottish accent, trapped in a lab, inadvertently clones hundreds of sheep because he's so engrossed in a $6.99 pizza offer; and a juggling infant balances the family dog on his head but fails to impress his pizza-obsessed father.

Most of those droll ads, with their exaggerated cheese pulls, suggested that Little Caesars pizza was cheesier and cheaper. "Training Camp" had a different mission (and no "cheese pull"). It was to announce Caesars' delivery service. Freeman opted for a mock-epic treatment that signaled fun.

"Pizza is a product that just screams for having fun," agency head Cliff Freeman said. Caesars introduced delivery long after its competitors, so "we had to make news by being overly big and dramatic," said Arthur Bijur, who was creative director on the spot. "It was an overwrought execution done in a very understated way."

Pizza Hut, which had been emphasizing quality, enlisted high-profile talk-show host Rush Limbaugh and New York's former glamour duo Donald and Ivana Trump to launch its stuffed crust. Ads where football fans stomp to the raucous song "We Will Rock You" for the home delivery leader insisted it's "Gotta Be Domino's." Against that tide, Little Caesars, the David up against Goliaths, went for the giggle.

Unlike its other ads, where oddball characters are put into off-the-wall situations (and where animals often steal the show), these were Caesars employees "so they had to be likeable and endearing—people you could laugh at, but not be mean about," said Bijur.

Before these commercials began in 1988, the $900 million Little Caesars was little known nationally. Denise Ilitch Lites, vice chair of Little Caesars Enterprises, said the fresh, original advertising was risky, but its humor built remembrance and helped drive up sales 138 percent from 1988 through 1993. But sales of the $1.8 billion empire soon slowed, and in February 1998 Little Caesars moved to a new agency.

HEY, YOU NEVER WIN

New lotto strategy says you won't win if you don't play

NEW YORK LOTTO
BOARD ROOM

DDB NEEDHAM, USA, 1993

The scene is a board meeting in a big brown room. Serious music establishes the somber nature of the session. The grim and greedy chairman leers in a sinister camera angle: "In short, gentlemen, our capitalization plan has paid hence dividends; Johnson here will fill you in on the details."

A gloating lackey takes the floor. "Thank you, J.P.; let me begin by saying . . ." but he is interrupted by a door opening to faster music.

A manager bursts in. "We've been acquired!" he tells the stunned assemblage.

J.P. asks, "By whom? The Omega Corporation?"

The manager tells him, "No. Chuck! From the mail room."

A door creaks open. "Hi, boys . . . Mr. Whitaker," drawls the tie-dye-shirted, jackpot-winning mail room clerk who has bought the company he works for rather than quitting his job.

Viewers hear a crash as the board members pass out . . . or away.
Voice-over and super provide the punchline: "The New York Lotto.
Hey, you never know."
Rock music plays softly in the background.
"Coffee, Johnson," Chuck orders his former, stuffed-shirt boss.

The New York State Lottery's "Hey, You Never Know" image campaign was launched in 1991. It replaced "All You Need Is a Dollar and a Dream," which portrayed Lotto players as "people like you and me and suggested that the dream of winning was as important as actually winning," said Aaron Schaeffer, account supervisor at DDB Needham.

But by 1990, after several years of steady growth, Lotto revenues had slumped. Sales were down 18 percent in the fiscal year 1991–92 and the lottery's annual survey identified part of the problem. The advertising slogan was sending the wrong subliminal message. The ads featured actors daydreaming about spending their lottery winnings—but none actually won.

Research suggested that the hidden message was that it was almost impossible to win. New advertising would have to take a different slant: it would have to express the idea that while the chances of winning are mathematically poor, you don't have a prayer if you don't play. Someone's got to win and it could be you. It had to include winners among the dreamers.

"Hey, You Never Know," the ad campaign developed to fix that problem, featured actors portraying ordinary people whose lives were changed when they won Lotto. Very carefully structured, it tacitly acknowledged the overwhelming odds against winning, but downplayed them. It was created to speak to whim and core player alike and was backed by a more than $40 million advertising budget. And while it shifted strategy slightly, it retained the core humor to which the theme of overnight riches lends itself.

"Boardroom," one of the first spots in the campaign, ran for two years on a rotation cycle and was ultimately eased out by dozens of other commercials designed with the same strategy. It was topical, seizing on workers' anxiety and fantasy at the apex of merger mania.

Critics contended that the fantasy approach overpromised. DDB Needham executive creative director Bob Mackle disputed that. Rather than promising players that they'd win, "Boardroom" and other spots in the campaign gave players "permission to believe that they could win," he said. Psychologists call this gap between reality and wishful thinking "cognitive dissonance."

Other spots touting the largest lottery in North America presented fictitious winners. In one, an engaging toll booth collector waves vehicles through, telling drivers, "Go ahead, it's on me," as he drops coins in and soaks up the drivers' startled expressions. There was the high-pressure car salesman, Happy Gary, who gave away his cars and headed for the Bahamas, and Mrs. Hazelwood, who liked talk shows so much she went out and bought her own. All the spots ended with the "Hey, You Never Know" theme line.

As a government-run monopoly, the Lottery had some distinct advantages. There was no competitive pressure and no need for its advertising to differentiate its brand from competitors. And lotteries, because they're run by states, don't have to adhere to federal truth-in-advertising regulations that require sweepstakes and contests to clearly state the odds of winning in each ad.

(In fact, the odds of winning the top prize in New York's Lotto are about one in 13 million, far smaller than the chance of being struck by lightning. A survey by two Duke University economists found only 20 percent of all lottery ads accurately report the odds. When ads do cite odds, it's usually the odds of winning anything, not the top prize.)

Still, in April 1996, New York Governor George Pataki ordered the "Hey, You Never Know" campaign scrapped, calling its prospect of instant riches misleading. He also objected to the commercial's appealing to poor and lower-middle-class people, who, research suggests, spend a greater portion of their income on the lottery than do middle- or upper-income citizens.

(New York's lottery director, Jeff Perlee, said the ads are designed to be "innocuous" and "general" without targeting any groups." DDB's Schaeffer says the average age of players is forty-two and their annual income is over $50,000.)

Ever since New York instituted a lottery in 1967 to divert money into the state treasury for education that might otherwise be gambled illegally, it has been surveying regular, occasional, and infrequent lottery players—learning everything about them: the time of day they buy tickets, why they buy them, how they pick their numbers, and how much a month they spend on which games.

Such research found that instant, or scratch-off games, are more frequently played by women, and that many people play in hopes of changing or improving their home or job situation. The best time to reach potential players, research found, is when they're depressed, and that they're most receptive during unpleasant parts of their day, like during their commute, sitting in traffic, or paying bills. Research also found that players don't care about the benefits the state receives through lottery proceeds—just about their chances of winning. New York is one of thirty-seven states, plus the District of Columbia, that runs a lottery.

"Hey, You Never Know" increased game awareness and pumped up sales from $598 million in 1991 to $839 million in 1995. From 1994 through 1995 sales increased 28.5 percent, awareness of the tag line hit an all-time high, and profits to the state Lottery for Education Fund totaled a record $1.26 billion for the year. State surveys show 90 percent of Lotto players and 80 percent of nonplayers know the slogan, which has become part of the vernacular.

DARKNESS FALLS

A bright idea for selling long-lasting lightbulbs

PHILIPS

SOUP COUPLE

CLIFF FREEMAN & PARTNERS, USA, 1988

A chubby, middle-aged couple sits at the dinner table. The rotund matron complains to her husband that "the magic's gone" out of her marriage. The overhead light reflects off his bald head, which is lowered in deep concentration over his soup as he attempts to ignore his wife. "Every time the lights go out you fall asleep," she whines. What happens next? The lights go out and from the darkened screen come snores and splutters, a splash, and then bubbling noises as hubby's face falls into his soup.

A split second elapses, a computer-generated bulb snaps to life on the screen, and a voice-over announces: "It's time to change your bulb to Philips. Philips longer-life square bulbs."

Let's face it, there's no good time for a lightbulb to blow. It's a nuisance whenever it happens; making it happen less often is an illuminating marketing opportunity. In the fall of 1986, North American Philips Lighting Corporation seized that opportunity with the most talked about advertising in the then 108-year-old history of the lightbulb.

The lighthearted campaign relied on humor to make a serious point: Philips square-shaped, soft-white lightbulbs burn 33 percent longer than the traditional round ones. According to its survey, long life is the one quality consumers look for in choosing a brand of lightbulb. "Lightbulbs are an indifferent category," said Jerry Preys, director of marketing operations at Philips. "People don't buy bulbs as often as they do coffee. And they've no emotional involvement with bulbs the way they do with beauty aids." In fact, even though the average American home contains twenty-eight lightbulb sockets, the only time people really notice lightbulbs is when they blow out.

"High-tech claims used to market lightbulbs don't work," Preys said. "People don't believe them because, essentially, this is pretty much the same product Edison invented one hundred years ago. The only issue people care about is putting off having to change a bulb. Though it was risky, we opted for humor because it was a chance to break through the clutter, to score a real home run."

Arthur Bijur, creative director on the account, said the challenge was to dramatize a negative. "As the number-two guy in lighting manufacturing, Philips had to do daring, dramatic work. We wanted noise and notice. We had a tangible problem—darkness—and a tangible product benefit, a way to ward it off longer. The solution came to us even before we knew we were going to work on the account." It was to warm people up with comedy, to get them to laugh at people's predicaments and their compromising positions so they'd pay attention to lightbulbs.

And so humor: In another spot in the campaign, a moon-faced night-shift maintenance man sits spellbound as his coworker reads aloud the exploits of Lord Klempston. But just as Lord K is "gazing at Lucretia's loveliness," a preamble to who knows what, *zap*—the lightbulb blows. Still another spot in the campaign portrayed a stumpy businessman in an elevator shyly admiring a statuesque blond fellow passenger. Taking refuge behind his newspaper, he fails to see the woman exit and a pudgy cigar-chomping workman take her place. When the elevator light fizzles, the business man, emboldened by the darkness, confides, "I guess you know I find you extremely attractive."

In yet another spot, a slightly blowsy looking homemaker steers her upright vacuum cleaner around her snoozing silver tabby. (The vacuum sounds were added later to keep the cat docile.) Suddenly, the lightbulb flickers, the screen goes black, and viewers hear the frenzied howl of the cat. Ooops! (Philips admitted it received angry letters from cat lovers who saw nothing to laugh at.)

The campaign results lighted up Philips management. Preys said sales grew 20 percent in the fourth quarter of 1986, 32 percent in January, and another 15 percent in February. In one year the company snagged two share points away from Sylvania and General Electric in the $2 billion category. Orders from retailers surged 50 percent in the first six months, with stores that previously had stocked only GE now carrying Philips as well. Within two years, major merchandisers like K mart, Wal-Mart, and Home Depot had put Philips on their shopping lists, and some, including Sears Roebuck, saw the light and picked Philips as their exclusive brand.

When the campaign first aired, nearly 20 percent of TV viewers thought it was a General Electric ad. Only 17 percent correctly identified North American Philips as the sponsor. A year later 67 percent of Americans knew the Philips brand name—though virtually no one had heard of it before. And 48 percent of consumers named Philips when asked to identify a brand of lightbulb, and 72 percent said they'd pick Philips the next time they bought bulbs.

BUVEZ ET PISSEZ

A French mineral water bottler says propriety be damned

VITTEL

DAME PIPI

CLM/BBDO, FRANCE, 1973

A ladies' washroom attendant at a fine restaurant is not having a good night. Only 15 centimes in tips are in her canister. But as music reminiscent of the can-can and circus plays, an idea begins to form. Dame Pipi (meaning wee-wee in French) tells the maître d' to serve Vittel mineral water to the diners. He passes the word down and soon every table has a bottle of Vittel atop it.

The old woman takes her place in the washroom, straightens her hair, and, before long, a never-ending stream of customers is entering her washroom, providing excellent tips.

A voice, followed by a super, announces (in French), "When Vittel cleanses the toxins from your cells, it cleans them all the way out of your body."

The risque and ever-so-French "Dame Pipi" was the first spot in a daring new campaign for Vittel mineral water, *"Buvez et Pissez"* (drink and piss). The campaign aimed to impose the Kellogg-ian idea that "elimination equals health" and that Vittel was an effective—extremely effective—mineral water diuretic.

It was a delicate subject, and CLM/BBDO knew it had to present the elimination story in a light, deftly humorous tone—not only not to frighten off possible consumers, but also to take on Contrex, which dominated the mineral water market at that time, recalled Olivier Bensimon, who with Jean-Claude Lacoste and chairman Philippe Michel conceived this execution. Vittel at first hesitated to follow the agency's whimsy, but then backed the concept fully.

The campaign did create a small scandal and the print component was even refused by certain newspapers for being too shocking, but the company nonetheless continued to run it for years, Bensimon said.

As much as the concept was charming, the casting of Laurence Treill was impeccable. After portraying the esteemed Dame Pipi she went on to a quite successful modeling career. And Dame Pipi wasn't the only one raking it in. The witty and surprising dramatization of Vittel's "benefits" carved out a defined and recognized territory for the brand. For many years after, Vittel was the brand leader, the best-selling mineral water in France.

WISE UNCLE

Volkswagen's fable of pennies saved and billions earned

A funeral procession passes by. As a voice announces the will of the newly departed, we see the various "mourners" in their large, fancy cars gleefully anticipating how they will benefit. But the deceased had other ideas. From beyond the grave his crotchety voice is heard reading his will: "I, Maxwell E. Snaberly, being of sound mind and body, do hereby bequeath the following: to my wife, Rose, who spent money like there was no tomorrow, I leave $100 and a calendar.

"To my sons, Rodney and Victor, who spent every dime I ever gave them on fancy cars and fast women, I leave $50 in dimes. To my business partner, Jules, whose only motto was spend, spend, spend, I leave nothing, nothing, nothing.

"And to all my other friends and relatives who also never learned the value of a dollar, I leave a dollar. Finally, to my nephew Harold, who oftentimes said, 'A penny saved is a penny earned,' and who also oftentimes said, 'Gee, Uncle Max, it sure pays to own a Volkswagen,' I leave my entire fortune of $100 billion."

Harold drives a lone black Beetle at the end of the procession and wipes away a tear.

VOLKSWAGEN

FUNERAL

DOYLE DANE BERNBACH, USA, 1969

Storyboard

While other auto marketers were showing artfully elongated cars in lush settings with models in diaphanous gowns draped over their hoods, and boasting of superior performance or suggesting visions of virility or romance, Volkswagen drove a different highway altogether—one of simplicity and wit.

In memorable counterculture commercials, it used self-deprecating humor to label itself "Lemon" and it nudged Americans to "think small." During the oil embargo of the early 1970s, a line drawing of a man with a gasoline nozzle to his head tersely illustrated the alternative to buying a VW.

But perhaps even more than its notoriously wry wit, VW's key to our hearts was its gentle, theater-of-the-absurd narrative commercials. "Funeral" typifies the genre—meting out vengeful justice from the grave with an irreverent chuckle. Legendary adman David Ogilvy called it the funniest commercial he'd ever seen, and credited "Funeral" with changing his mind that people don't buy from clowns. "Funeral" also talked up the car's principal benefit—its economy—in a novel, arresting, and subtle way that did not insult the consumer's intelligence. And it provided a new hero and status paradigm—along with the obligatory car-on-the-highway shots.

Written by Bob Levinson and Roy Grace and art directed by Grace, "Funeral" was shot by Howard Zieff. Grace came up with the idea as he was driving alongside a funeral procession on the Palisades Parkway. The

191

client approved it on the day of his own brother's funeral. VW eschewed what Levinson called the "I'll try it, I'll buy it, I'll switch, I'll put it on top of my shopping list" commercial. "We wanted to present the fact that VW is an intelligent purchase in an irreverent, anti-establishment VW manner," he said. VW sales in the U.S. peaked a year later as Americans snapped up the goofy-looking car they understood to be practical and fun. But eventually the Beetle was left in the dust of better equipped, more comfortable, cheaper Japanese cars and more stringent U.S. safety standards.

In 1979, the German car company stopped selling the love bug, for which advertising had created an almost human personality, in the U.S. Over the years, more than 21 million Bugs sold around the world and its helmet-shaped body may be the most famous silhouette in the world.

CHAPTER FOURTEEN

SOFT TOUCH, HARD SELL

In a 1975 commercial for the insurance company Mutual of New York, a young man looks sincerely into the camera lens and brightly recalls how his dad opened a savings account for him on his tenth birthday. "Brian," the son recalls his dad's announcement, "you're gonna have it better than me. You're not gonna have to stand on your feet all day just to make a buck. You do the studying and I'll do the saving." The earnest young man enters a luncheonette and slips on an apron. "He had it all planned," he continued. "There's only one thing he didn't plan. He didn't plan on dying."

It wasn't just then-unknown John Travolta's soliloquy that captured viewers' attention, it was the sudden invasion of death and its devastating impact on those left behind. Adam's apples needed to bob before people could overcome their natural resistance to facing their own mortality—and discussing life insurance. "Sometimes the saddest thing about a man's death is to watch his dreams die with him," its announcer zeroed in on our emotional wellsprings.

Manufacturers have long believed that people purchase products because of their "rational" benefits. They now know that the more potent persuader is emotion—how the experience or even the advertising makes a viewer feel. Almost two decades ago, AT&T's heartrending "Joey Called" prompted people to "reach out and touch someone." Nowadays, MasterCard's "Priceless" commercials remind us that even the most seemingly rational nuts-and-bolts money decisions are tilled by emotional hoeing. Every car company concedes

that what's under the hood makes the car move, but it's the emotional message about the driving experience that moves car buyers.

Campbell Soup Company has long known the emotional power of the family and how it can be harnessed to sell. Campbell used a mother and small son to position soup as more than the mere contents of the can. The misty setting, the parental halo, the child's-eye perspective, the melancholy music, and the conveyed sense of paradise lost raised Campbell Soup to an icon of maternal warmth and caring, and a conduit to paradise found.

Volvo showed parental passion for a teen can be equally highly charged. Rather than disallow his daughter from going out during a frightful thunderstorm, a doting father pleads with her date to take his (presumably safer) Volvo. How direct an assault to the Swedish car maker's target audience, that they so loved their begotten daughter they gave their car for her!

Advertisers have mined emotional lodes other than the rich vein of parent and child. The Spanish Ministerio de Sanidad used the ideals of selfhood and honor in a condom commercial that portrayed teens in a gymnasium standing up to authority and individually claiming ownership of a condom the furious principal has found. Emotionally seductive, the spot had us rooting for principle over principal. And the Partnership for a Drug Free America's empathetic salute to a young ghetto boy who must take the "long way home" from school, through backyards and alleys, past gangs and dealers, elevates his just saying no and makes his struggle heroic and moving.

While evermore-jaded viewers disregard emotional advertising or dismiss it as too blatant a sell, sometimes sentiment is the only card to play. The mission of the ad campaign for the Church of Jesus Christ of Latter-day Saints was to remind families of the magic of life's moments and to look at everyday events with new eyes. Happiness, the announcer reminds viewers, isn't about purchasing so much as repositioning—opening our hearts and minds.

PARADISE REVISITED

Campbell's says a cup of soup is the ticket to better times

A mother's son runs home with a potted flower and rings the bell. In a soft song we hear the theme of the ad:

> *"Kids grow up and they leave so soon*
> *But we like to think they will always recall*
> *the little things, the loving things*
> *The very special giving things*
> *we do for them when they are small.*
> *There are very special soups that kids remember*
> *'cause they're made with extra care."*

Voice-over: "Soup is a giving thing—full of warmth, nourishment, and good psychology. To folks big and little, Campbell's soups have a way of finding and filling the cold and empty places. Good to give and good to get—happy, homey soup."

Mom opens the door and views the broken flowerpot. She hugs her son to comfort him as he holds the flower without the pot. A sad little boy sits at the table. Mom goes to the kitchen to bring cheer to her loved one. She reaches for the Campbell's and brings a bowl full of warmth and love to her boy. Mom then places the flower, repotted in a mug, next to her son and he smiles.

> *Lyrics: "The very special soups—prepared by Campbell's."*

Voice-over: "In the can with the famous signature—serve your family soup often. From Campbell's."

CAMPBELL SOUP

FLOWER POT

LEO BURNETT, USA, 1965

Perhaps more than anyone, the Campbell Soup Company knows the selling power of nostalgia for home, childhood, and Mom's love. In its mythic advertising world, the family equals paradise. The setting is pure Norman Rockwell: the warm color scheme, the light glow around the parents, the kid's-eye perspective. Add the sentimental music and the paradise-lost subtext is clear: long ago things were perfect—and Campbell's soup is the way to get back to those times, to go home again.

Thanks to Andy Warhol, Campbell's red and white can may be the most-recognized product in the world, but in 1965, when the then-hundred-year-old Campbell Soup Company served up "Flower Pot," soup sales were lukewarm. The Camden, New Jersey–based company tried to heat things up by positioning soup as nurturing and nourishing. At the time, Campbell sold 90 percent of canned soup in the U.S., so the concern was less increased market share than increasing the overall market for soup.

"Flower Pot" and other commercials then in Campbell's cupboard equated giving soup with a mother's love for her child. "Soup has great emotional appeal as a warming, comforting food served when you're ill or

195

cold or unhappy or just plain hungry," said former Campbell president Herb Baum. "It's a rare food served as a complete meal or part of one and its advertising represents warmth and friendliness. Sympathy along with a little hot soup brings the boy's world back to livability."

The spot was designed to appeal to mothers, copywriter Gene Kolkey said. "The story was developed so as to make the child seek comfort or help from his mother, with the serving of soup part of Mother's comforting gesture." Kolkey originally shot the commercial with a 16mm Rolex camera using his own three-year-old son as a model to show what he envisioned. When it was ultimately produced, viewers said that the last scene looked spontaneous, with the boy looking truly surprised when he sees his flower replanted by his mother. But director Howard Zieff took fifteen takes to get that final expression, acting it out for the child each time. He actually shot three different boys doing completely different footage with each boy reacting in his own way to the situation. Then Zieff chose on the Moviola the one he felt came closest to what Campbell Soup wanted.

In America, 98 percent of homes stock cans of soup—more than use bathroom tissue. The average American household stores six to eight cans of soup in its cupboard. The problem of late has been getting people to dust off the cans and use them.

In February 1998, with Campbell Soup sales down slightly from the year earlier and with 74 percent of the then $3.5 billion canned soup business in the U.S., Campbell returned to the theme that had served it so well in the past with the largest advertising campaign in the company's history. After years of focusing on health benefits, the company launched a $130 million campaign called "Good for the Body, Good for the Soul," a series of stories designed to promote its soup as comfort food that brings families together.

In one of the commercials, a young child arrives at her new foster home and, overwhelmed, withdraws within herself, unable to speak until her foster mother brings her a steaming bowl of Campbell's soup. Then she opens up: "My mommy used to fix me this soup," the child says quietly. The foster mother, fighting back tears, responds, "My mother used to make it for me too." The commercial closes with mother and child sharing memories. In another spot, six children from two families plot to persuade their single parents to marry by secretly preparing a romantic dinner for them with a recipe from Campbell. They're too late: seems dad's already popped the question.

"The charm of these spots are their nurturing aspects. They associate soup with feeling good and conjure up warm, comforting images. It's an emotional sell," said Phil Dusenberry, chairman of Omnicom Group's BBDO/New York ad, which created the new work.

DON'T GET MAD, GET GLAD

A church sells kindness in an ongoing series

Three country kids are having a good, messy fight in the yard of their rural home, throwing buckets of mud, rolling and wrestling in it, squirting each other with a garden hose. A voice-over sings, "Don't let the magic pass you by. You know . . ."

Suddenly, the fight stops as a pickup truck pulls up. The song continues, ". . . the greatest moments are not the kind that you buy. You've got to open up your heart and mind. Magic won't be hard to find. So don't let the magic pass you by."

The brakes squeal, doors slam, and grim-faced Mom and Dad get out of the truck. "Joan, look at this . . . don't anybody move," Dad says sternly as he marches toward the house. "I'll be right back."

Mom is equally tight-lipped. "I think you've finally done it," she tells her trio. Dad, arriving back from the house, breaks into a big grin and brings out the camera. "All right, everybody . . . smile," he says.

The song concludes, "Don't let the magic pass you by."

Mom then turns the hose on Dad.

The voice-over, this time an announcer, drives home the message, "Small moments often bring the greatest memories. Don't let their magic pass you by. From the Mormons, the Church of Jesus Christ of Latter-day Saints."

Super: "The Church of Jesus Christ of Latter-day Saints."

THE CHURCH OF JESUS CHRIST OF LATTER-DAY SAINTS

WATER FIGHT

BONNEVILLE COMMUNICATIONS, USA, 1984

"Water Fight" was the twenty-second installment of an ongoing public service campaign called "Home Front" for the Church of Jesus Christ of Latter-day Saints (i.e., the Mormons). The strategy for all the spots was to stress the importance of the family unit by giving the target audience—families, especially parents—concrete and simple ideas and attitudes they can use to forge a better home life.

There was no strident fundamentalism here, no presenting the Mormon Church as a source of inspiration, no call to the faith to lapsed or first-time Church goers. In fact, there was no mention at all of the kind of worship the Church offers. Instead, it showed values other than raw consumerism that reflected the Latter-day Saints' worldview. "We tried to relate to the audience that some small frustrating moments can actually be made memorable and positive if they are just looked at differently," said Curt Dahl, creative director at Bonneville, who wrote and produced "Water Fight." From this came the tag line: "It's often life's small moments that bring the greatest memories. Don't let the magic pass you by."

197

Inspiration for the commercial came one afternoon as Dahl looked out-side his back window and noticed a few young children playing in a pile of topsoil. "In a short time they had supplemented the dirt with water from the hose and soon began to make a big mess in the mud," he remembered. "It wasn't long before they were all covered in muck. Their parents weren't home at the time and I figured the kids would be in big trouble when they returned. But when Mom and Dad arrived on the scene, I watched in amazement as Dad walked into the house and returned with a camera to capture the moment. I knew then it would make a great scene for 'Home Front.' "

The spot was originally conceived for a suburban setting, but during lo-cation-scouting director Rick Levine suggested a middle-American farm set-ting would give it a warm feeling and timeless look. Levine added the grace note at the end, where the parents get to turn the hose on each other. (His team also produced the mud for the yard.)

During casting, agency representatives asked the children if they would enjoy playing in water and mud and everyone was excited and enthusiastic about it. "And then we arrived at the set," recalled Levine. "The little girl simply did not want to get dirty." Her reluctance was palpable. "I kept of-fering her money—I was up to $5—if she would just participate," said Levine. The two boys, he said, willingly and energetically did anything asked of them—even though they were out romping in the mid-December chill of Southern California. (There were two giant space heaters just out of view of the camera.)

Most public service advertising runs for only a brief time, as did "Water Fight." It ran for about four months, but because of its original success was re-released in 1996 as part of a special classics 50th Home Front campaign. Then it also ran for four months.

There were no sales associated with this commercial, and brand aware-ness wasn't measured, but Dahl said the Church felt that based on the amount of unpaid airtime it received and the glowing comments from the public service directors of the TV stations throughout the country, it was one of the most successful commercials they had ever aired.

OWNING UP

A Spanish public service spot turns condom usage into an issue of honor

The camera cuts between a high school gym class and a school principal roaming the locker rooms. While the kids jump rope, bounce basketballs, and career off the balance beam, the principal has found a condom among some clothes. A whistle is blown and the class assembles. "I found this in your dressing room. Whose is it?" he demands (in Spanish). When no culprit owns up he grows sterner: "I said whose is this?"

Finally one boy stands and declares, "It's mine."

But another boy says, "It's mine," and he's on his feet.

A girl's voice claims, "It's mine," and she stands too.

The rest of the class stands up, confronting the principal, claiming to be the owner.

Super: "The condom is the most efficient method for preventing unwanted births and sexually transmitted diseases. Put it on. Put it on him."

MINISTERIO DE SANIDAD GYMNASIUM

CONTRAPUNTO, SPAIN, 1991

"Gymnasium" would have been courageous in any context, but to be approved by a government agency and aired in a Catholic country not long out of the shadow of a repressive dictatorship makes its existence, not to mention its enormous success, all the more remarkable.

Americans talk about persuasion, said Contrapunto chief executive Teofilo Marco, but in Spain they think about seduction and produce ads that are clear, direct, and emotional. This gutsy spot in which youth rebels against authority is certainly emotionally seductive. Unlike most other condom advertising, which hides behind humor, "Gymnasium" made a timely statement about honor and honesty. It took an embarrassing topic and forthrightly declared it not only unembarrassing, but a source of pride. And it did so without preaching or hectoring.

In 1991, Spain had the second-highest incidence of AIDS-related illnesses in Europe, according to the World Health Organization. While stern "cod-liver" warnings about unwanted pregnancies and sexually transmitted diseases have been the conventional way to sell condoms, many marketers had begun to recognize that preaching didn't work, especially with young folks, who feel immortal. This table-turning tale, wherein the teacher is taught a lesson, reached across that chasm and became a pop culture sensation. It ran in print, on radio, and on billboards. The "It's Mine" slogan appeared on buttons, stickers, and T-shirts, and Spanish pop stars incorporated the line in their songs. And the ministry distributed a million free condoms via pharmacies and schools—instructions included.

WE HEAR YOU

An anti-drug campaign honors those who just say no

**PARTNERSHIP FOR A
DRUG FREE AMERICA
LONG WAY HOME**

GOODBY SILVERSTEIN & PARTNERS, USA, 1992

A black-and-white spot shows a young boy running home from school—the long way. As somber piano music plays, he climbs over high fences, cuts through backyards, sprints through alleys, and darts past drug dealers. A voice-over explains, "My teacher tells us all we gotta do is 'just say no' and the other day a policeman came to our class talking about 'say no,' too. Well, my teacher doesn't have to walk through this neighborhood." (We see the boy run quickly by a gang hanging out on a street corner.) "And maybe the dealers are scared of the police, but they're not scared of me. And they sure don't take no for an answer."

Voice-over: "To Kevin Scott and all the other kids that take the long way home, we hear ya. Don't give up."

Super: "Partnership for a Drug Free America."

In 1987, the Partnership for a Drug Free America, a coalition of volunteers formed in 1985 by the American Association of Advertising Agencies, launched an effective series of spots designed to "unsell" drugs to the American public. The message would be that illegal drugs are dangerous; the goal was to reshape societal attitudes about their acceptance.

One of the very first spots, from the the Keye/Donna/Pearlstein agency, was a milestone tough-love public service commercial: "Fried Egg." In perhaps the most famous commercial in the Partnership's history, an announcer likened viewers' unadulterated brains to an intact egg, then compared a sizzling egg to "your brain on drugs." In the same year, "Tricks of the Trade" showed mechanistically how drugs become part of our youth culture, how kids get hooked.

Since those Partnership messages began, America has become increasingly hostile to drugs and usage has dropped on a national basis. In 1991, the Partnership had found that children and adolescents in areas of urban poverty were at specific risk of involvement in the drug culture. Meetings with more than 175 experts helped identify vulnerability and attitudinal differences specific to low-income, urban children. Although many of the children were defiantly anti-drug, many feared they'd be pressured into using drugs. At the same time, some of these children's perceptions of dealers were rather positive.

Despite critics who argued that these children were hopelessly alienated and could not be reached or influenced with mass media messages, the Partnership decided to launch a series of public service spots aimed directly at them, focusing specifically on African-American and Hispanic children ages six to twelve. The goal was to fortify their ability to resist drugs and to reinforce their negative perceptions about the drug culture and dealers by deglamorizing them.

200

The gut-wrenching "Long Way Home" spot, overseen by Jeff Goodby, written and art directed by Jeremy Postaer, and produced by Cindy Fluitt, was one of sixteen television messages in the highly targeted anti-drug effort. "Instead of trying to force the idea of not taking drugs, 'Long Way Home' aimed to say we see you, we hear you," Goodby said.

The Partnership surveyed 7,288 New York City elementary school kids in 1992 about drugs and again in May 1993 and found changed attitudes. Before the commercial, 18 percent of second and third graders were afraid they might want to try drugs sometime. After, 15 percent did. The number of fourth through sixth graders who would walk away if offered drugs increased from 78 percent to 82 percent; at the same time their confidence in their resistance skills rose from 11 percent to 14 percent. Their images of drug dealers were also sharply less glamorous. Eight percent more concluded that a dealer was scared all the time.

In 1995, the Partnership shifted emphasis again. Heroin's lower prices and higher purity made it a drug of choice for a new generation. With such purity, users could now snort it like cocaine, eliminating the injection-by-needle barrier. And the stigma against drugs abated with Hollywood models, actors, musicians, and the club scene embracing the glamour of self-destruction. In 1995, an estimated 90 percent of new users were under twenty-six; 77 percent had never tried heroin before. (Between 1990 and 1995, according to the Partnership, heroin-related hospital emergency room episodes more than doubled from 33,900 to 72,200.)

With the glamorization of death, the Partnership decided that a message that said heroin can kill you could backfire and attract risk seekers living on the edge. The new advertising must emphasize the severe risks of experimentation and shatter images of heroin as hip, cool, and attractive. In one spot, an attractive woman removes her earrings, eyelashes—and teeth. "It's hard to face what heroin can do to you," declared the tag line.

COUCH POTATO

The tale of a TV that will outlive you

SONY
LIFESPAN

BOASE MASSIMI POLLITT, U.K., 1984

The spot opens on an empty sofa with the back of a TV set in the foreground. Country music plays, as the successive phases of one man's life is revealed. Through a series of cuts, he is shown growing from a baby to a man to a husband to a father to a grandfather to a decrepit old man. Finally, all that's left are his shoes and pipe as the picture of a flower (which itself has grown into full bloom) falls off the wall.
Super: "Sony Trinitron. Designed to last."

In 1984, color television was no longer a novelty, but the sets themselves were renowned for being unreliable. The color was inconsistent and the machines had high malfunction and repair rates.

Sony's advertising had touted its excellent picture quality, but its competitors were attempting to enhance their reputation for reliability. Market research suggested that such positioning was more compelling than one focused on clarity and tone. Sony switched gears.

John Webster conceived "Lifespan"—an unusual commercial in that both the camera and its subject were static—a device intended to both grab viewers' attention and drive home the TV's longevity claim.

Before the commercial was produced, the concept was tested against a group of twenty-one- to forty-four-year-old men with at least moderate incomes who were deemed to be the TV purchasing decision makers. They indicated that the commercial clearly communicated the "extra life" benefit of Trinitron.

"Lifespan" was very popular with viewers and was one of the most widely recalled commercials of its time. Even more significant, it dramatically increased consumer confidence in the reliability of Trinitron and piloted a switch away from the until then flourishing rental market into the direct purchasing of Trinitron.

Another Sony spot in 1984 was equally unusual. In that one, Sony's compact disc player, videocassette recorder, and TV were all introduced by a lovable Giacomettish robot with the voice of John Cleese, who has been used on other Sony commercials. The robot played laser discs, tapped his metallic leg to the music, asked a lamp to dance, and mused that the videocassette recorder might be better looking than his wife, a vacuum cleaner.

FIRST LEER

Sex sells, but the soft sell sells sex better

This romantic, sepia-tone spot set to the strains of a Puccini opera overture opens in a gym. Our twelve-year-old heroine is doing arm raises knowing she's the only one without a bra, an embarrassing fact that is confirmed in the changing room. At home she's disconsolate on her bed with a favorite doll. Then she sees a gift package on the bed. She opens it; it's a junior bra. She pulls it on before her mirror. Out in the street her new bra is visible beneath her crisp white shirt. A boy passes and ogles her breasts. She holds her schoolbooks over them in false modesty. She's feeling like a woman.

Voice-over: "The first Valisere. We never forget our first bra."

VALISERE
FIRST BRA

W/BRASIL W/GGK, BRAZIL, 1987

Valisere was a traditional manufacturer of female undergarments, especially nylon lingerie. But at the end of the 1980s, consumer preference had switched to cotton underwear. The image of nylon bras and underpants, which were less expensive and not as sophisticated, was associated with lack of taste. Valisere had to do something to reverse this image.

It did so with one commercial—virtually overnight—by taking a totally different tack than most Brazilian underwear ads, which typically are obsessed with sex and show a lot of flesh. Agnelo Pacheco, a Brazilian creative executive from the Agnelo Pacheco Criacao e Propaganda agency, said eroticism is essential for Brazilians. A typical Brazilian ad shows a close-up of a woman's breast in a black bra next to the orange juice ostensibly being advertised. "There are better things to squeeze than oranges," explains the voice-over.

Valisere made its point with a sweet, humane, real film and gentle nostalgia. There is a brief nude shot, as the adolescent excitedly tries on her new bra, but creatives Rose Ferraz and Camila Franco insist this wasn't the spot's focus. "The moment is so true that you can't see it as sex," said Ferraz. "Brazilians are already so used to the sexual approach, you can go beyond this and take a totally natural approach" to command attention.

The commercial's slogan, "We Never Forget Our First Bra," became a popular expression in Brazil the way "Where's the Beef?" did in the U.S. Formula 1 champion Ayrton Senna, Brazil's racing car idol, made newspaper headlines when he declared, "We never forget our first Ferrari," in an interview with *Playboy* magazine. Less fortunately, Patrician Luchese, the actress in the film, who was thirteen at the time, was so closely identified with her role in the film that she couldn't get her TV career off the ground. "Audiences could only relate to her as the girl in the first-bra commercial," said creative director Washington Olivetto.

203

"Primeiro Sutia" conveyed a new image to the public. What used to be seen as a somewhat unpopular product, even a bit vulgar, was now seen as something sweet, delicate, and very feminine. Eleven years after the commercial first aired Valisere still uses the theme and is a market leader.

TAKE MY CAR, PLEASE

From compact to safe, Volvo drives home its message

VOLVO

TAKE MY CAR, PLEASE

SCALI, MCCABE, SLOVES, USA, 1976

A worried father and his wife pace the living room while a thunderstorm rages outside. The father frets about his daughter going on a date in such horrible weather. "It's crazy to let them go out on a night like this," he grumbles agitatedly to his wife. "But she waited months for tonight," the mother replies understandingly.

The doorbell rings. "Mom, is that Jeff?" the young girl asks expectantly.

Indeed it is and Mom greets him with "Hello, Jeff."

Jeff greets the parents: "Mrs. Stewart. Mr. Stewart."

After some feet-shuffling greeting, Dad makes a decision—the next best thing to preventing his daughter from going out.

"Jeff, do me a favor, will you?" he says. "Take my Volvo."

Voice-over: "Over the years, safety has been an obsession with Volvo. Because of all the things that go into a Volvo, the ones we've always valued most are people."

Super: "Volvo."

Mother has the last word: "Be careful," she calls as they leave the house.

At a time when Detroit was creating its standard car-on-a-curvy-road advertising, Volvo created a commercial daring for its time in that it didn't talk about the car's attributes; it assumed that people already understood them. "Take My Car, Please," written by Mike Dazen, art directed by John Danza, and shot by director Rick Levine, was the first commercial ever done for Volvo that focused on dialogue and humanity.

This thirty-second slice of life sold the Swedish car maker's reputation for safety. That reputation was so ingrained that advertising could safely avoid making claims and instead focus on the simple idea of a parent's concern over his child going out on a date in bad weather. The car maker and its agency believed that no other car company could put its logo at the end of this spot and be believable.

The one-day shoot, which took place in Englewood, New Jersey, relied on fire hoses to create the rain effect. "The scripting was very tight," said Levine. "It was critical that every nuance be there with perfect timing; that every glance be scripted to achieve an emotional pull in thirty seconds. We were careful to cast people that were very real and not use any that were beautiful," he said.

Car commercials usually run for a year because new spots introduce car model changes. The marketing objective was simple, said Ed McCabe, former creative director at Scali, McCabe, Sloves. "We wanted to sell *all* the cars Volvo imported to the U.S. to a waiting list of customers at full retail price. The primary objective of the advertising was to position Volvo as the most well-made, durable, and reliable cars available for the price. A secondary objective was to communicate Volvo's commitment to safety and the car's safety features."

That the commercial succeeded is incontestable. In 1967 Volvo sold 6,000 cars; it increased its sales every year for the next twenty, and in 1986 sold 158,000 cars in the U.S. But even more magical than the obvious sales increases was the building of a gilt-edged image that cut across all models and prices.

In the early 1960s, Volvo had been positioned as a compact car. Advertising such as "Take My Car, Please" "unpositioned" it by size and solidly repositioned it for quality, says McCabe. By 1987, Volvo models were much more expensive than they had been. They were competing with luxury cars and had to communicate beauty and style. McCabe says Volvo was the only automaker in history that was able to migrate from economy car to compact car to full-sized sedan to performance car to luxury car with a single nameplate.

Volvo was able to accomplish this while delivering full gross profits to its retail dealers with the lowest advertising cost per car in the imported car business, says McCabe. BMW and Mercedes-Benz, for example, spent nearly double per car on advertising.

YELLOWED PAGES

A phone directory lets family ties do the selling

YELLOW PAGES

J. R. HARTLEY

ABBOTT MEAD VICKERS, U.K., 1984

The commercial opens in an old cove in a secondhand book shop. As a piano plays, an old man asks the clerk: "I don't suppose you have a copy of Fly Fishing *by J. R. Hartley? It is rather old. It's by J. R. Hartley."*

The clerk doesn't. The spot dissolves into a second bookstore, where the man again tries his luck. "It's by J. R. Hartley."

Defeated again, the old gent arrives home disappointed but his pleasant daughter brings him a nice cup of tea and the Yellow Pages. "No luck, Dad? Never mind," she says. "There's still a few more to try."

Announcer: "Good old Yellow Pages. We don't just help with the nasty things in life like a blocked drain. We're there for the nice things, too."

The man is now in his stuffed armchair on the phone: "You do?"

The daughter looks up from her needlework. "Oh, that's wonderful," he continues. "Eh, eh, can you keep it for me? My name? Oh, yes, it's J. R. Hartley." Freeze on the old boy as he sits back with a twinkle—concluding the neat little narrative with a kicker.

Super: Yellow Pages logo.

A 1983 study showed that, although virtually everyone in the U.K. had heard of the Yellow Pages, they associated the directory only with the nasty things in life—like finding a plumber or electrician in an emergency, said David Abbott, the writer on "J. R. Hartley" at Abbott Mead Vickers. Consequently, the directory was at the back of people's minds until their next catastrophe occurred. Abbott's task, along with that of art director Ron Brown, was to make the Yellow Pages mean something more in people's lives than a yellow book full of company names and addresses. The way to do that was to touch them—to tug at their hearts.

The "Let Your Fingers Do the Walking" campaign had run for thirteen years before, establishing the Yellow Pages as a valuable and easy-to-use resource that saved time, trouble, and money, said John Condron, then marketing controller and now managing director of the Yellow Pages. "J. R. Hartley" was the first commercial in a new campaign designed to turn the brand into something more—a really helpful friend of the family for nice things, too, such as ordering flowers. Or finding a book.

Originally J. R. Hartley was looking for a book on British butterflies but research showed that pursuit to be a little too esoteric to ring the right bells with viewers. So his mission was changed to fly-fishing. The agency actually won the Yellow Pages account by insisting on developing a warmer, more emotional approach. "I remember David Abbott interrupted an early planning session to say we had to concentrate on the relationship between the book and its users in a way that warmed the cockles of the heart," said Condron.

In another spot in the campaign, a contrite boy looks to the Yellow Pages for a polish to mend his parents' coffee table after a riotous party. In others, a cherished gardener is bought a motorized lawn mower by his employer with an assist from the Yellow Pages, and the ex–England football managers buy Terry Venables a cake to wish him good luck in his new job.

"J. R. Hartley" has been one of the longest-lived commercials on British TV. It's run regularly for twelve years and become a national institution.

Awareness of the commercial was extraordinary, said Condron. So was recall—documented at 80 to 85 percent—with research groups playing back every detail of the execution. The spot has been mimicked on many comedy shows in the U.K., a sure sign it has become part of the culture. Norman Lumsden, the actor who played J.R., went on to do chat shows, supermarket openings, and other promotional gigs. "This commercial encapsulated all our brand values and has created a goodwill halo around our business," said Condron.

In 1991, eight years after this ad first appeared, Yellow Pages sponsored the writing of the book *Fly Fishing* by "J. R. Hartley." It became the number-one best-seller that Christmas—the time of year, interestingly, when Yellow Pages is used most heavily—and may have been the first example of "the book of the commercial." "Hartley" also ghosted the book *Golf*, written to coincide with an ad in which he used the Yellow Pages to find a golf instructor.

CHAPTER FIFTEEN

KANNER'S PICKS
(A Dozen More)

Burnett's "100" list does what it set out to do: identify fresh concepts that were superbly executed and raised the bar on what advertising could be. The commercials on it are indeed worthy of the applause they generated.

But so are many other outstanding commercials worthy of recognition—including dozens that were finalists on Burnett's list and a few that escaped their eye. Some were just whimsically seductive and engaging—like the 1986 California Raisin Advisory Board's sun-dried Claymation critters who conga-danced off the vine into America's hearts and pantries, making the prune-faced morsels hot, hip, and fun. Others broke the rules and overturned conventions. Copywriter Shirley Polykoff broke the rules by provocatively asking "Does she or doesn't she?" for Miss Clairol, a hair color "so natural only her hairdresser knows for sure!" Despite widespread derision, Polykoff played to a suppressed truth: that even nice girls reared to regard blondes as peroxide trash wishfully dreamt of becoming one.

Still others played by the rules, albeit ingeniously. In a 1965 silent slapstick commercial for Cracker Jack, Jack Gilford, a master of gentle comedic nuance, did a role reversal, acting like a child for Cracker Jack. A year later, Burlington Mills socked home the unique selling proposition of its new Lycra stay-up socks in a totally charming way: a man stomps, jumps, and bops to a flamenco-type tune to try to make his socks fall down.

Some went where few tread before them. Hebrew National, for

example, went to the top of the heavenly hierarchy, implying superiority for hot dogs that "answer to a higher authority." Some, like Frank "It Takes a Tough Man" Perdue, relied on the power of a spokesman to imply if not divinity, at least superiority.

Some ran in a single market only once: Others spanned continents and decades—even products. The Hepburn-Tracy style romance of Nestle Beverage Company's chic Taster's Choice couple started to percolate in late 1990 as a series for Nescafe Gold in England. Their brief encounter that began when an attractive woman rang the doorbell of her neighbor, a handsome single man, to borrow coffee left them (and us) . . . interested— and bloomed along a different track for a different product in America.

Even B.C. (before computers) inventive advertising struck a chord. In 1956, Young & Rubicam demonstrated the sticking power of Johnson & Johnson Band-Aids by picking up an egg dunked in boiling water with one. Eighteen years later it held the fort against Curad's "ouchless" strip and low-priced generics with wet people crooning out why they're stuck on Band-Aid (" 'cause Band-Aid's stuck on them"). Twenty-two years later, a redo of the jingle was back on the air.

More recently chimpanzees being studied by scientist Jane Goodall (supposedly an HBO viewer since 1978) starred in the first commercial to ever win an Emmy. Special effects made it seem as if the chimps were speaking familiar lines from *The Godfather, Network,* and other Hollywood films they'd glimpsed on the anthropologist's TV set. Critics sniped that Goodall (who never appeared in the spot) had sold out and that she didn't even get HBO in the Gombe desert. They missed the point—and the spot's hyperbolic humor.

Advertising has a license to disarm—as long as it charms. Here are a few more "winners" that, like those cited above, drive home a powerful sales message that ambushed us.

DO YOU KNOW ME?

A decade of celebrities lending recognition to American Express

As fog sifts through a ghoulish old mansion (actually the Gould mansion on the North Shore of Long Island), and spooky organ music plays, horror novelist Stephen King emerges. Lightning flashes, doors bang, and disembodied human arms and hunchbacks scurry past.

"It's frightening how many novels of suspense I've written," he says, a lighted taper in one hand, a sinister black raven in the other. "But still, when I'm not recognized it just kills me. So instead of saying I wrote Carrie, I carry the card." King gestures toward a table strewn with Amex applications. "Without it, isn't life a little scary?" he asks archly.

A voice-over suggests, "The next time you visit your favorite haunt, why not apply for an American Express card?"

AMERICAN EXPRESS

STEPHEN KING

OGILVY & MATHER, USA, 1984

Back in 1974, when American Express began to feature high achievers whose names were often better known than their faces, only 6 million people owned Amex cards. Today more than 20 million do so.

Partial credit must go to Ogilvy & Mather's ingenious strategy of using nonrecognizable celebrities who rely on the widely accepted card to get them what they need—and to associate their status with that of the card's users. King was the sixty-first "invisible" celebrity in the series and perhaps the most flamboyant. The inaugural spot featured character actor Norman Fell (from *Three's Company*), followed by 1964 vice-presidential aspirant William Miller. With the card, people "treat me as though I'd won," he exclaimed.

Mel Blanc asked if viewers knew him as the voice of Bugs Bunny—"because without the card, the only way I'd get any attention is by saying, 'Ebe, eh mebe, eh mebe . . . that's all, folks.' " Benny Goodman played along because "without my clarinet a lot of people don't know me." Paloma Picasso packed it to be as recognizable as her jewelry creations. Robert Ludlum toted it because while his books were known, his face remained a mystery.

As the campaign evolved, the card promised more than recognition. It promised membership in an elite society. Tom Peters, who wrote the book on America's best-run corporations, claimed it "always put him in the right company" and Itzhak Perlman used it "for the same reason I use a Stradivarius."

Advertising evolved to promote specific benefits. Jesse Owens, who won the Berlin Olympics in 1936 and now traveled at a much slower pace, found that even if "I come in last" the hotel room is guaranteed. And pollster George Gallup touted the complete monthly billing record as very important . . . "at least in my opinion."

Ad director Glen Gilbert said the endorsers were paid peanuts and did it largely for the publicity. Jim Henson used to claim he was better known for his "Do You Know Me?" than for creating the Muppets.

"Do You Know Me?" ended in 1985 after an eleven-year run. "The premise had played out and though people only needed a fifteen-thousand-dollar annual income then, many felt unworthy of the card," Gilbert said.

POURING IT ON

Making even the lactose intolerant yearn for a milk mustache

CALIFORNIA MILK PROCESSOR BOARD

HEAVEN

GOODBY, SILVERSTEIN & PARTNERS, USA, 1996

A smarmy, soulless businessman (actor Kenny Moscow) cruelly and arbitrarily fires an employee and moments later, stepping off a curb, is run over by a truck. He arrives in a white-on-white world replete with gigantic, irresistible chocolate-chip cookies and an enormous refrigerator. After gobbling some of the cookies he opens the fridge and grabs milk carton after milk carton, discovering that all are empty. "Wait a minute," he says as the realization of his eternal damnation in as hellish a circle as any Dante envisioned dawns on him, "where am I?"

A flaming "Got Milk?" logo appears.

Historically, milk ads have tried to remind people in wholesome ways about the ingredients that do a body good or change milk's image from boring and fat-laden to fun and healthy. The "Got Milk?" campaign was a hilarious, brilliant, strategic departure that ignored nutrition and fun in favor of showing the dire effects of milk deprivation and how we'd better have some around for those times we need it.

The milk board almost nixed the imaginative and uproarious "Heaven," written by Harry Cocciolo and art directed by Sean Ehringer, uneasy about the complexity of the spot and its focus on death. Agency principal Jeff Goodby directed the spot himself. "Heaven" was just one of a series of spots that showed people suffering the consequences of not having milk to go with partner foods like cookies, cereal, chocolate cake, or peanut butter. In "Aaron Burr," for example, an Alexander Hamilton buff can't name Hamilton's murderer (Aaron Burr) to win a radio quiz jackpot—because his mouth is stuffed with peanut butter and he's out of milk to wash it down.

Research showed that people only gave milk a second thought when they didn't have any, said Jeff Manning, executive director of the milk board. And as a thirst quencher, most people opted for a soda, iced tea, or water. Rather than show milk consumed alone, as most milk ads had done in the past, Manning pushed for it to be shown with certain foods where only milk will do. And rather than focus on nonusers, the team opted to target milk drinkers and encourage them to drink more.

"Got Milk" got results. Milk sales in California had been declining 3 percent a year. Since the campaign started in 1993, per capita consumption increased slightly. And a line of licensed T-shirts, cups, and other merchandise materialized, perhaps a first spawned by ads for a generic food.

In 1997 Goodby pulled up stakes on the familiar scenes of milk deprivation to move to a fictional town called Drysville, where milk is outlawed and everyone's morose. The cats have run off, bakeries gone out of business, and folks wet their breakfast cereal with tap water.

In one black-and-white spot, a heartbroken mother reads a wistful letter from her son, who's left home because he "can no longer live in a town that holds no milk for me." In another, Drysville police apprehend a car of teens trying to sneak contraband milk and cookies home from a party in a nearby town. Over a megaphone the sheriff orders them to put their straws down. "With 'Got Milk,' people could see what was coming around the corner," said Manning. "We wanted to keep the element of surprise."

BACK IN THE U.S.S.R

Dannon proposes yogurt for those who think young

The Soviet Georgia Centenarian choir of old men are singing. "In Soviet Georgia, where they eat a lot of yogurt, a lot of people live past one hundred," an announcer explains as the camera pans past a series of weathered citizens smiling, dancing, and eating yogurt. "Of course many things affect longevity and we're not saying Dannon yogurt will help you live longer," the announcer continues with the mandatory disclaimer. "But Dannon is a wholesome, natural food that has active cultures. Many other yogurts don't. By the way," adds the announcer as the camera closes in on one man in a long-haired cloak and lamb's-wool shawl happily spooning up the yogurt: "Temur Vanacha thought Dannon was really fine yogurt. He ought to know. He's been eating yogurt for 105 years."

DANNON
OLD RUSSIANS

MARSTELLER INC., USA, 1976

The world's top-selling yogurt, founded in Spain in 1917, didn't arrive in America until 1942. It didn't arrive in America's consciousness until the 1960s, when Dannon chairman Juan Metzger began marketing yogurt as a food rather than a medicine.

At first Dannon tried a hard sell, reminding Americans who "don't always eat right" that its low-fat, no-artificial-anything yogurt was "the right thing to eat." At that time, less than 10 percent of Americans ate yogurt at least once a week; nearly half never touched the stuff. Metzger blamed yogurt's "ugly taste" but decided that the way to plant Dannon in the refrigerators of young, upper-income consumers—the target he identified—was to build its image as a health food in keeping with the hip, flower-power times. The Soviet Georgia centenarians spots did that and implied (strongly) that the secret to the centenarians' good health and long life was yogurt.

In 1975, Peter Lubalin, creative supervisor at Marsteller, had read an article in *National Geographic* magazine about the longevity of the Soviet Georgians. He and partner Arlene Hoffman got contacts, visas, and client approval to make the first American commercial shot in Soviet Russia.

In Kutol, a dilapidated small town on the Black Sea, Hoffman located eighty-nine-year-old Bagdah Dacvholovich—and his 116-year-old mother. Lubalin's gifts of ballpoint pens and American dungarees won the "talent" over, including a 98-year-old man filmed tending his vineyard, a 107-year-old-woman feeding her chickens, a 130-year-old woman smiling broadly, and a 96-year-old man chopping wood like a logger. To maintain warm relationships, each American had to drink a bottle of vodka a day, Lubalin estimated, and "that left a very short window for clear heads."

The ads ran for years before wearing out—but not before helping to push up yogurt consumption more than 120 percent between 1975 and 1990. Sales rose every year, until 1989, when consumers balked at price hikes. Dannon grew despite intense competition and the fact that yogurt was hard to position. (Deeming it a snack food would put it in an intensely competitive industry; dessert is "a dirty word today," and "frankly [yogurt] makes for a *very* light lunch" Metzger said at the time.)

FLOWER POWER

Extremism in the defense of incumbency proves to be no vice

DEMOCRATIC NATIONAL CONVENTION

DAISY

DOYLE DANE BERNBACH, USA, 1964

As birds chirp merrily in the background, a little girl idly plucks petals from a daisy, counting, not entirely accurately, each petal she picks. Her childish voice is replaced by an ominous voice-over counting down from ten to zero as the camera zooms into an extreme close-up of the girl's eye. At "zero," her pupil dissolves into the image of an exploding mushroom cloud. President Lyndon Johnson, in a voice-over, pleads: "These are the

214

stakes: to make a world in which all of God's children can live or to go into the dark. We must either love each other or we must die."

Super: "Vote for President Johnson on November 3."

Voice-over: "Vote for President Johnson on November 3. The stakes are too high for you to stay home."

Negative political advertising is as old as politics itself, but "Daisy" was a landmark in campaign history nonetheless, both for its brutal simplicity and the shameless way it used a child as an ideological weapon. The sixty-second spot, masterminded by media guru Tony Schwartz, proved that fear is every bit as potent a persuader as love.

The 1964 race for the White House between incumbent Lyndon Johnson and Arizona Republican Barry Goldwater was a bitter one, and fears generated by the Cold War and the steadily increasing U.S. involvement in Vietnam made Goldwater's no-holds-barred conservatism an irresistible target. Although "Daisy" never mentioned Goldwater by name, it was nonetheless a devastating reminder of the ultimate consequences, in Johnson's view, of Goldwater's extremism. It implied, simply, that a vote for trigger-happy Goldwater was a vote against our children's future.

"Daisy" officially aired just once, two months before Election Day, 1964. But its publicity aftermath (it was on the cover of *Time* and ran on the evening news dozens of times) infuriated the Republicans, polarized the country, and forever changed the balance of power from the whistle-stop to the television. Goldwater managed to win only six states and 38 percent of the popular vote, the worst loss ever by a presidential candidate.

SEATTLE FOOT

An amputee shows the low-tech benefits of high-tech Du Pont

As a young man limps to an urban school yard where a basketball game is in progress, a voice-over tells his history:

"When Bill Demby was in Vietnam he used to dream of coming home and playing a little basketball with the guys. That dream all but died when he lost two legs to a Vietcong rocket." Demby arrives at the school yard, where friends greet him. As he sits on a bench to remove his sweatpants, the camera pans to a teammate glancing sideways at his legs: prosthetic limbs.

The voice-over continues. "But then a group of researchers discovered that a remarkable plastic from Du Pont could help make artificial limbs that were more resilient, more flexible, more like life itself."

DU PONT
BILL DEMBY
BBDO, USA, 1987

215

Demby goes for a shot, falls, and softly groans. But he refuses help and pulls himself up as if he had legs of flesh and bone.

The announcer continues, "Thanks to these efforts, Bill Demby is back. And some say he hasn't lost his step. At Du Pont, we make the things that make a difference."

A friend says, "Hey, Bill, you've been practicing."

Voice-over: "Better things for better living."

Super: "Du Pont. Better things for better living."

A Du Pont department head had read about the Seattle Foot, an artificial limb that mimicked the springing action of the muscles and bones of a real foot more faithfully than anything before. The inner spring of this device was made of Du Pont's plastic resin. What better way to demonstrate the "better things for better living" corporate motto, he reasoned.

Vietnam vets were among the first people to use the Seattle Foot. Du Pont's team—BBDO copywriters Rick Meyer and Ted Sann, art director Len McCarron, and agency producer Regina Ebel—decided to show a disabled one returning to his old haunts. But they couldn't find one who looked good on TV and was athletic enough to demonstrate the capabilities of the prosthesis, recalled director Rick Levine.

Finally, at the Disabled Games (akin to an Olympics for the handicapped) they found thirty-nine-year-old Bill Demby. The Mitchellville, Maryland, native had dreamed of playing pro basketball as a kid, but lost both legs below the knee when a Vietcong rocket hit the Jeep he was driving outside Quang Tri in 1971. His left leg was blown off; the right one was severely crushed and had to be amputated.

This gripping sixty-second spot, shot on a Manhattan basketball court, packed in information and emotion without any actors, special camera angles, or tricks. (Demby nixed camera angles that would make it look as if he were jumping ten feet—and a stuntman to do the scripted fall, even though he hurt his hip doing it himself.)

"Demby," intended as a short-term corporate ID, became a corporate image spot and ran for two years. It attracted the attention and interest of key business prospects while changing people's perceptions about Du Pont. "After 'Demby' they saw Du Pont as an innovative, socially minded, humanized company," said Jack Comfy, Du Pont special events manager.

Du Pont subsequently hired Demby to give motivational speeches. In 1989 he became a nationally ranked track and field competitor and certified ski instructor. Demby went on to work with the Disability Awareness Project based in Maryland, play on a wheelchair basketball team, and break national amputee records in the shot put, javelin, and discus.

PUTTIN' ON THE DOG

Hush Puppies barks up a different tree

Jason, the basset hound and Hush Puppies' canine symbol, sits on a side-walk grate amid car horns and other city sounds. A subway train rumbles underneath, its whoosh causing his great ears to blow up and puffing out the pooch's ample cheeks.

"Ventilated Hush Puppies," declares a title card next to a pair of Hush Puppies sandals.

HUSH PUPPIES
VENTILATED HUSH PUPPIES

FALLON MCELLIGOTT, USA, 1988

The fifteen-second, voiceless "Ventilated Hush Puppies" was intended to plug the gap until Wolverine World Wide could roll out the next campaign for its Hush Puppies line of shoes. Instead, this new trick with an old dog—the sad-eyed hound with droopy ears had been its icon since 1958—fetched younger customers and restored Hush Puppies' luster and sales, recalled copywriter Jart Olsen.

Hush Puppies' reputation was built around the classic loafer and suede oxford—its mainstay since 1958. By 1985, those styles had lost their appeal and Hush Puppies was branded a fusty has-been. Advertising had to turn a staid, old-fashioned, down-market product into chic, contemporary, up-scale footwear and to convince people it had a lot more in its warehouse than the loafer.

Originally, the advertising was meant to be simple product shots with headlines but the basset hound—a pet picked from a casting call—was so enchanting that art director Bob Barrie and Rick Dublin Photography began to play around with it. To get his ears to do that Marilyn Monroe *Seven-Year Itch* swoosh, the agency taped fishing line to them.

Wolverine at first resisted. The dog was associated with the past they were trying to shake. The fact that the ad was charming—and so cheap to produce—ultimately swayed them. The "orphan" commercial was a hit that led to others. In one spot, a woman poured Perrier into the dog dish while the stoic basset hound looked on. Below were women's pumps and the headline: "Sophisticated Hush Puppies." For another spot, "Corporate Hush Puppies," a pooch licked the boss's shoes.

The spots got Hush Puppies astronomical recognition but they essentially barked up the wrong tree by disavowing the company's classic shoes, said Hush Puppies president Louis Dubrow. "We spent millions trying to convince people we didn't make that shoe anymore," he said ruefully. In 1994 Hush Puppies again flourished by doing the unconventional. "We've walked our dog on the other side of the street," Dubrow said. "We ran our shoes out in all kinds of bright colors when the entire footwear industry was a sea of black shoes. Interestingly, it's that same shoe in bright oranges and greens at seventy dollars, not forty dollars that has resurrected this company."

217

LIAR, LIAR

Can you believe it? Isuzu scores without selling

ISUZU

THE LIAR

DELLA FEMINA, TRAVISANO & PARTNERS, USA, 1987

A seemingly trustworthy announcer stands beside a car, which he introduces as "The amazing Isuzu I-Mark, rated one of the best of the best by Car & Driver magazine. It gets 94 miles per gallon city. One hundred and twelve highway."

That outrageous claim is corrected by a super: "He's lying: 34 miles per gallon city, 40 highway."

The salesman continues, "Its top speed is 300 miles per hour."

The super again corrects the overstatement: "Downhill in a hurricane."

The dissimulating car man rolls on, "And Isuzu dealers have millions in stock."

The super sets it straight: "Close. We have hundreds."

Liar: "So they're selling them for $9."

Super: "Wrong. Prices start at $6,999."

The seamy salesman's claims become increasingly outlandish—and entertaining: "And if you come in tomorrow you'll get a free house. You have my word on it."

Super: "House not included."

Voice-over: "The Isuzu I-Mark. Now at your local Isuzu dealer."

Super: "See your local Isuzu dealer."

"Liar" may have been the first emperor-has-no-clothes advertising. It admitted what people already knew: that hard-sell, oily salesmen, especially those who sell cars, often stoop pretty low to make the sale.

American Isuzu Motors says its Liar commercials don't fit with Isuzu's currently desired imagery. But in their day, "Liar" was an unparalleled pop-culture phenomenon.

Isuzu didn't import cars to the U.S. until 1981, long after rivals Toyota and Nissan had parked here. And its $45 million ad budget was a fraction of others in the hypercompetitive auto market. Della Femina initially tried to build name recognition with funny ads—in one spot an American tries to pronounce "Isuzu" and a Japanese salesman likewise mangles "Chevrolet"—and traditional ones about Isuzu's long heritage in Japan.

"Liar" lightning ignited in early 1986 when associate creative director Rick Carpenter asked copywriter Matt Bogen and art director Jeannie Marie Obeji to create a spot for Southern California Isuzu dealers. Rather than do the conventional running shots of the car, Carpenter proposed enlisting an unctuous prevaricator to pitch it. He envisioned a parody of all TV car commercials with exaggerated claims about gas mileage, performance, accessories, and financing, corrected with superimposed captions. He and associate creative director John Armistead helped develop the scripts that, in a plucky way, presented the cars' relevant selling points.

Isuzu's ad team, figuring this would cut through clutter and be memorable, swallowed their misgivings that it cut too close to the truth of their business and approved it unanimously as a dealer promo.

The original inspiration for the star, *Saturday Night Live* cast member John Lovitz, wanted too much money, so they cast David Leisure (an underemployed actor living in his 1964 VW bus) as the self-important reptilian announcer because he oozed like a punctured tube of toothpaste. After two months airing locally, the pathological liar was ready for prime time. But when Leisure showed up to shoot new spots, he was in a cast: he'd broken his ankle ice skating. The ad team tucked him behind the car for one spot and concealed the cast behind a rock for another. But they also rewrote one script so Leisure appeared with cast, crutches, and a Formula 1 racing suit, standing beside an amusement park bumper-car ride talking about "a little problem" he'd had at Monte Carlo. The super explained: "He slipped in the bathtub."

In a subsequent "hoax," Isuzu tried to demonstrate the high performance of its I-Mark by having Leisure in the car miraculously overtake a bullet he'd fired from a .357 Magnum. In other scenes, the salesman proclaims that the Trooper II has "enough cargo space to carry Texas." (The overlay clarifies: "seventy-nine cubic feet of it.") Flashing his trademark shark smile, the huckster deadpans that "Isuzu will accept marbles and seashells as payment." (The super provides the real price.) Mr. Unbelievable also contended as he stood in front of Buckingham Palace that he sold an I-Mark to the Queen. ("He telleth a lie," corrected the script.)

Joe Isuzu tickled America's funny bone and implanted the Isuzu name in our consciousness. The public relations firm that tracked publicity reported more than 150 million individual exposures of press coverage. Joe Isuzu became a touchstone of sleaze. Ronald Reagan once compared Nicaraguan leader Daniel Ortega with "that fellow from Isuzu." George Bush as well as presidential wanna-be Michael Dukakis made public references to him. And Chrysler chairman Lee Iacocca in ads once contended, "If Chrysler isn't the performance company, then I'm Joe Isuzu." "Now everybody pronounces our name right," one executive said at the time.

But scattered news reports claimed Isuzu actually sold fewer cars in the first half of 1987 than during that period in 1986. Critics theorized that the "Liar" ads were too funny to take the car seriously. In 1991 Isuzu moved away from "Liar." Dick Sittig, associate creative director at Della Femina, said that when the campaign began, "lying on TV was enough to get people's attention. But once people got used to the character telling lies, we had to do something more."

David Leisure went on to do movies. In *The Martini Project*, he starred as a corrupt adman and in an NBC special, *If It's Tuesday, It Still Must Be Belgium*, he was a comic spy. He is probably best remembered as the neighbor in NBC's long-running sitcom, *Empty Nest*. His "You have my word on it" line de résistance remains part of the vernacular.

TOO REAL TO BE FAKE

John Hancock Financial Services writes the book on real

JOHN HANCOCK

BILL HEATER

HILL HOLLIDAY CONNORS COSMOPULOS INC., USA, 1986

A father rocks his baby daughter to sleep. The camera cuts to type on a black screen, which presents his situation.

"Bill Heater, thirty, married, two children, income $35,000."

Subsequent screens present his expenses, needs, and solutions.

"I love you, little Jenny Catherine," Dad coos. "I've got something very, very important to tell you. Daddy got a raise. [Pause] Are you listening? I got a raise."

His "estimated expenses" (income tax, rent, et al.) flash on the screen.

Dad murmurs, "That means, uh, that I can buy you a sandbox, playhouse . . . It means I can buy you a sliding board, a little bicycle, a diamond ring."

Super: "Needs long-term security for his family to build investments."

Dad continues, "It means I can buy you a mink coat. [Pause] Maybe we could buy a . . . or maybe we should put some of it away?"

Super: "Answer: John Hancock Variable Life Insurance with five investment options: Stocks. Aggressive stocks. Bonds. Money market. Total return."

Dad: "Huh? What do you think about that? What do you know about the stock market? I love you, little Jenny Catherine—very, very much. Guess what? Daddy got a raise."

Super: "Real life. Real answers," followed by the John Hancock logo.

While other financial services companies boasted about what they could do for you or relied on such "feel-good" symbols as the Rock of Gibraltar or Snoopy to suggest security, John Hancock convinced us it understood people and their needs. Its emotional dramas combined reality with sentimentality, gripped the head and heart, and helped transform a simple mutual life insurance company known for a sweeping signature and its "Put your John Hancock on the John Hancock" song into a respected financial services provider.

220

The characters who populate this series seem so real you'd swear they weren't actors and that their lines bubbled forth from their heads, not from a script. They didn't look at the camera; indeed, they looked away. They mumbled and shrugged. Their voices overlapped; background noises distracted. This was hard-sell advertising served up in the softest, most palatable way.

In 1980, the venerable, 124-year-old life insurer was under siege from banks and brokers. Life insurers managed 21.2 percent of U.S. household assets in 1950, but only 11.9 percent by 1980. John Hancock had expanded its services and needed to let the world know what its buffet included. The voyeuristic but quiet spots with the texture and look of a documentary cost, on average, a scant $125,000 to produce.

The names used belonged to real agency employees and the financial dossiers were composites of Hancock policyholders. Hill Holliday art director Don Easdon and writer Bill Heater conceived the campaign during long walks along the Boston waterfront and visits to a nearby bar, where they saw the kinds of people they were targeting. The agency rewrote the lines to fit the actors' speech patterns. Joe Pytka directed. Footage seemed unedited, to make consumers think they were eavesdropping on real families working out financial plans.

There is no pitch. The John Hancock name is used only when the ads are nearly over. "A voice-over would have been too commercial," said Easdon, who expected viewers would need to see the ads three time before they absorbed the message. President David D'Alessandro needed to see it only once: Hill Holliday won the account with this pitch.

Ironically, agents in the field initially spurned the ads, but D'Alessandro plowed ahead. After the campaign broke on the Super Bowl, calls poured in and agents got behind it. Later it was adapted to print ads.

The ads changed people's perception of John Hancock and briefly made it a market leader. Awareness of the name was up along with attributes such as "honest" (up 11 percent), "accessible" (up 19 percent), and "provider of a broad range of financial services" (up 23 percent). Sales that year soared 17 percent—the largest increase in Hancock's history.

The low-key sort of family photo album also made people aware of their insurance needs—not forcing them into denial and psychological withdrawal, or treating the subject too flippantly so viewers didn't take it seriously. Many advertisers credit "Real Life, Real Answers" with sparking the revolution of "realism" in advertising.

After a ten-year run, in 1995, Hancock canned the campaign. D'Alessandro said it "was a little too tied to life insurance" and other advertisers had copied its style, leaving John Hancock without a clearly differentiated look. In its place it crafted the lyrical "Insurance for the Unexpected. Investments for the Opportunities" campaign. One spot asks a middle-ager to choose between educating her children and taking care of her parents. Narrator Sigourney Weaver asks, "Whose eyes can you look into and say you just can't help? For in both, you will surely see your own."

NATIVE GROUND

The most-seen ad in TV history reminds us to watch what we drop

**KEEP AMERICA
BEAUTIFUL**

CRYING INDIAN

MARSTELLER INC., USA, 1970

From print campaign

A dramatic drum rhythm pulses as Iron Eyes Cody paddles his canoe past smokestacks through debris-infested waters, beaching on a litter-strewn shore.

"Some people have a deep, abiding respect for the natural beauty that was once this country," says the voice-over. "And some people don't." A passenger in a car on a congested highway tosses the remains of a meal out the window at Cody's feet.

"People start pollution; people can stop it," the announcer adds, as the camera zooms in on a single tear rolling down the Cherokee Indian's weathered face. The announcer urges viewers to write for a free booklet on how to help.

"Crying Indian," created by Young & Rubicam's Marstellar Inc., has been called the most famous public service commercial of all time. It moved people emotionally to consider how small, thoughtless acts add up, and sparked the environmental consciousness of millions of people.

Before Cherokee Indian Iron Eyes Cody and his single tear played on our collective guilt of deposing a people and then despoiling their land, the Stamford, Connecticut–based Keep America Beautiful advocacy group had used an animated "Suzie Spotless" and spokesdog Lassie to remind people not to pollute. "Nothing came close to the impact of 'Crying Indian,' " said Roger Powers, former chairman of KAB.

Cody, who appeared in many Western movies with John Wayne, originally turned down the job. He relented at the urging of Lady Bird Johnson: pollution control was then a priority of President Lyndon Johnson. Two years before, Richard Nixon had created the Environmental Protection Agency.

Cody could not swim and wore a life preserver for the spot. "There was talk of an onion used to get that tear," added Powers.

"Crying Indian" aired at the discretion and expense of individual stations and became what is likely the most-viewed public service advertising of all time. Since its release, it has amassed 24 billion-plus household impressions, more than any other single TV spot—both commercial and public service—in the history of television. Research showed that during the 1970s, 94 percent of viewers recognized the spot (which received more than $700 million in donated network airtime) and associated Cody with pollution control.

"Crying Indian" ran for more than ten years. Cody served as a Keep America Beautiful spokesman for decades after that. He died in 1999. After "Crying Eyes," KAB tried other approaches to deliver its "It's up to us" message. But Cody's reaction to pollution was so hauntingly memorable that in April (Keep America Beautiful month) 1998, KAB launched a follow-up commercial featuring him. In it, real people at a bus stop munch on a doughnut, read a newspaper, and drink coffee while waiting. When the bus pulls up, they leave their litter behind, having aimed for the trash receptacle but missing. The camera pans back to reveal the filthy landscape, then zooms in on the bus shelter, where a poster of Cody hangs, but this time with a "real" (computer-generated) tear emerging from his eye.

TRUTH TEST

Memorex asks for proof of love

A James Dean type in jeans and T-shirt wistfully takes leave of a pretty blond girl. "Look, I'll be seeing you around, okay?" he tells her. He jumps into a red Porsche and zooms off as she sobs, watching him grow smaller in the distance.

Suddenly, Romeo's car is in reverse, and he's moving back down the highway as quickly as he left. The camera cuts to a finger on a rewind button and then to "Juliet" popping out a tape and clutching it to her chest as the guy says, "Look, I'll be seein' you around, okay?"

Voice-over and super: "Is it love or is it Memorex?"

MENTEX

IS IT LOVE?

LEO BURNETT, USA, 1986

Mentex's Memorex-brand cassette tapes have identified themselves with the "Is It Live" motto since 1971, when opera singer Enrico DiGiuseppe shattered a glass live—and on tape. The spot executed Memorex's strategic message, that the audiotape's reproduction was as close to real as possible—and thus established it as the highest quality available at the time—"but people didn't know Enrico," recalls Murray Kalif, who conceived the early campaign. So in 1972 Memorex enlisted the jazz legend Ella Fitzgerald for the first "Is It Ella or Is It Memorex?" spot.

"We bought champagne glasses at Woolworth's and measured the frequency response of each so Ella would bring her voice to that range," recalled Kalif. "We'd hit the glass and she'd listen and get the pitch and we watched as the glass started to vibrate, then shake and then blew. She knew where to reach and could belt it out in one take though we often did a few extras for safety."

A problem, he said, was finding two glasses with virtually identical pitches, because when they replayed Fitzgerald's voice over the Memorex it had to sound the same. Lawyers were on the set—a sound studio stage in Burbank—to make sure there was no hanky-panky. Francesco Scavullo, who later became a famous fashion photographer, directed the spot.

Memorex never declared quality superiority—just that it reproduced the human voice so perfectly you couldn't tell whether it was live or Memorex. "The implication was certainly that you couldn't get a better tape," Kalif said.

At the time, competitors TDK and Maxell were targeting young consumers with technical claims or a guy in a chair being blown away by the sound. Memorex aimed for more of a mass audience. The "Ella" spots ran intermittently through 1987, when Memorex decided advertising was too costly in a low-profit business. And the advertising had done its work. People still remember the concept, which is still used—along with the shattered-glass icon—on all Memorex packaging.

The "Ella" spots exploded sales, but the revival of the concept was an especially smart bit of packaging. When Memorex launched a new video-tape line in 1986, it borrowed the by then universally recognized "Is It Live" line to convince viewers of the quality of its pictures, recalled Ted Bell, now creative chief of Young & Rubicam, who was creative director, writer, and art director on the spot at Burnett. In addition to borrowing interest from the original tag line, "Is It Love?" turned "a staid, faded product image into one that was sophisticated, hip, and contemporary," said Bell. "It broke the rules by not telling the technical story . . . and by not shattering glass."

INSTANT CLASSIC

A "marital" spat helps Garner and Hartley pitch Polaroid

Upbeat music plays as Mariette Hartley works on a car while James Garner explains to the camera that "Polaroid's One Step is so simple to operate, even a woman can use it."

"How'd that go again?" asks Hartley.

Garner says conspiratorially, "I thought that would get her attention."

Mariette is not amused. "I can have one thousand women here in half an hour . . . all marching with big signs," she threatens.

Jim is undeterred from explaining the ease of using the camera. "You never focus. You just point it and press the button," he says and snaps her picture. "The sharp clear color develops in minutes," he says and then ribs her. "You're beautiful when you're angry."

Mariette continues the verbal reprimand. "You had a nice career there for a while."

Jim stays the course: "Get the One Step. This may be my final appeal."

Mariette finally breaks her cold war seriousness with a laugh.

Super: "Polaroid"—as the camera clicks.

POLAROID

IT'S SO SIMPLE

DOYLE DANE BERNBACH, USA, 1977

Imagine this lighthearted marital sparring in 1977! Rather than fuss over the mechanics of picture taking and the technologies involved, Polaroid focused on the "emotional benefit of love," said Bob Gage, who was art and creative director on the series. (Jane Liepschutz was producer, and Jack Dillon, copywriter.) "People take pictures of people they love. We sold love."

They sold it with a captivating and breezy battle of the sexes that effectively teamed a pair of sparring, flirting celebrity endorsers. James Garner and Mariette Hartley's relaxed, informal relationship seemed so authentic that many viewers believed they were really married. Fans nicknamed them the Bickersons. (Hartley took to wearing a T-shirt inscribed "I am not Mrs. James Garner" while the real Mrs. Garner began wearing one declaring that she was.)

Garner, who was then starring in the *Rockford Files* TV series, hadn't done a commercial since 1954, when he pitched Winston cigarettes. Hartley was recruited after the woman featured in the first promotion was unavailable for a sequel. Gage remembered Hartley from a Pillsbury spot and cast her. Management at Polaroid reluctantly approved the spot: they didn't think it was funny.

But the rest of America did and the ad—and campaign—took off. Women applauded Hartley's "giving as good as she got" exchange. Viewers got the point that the camera was easier to use and more convenient than any camera on the market. And the One Step went on for a time to become the fastest-selling instant or conventional camera in America.

In another spot, Garner claimed, "There's just one step," and Hartley contended that she thought "pointing is a step." He said it wasn't and she said, "Well, I think it should be," and he countered that "We don't count it" and she snipped back that "You should."

The spots—there were eventually more than sixty—ran for four years. Hartley said Polaroid gave her more notoriety than any of more than one hundred other ads she'd done. It gave Polaroid awareness too, but the camera that Dr. Edwin Land first released in the mid-1950s needed more than that to compete against inexpensive 35mm point-and-shoot models from Kodak, Nikon, Minolta, Olympus, and Canon, whose marketing departments were fierce and well funded.

Years after Polaroid stopped running Garner and Hartley, Americans remembered them. But they also thought of Polaroids as bulky, inconvenient cameras that required expensive film and produced inferior pictures compared with those of 35mm cameras. What's more, despite the duo's appealing banter—or perhaps because of it—Polaroid had low "social approval." People just didn't consider it "serious."

HE LIKES IT!

Young Mikey guilelessly endorses the benefits of good-tasting cereal

QUAKER OATS

MIKEY

DOYLE DANE BERNBACH, USA, 1972

Two brothers sit around the breakfast table, eyeing a box of Life cereal. "What's that stuff?" the older one, perhaps seven, asks.

"Some cereal," the younger brother (maybe five) replies. "Supposed to be good for you."

"D'you try it?" the older inquires.

"I'm not gonna try it. You try it," the younger snaps.

The older of the Dennis-the-Menaces gets an inspiration: "Let's get Mikey!" an idea with which his sibling concurs.

The younger predicts that their guinea pig—adorable, finicky Mikey—will spurn the cereal. "He won't eat it. He hates everything," he declares.

"Hey, Mikey!" the scheming lads call.

But the chubby-cheeked three-year-old surveys the offering and gingerly puts a spoon into it. Then he puts in another—and another. "He likes it," his astonished brothers cry. "He really likes it! Hey, Mikey!"

226

A voice-over chirps: "When you bring Life home, don't tell the kids it's one of those nutritional cereals you've been trying to get them to eat. You're the only one who has to know."

The conspiracy theory applied to cereal! "Mikey" breathed new life into Life. The high-protein oat-based cereal, which had been introduced nationally in 1961, grew for its first few years and then plateaued. After ten years, it had roughly one share point of the cereal market. In 1969, Quaker president Robert Stuart Jr. testified before a U.S. Senate committee on nutrition that the company had spent $15 million in seven years advertising the nutritional value of Life—but found only 9 percent of consumers got the message.

At that time, most women (the key cereal purchasers) were unconcerned with nutrition, noted Jack Young, then vice president of marketing at Quaker. "Mikey" downplayed the nutrition while playing up the good taste. When DDB presented the ad, Quaker's marketing team did a first: they put it on the air without testing it.

Mikey, played by three-year-old John Gilchrist and his real-life siblings, was an immediate hit. Americans ate up the young boy who showed such confidence and independence in the face of two brothers who seemed to be getting the best of him—and the cereal. In its first year, Life sales went up 20 percent. Within three years the brand had grown two and a half times what it was pre-Mikey, said Keith Neumann, brand team manager for Life.

"Mikey" ran sporadically for twelve years—even after Quaker moved the account to BBDO in 1974—but ultimately grew tired and dated. "It had lost some magic," Neumann said. In 1986 Quaker brought back the now teenage Mikey in a promotion. It fizzled, Quaker theorizes, because people identified more with the adorable young icon from memory than they did with the fully grown Mikey, so unlike his younger self. Undaunted, in 1998, Quaker tried again with a contest that determined that Mikey II would be . . . a girl. In the spot, four-year-old Marli Brianna Hughes from Tampa, Florida, shared with her classmates her experience of being chosen as the new Mikey.

IMAGE CREDITS

Chapter One American Tourister "Gorilla" courtesy of Roy Grace; Araldite "Hammer and Nail" © Ciba Speciality Holding, Inc.; Cheer "Diva" courtesy of Procter & Gamble; Timex "Acapulco Diver" courtesy of Timex

Chapter Two Chevrolet "Baseball, Hot Dogs, Apple Pie" courtesy of Chevrolet; Coca-Cola "Mountain Top" courtesy of The Coca-Cola Company; Courage Best "Gertcha" courtesy of Scottish & Newcastle; Kellogg's "Vesti" © 1969 Kellogg Company; KELLOGG'S, RICE KRISPIES, and SNAP, CRACKLE, POP are registered trademarks of Kellogg Company. PUT SOME SNAP, CRACKLE, POP INTO YOUR LIFE and SNAP, CRACKLE, and POP are trademarks of Kellogg Company. Levi's "Launderette" courtesy Bartle Bogle Hegarty, Ltd.

Chapter Three Federal Express "Fast-Paced World" © courtesy of FedEx; Mates Condoms "Chemist Shop" courtesy of Mates Condems Limited; MCI "Parents" courtesy of MCI Corporation; Parker Pens "Finishing School" courtesy of The Gillette Company

Chapter Four Chanel "Pool" courtesy of Chanel; Chanel "Share the Fantasy" courtesy of Chanel; Dunlop "Tested for the Unexpected" courtesy of Abbott Mead Vickers/BBDO; Perrier "Le Lion" courtesy of The Perrier Group

Chapter Five Apple "1984" courtesy of Apple Computer, Inc.; British Airways "Face" courtesy of British Airways; Citroën "Le Clemençeau" courtesy of Euro RSCG

Chapter Six Audi "Procon Ten" courtesy of BBDO/Europe; Clark's "Blueprint" courtesy of Clark's Shoes; *Folha de São Paolo* "Hitler" courtesy of W/Brasil; *The Guardian* "Points of View" courtesy of BMP/DDB, Ltd.; McDonald's "Sign" courtesy of McDonald's

Chapter Seven Camay "Small Store" courtesy of Leo Burnett, U.S.A.

Chapter Eight Barneys "Men of Destiny" courtesy of Barneys New York; Hallmark "Dance Card" © Hallmark Cards, Inc.

Chapter Nine Ambipur "Cat and Fish" courtesy of Saatchi BCN; John Smith's Bitter "Dog Tricks" courtesy of Scottish & Newcastle

Chapter Ten Bartles & Jaymes "Yuppies" © 1986, E. & J. Gallo Winery. Used with permission. Coca-Cola "Mean Joe Greene" courtesy The Coca-Cola Company; Diet Pepsi "Ray Charles" courtesy of BBDO/NY Pepsi Group

Chapter Eleven Norwegien Book Club "Train 1" courtesy De norske Bokklubbene A/S; Southern Airlines "Orgy" courtesy Sedelmaier Film Productions Incorporated

Chapter Twelve Energizer "Bunny" used by permission of Eveready Battery Company, Inc. Energizer Bunny® is a registered trademark of Eveready Battery Company; Xerox "Monks" courtesy of Xerox Corporation

Chapter Thirteen Alka-Seltzer "Spicy Meatball" courtesy of Roy Grace; Centraal Beheer "Hedgehog" courtesy of Centraal Beheer; Volkswagen "Funeral" courtesy of Roy Grace

Chapter Fourteen The Church of Jesus Christ of Latter-day Saints "Mud Fight" © 1983 Bonneville Communications. Used by permission of The Church of Jesus Christ of Latter-day Saints and featured talent; Partnership for a Drug Free America "Long Way Home" courtesy of Partnership for a Drug Free America; Valisere "First Bra" courtesy of W/Brasil; Yellow Pages "J.R. Hartley" courtesy of Abbott Mead Vickers

Chapter Fifteen American Express "Stephen King" courtesy of American Express; Dannon "Old Russians" courtesy of The Dannon Company, Inc.; Hush Puppies "Ventilated Hush Puppies" © The Hush Puppies Company. Hush Puppies is a registered trademark of Wolverine World Wide, Inc. Used with permission. No further republication or redistribution permitted without the consent of Wolverine World Wide, Inc.; Keep America Beautiful "Crying Indian" reprinted with permission from The Advertising Council; Polaroid "It's So Simple" courtesy of Polaroid

GENERAL INDEX

INDEX OF 100 BEST ADS PLUS KANNER'S PICKS

PRODUCT INDEX

BERNICE KANNER wrote the "On Madison Avenue" column for *New York* magazine for thirteen years. Her first-person adventures there as a cabdriver, traffic cop, Tiffany's temp, Wendy's counterman, and census taker are among the magazine's most celebrated pieces. She has been a marketing correspondent for CBS News, a marketing commentator for Bloomberg News (print, radio, and television), and a columnist for *Working Woman* magazine. Her previous books include *Are You Normal?*, *Lies My Parents Told Me,* and three children's books endorsed by the National Center for Family Literacy. She lives in New York City and Bridgewater, Connecticut, with her husband, son, daughter, and menagerie of animals.